As a chef, Ian Walker has a multitude of experience: he has worked in top London restaurants, consulted for major food retailers and run a successful farmers market enterprise. His exploring credits include cycling through the Democratic Republic of Congo, travelling across Mongolia on horseback and venturing into the remote regions of Northern Vietnam.

D1323300

Hcc   C000850258

BY THE SAME AUTHOR

Thirty Miles: A Local Journey in Food

AGAINST THE FLOW

Culinary Adventures up the Mekong River

Ian Walker

Copyright © 2009 Ian Walker

The moral right of the author has been asserted.

Apart from any fair dealing for the purposes of research or private study,
or criticism or review, as permitted under the Copyright, Designs and Patents
Act 1988, this publication may only be reproduced, stored or transmitted, in
any form or by any means, with the prior permission in writing of the
publishers, or in the case of reprographic reproduction in accordance with
the terms of licences issued by the Copyright Licensing Agency. Enquiries concerning reproduction
outside those terms should be sent to the publishers.

Matador
9 De Montfort Mews
Leicester LE1 7FW, UK
Tel: (+44) 116 255 9311 / 9312
Email: books@troubador.co.uk
Web: www.troubador.co.uk/matador

ISBN 978 1906510 879

The identity of some individuals mentioned in this book has been changed.

Typeset in 11pt Sabon by Troubador Publishing Ltd, Leicester, UK
Printed in the UK by TJ International Ltd, Padstow, Cornwall

Matador is an imprint of Troubador Publishing Ltd

To Alison,
for allowing the
freedom to express

Contents

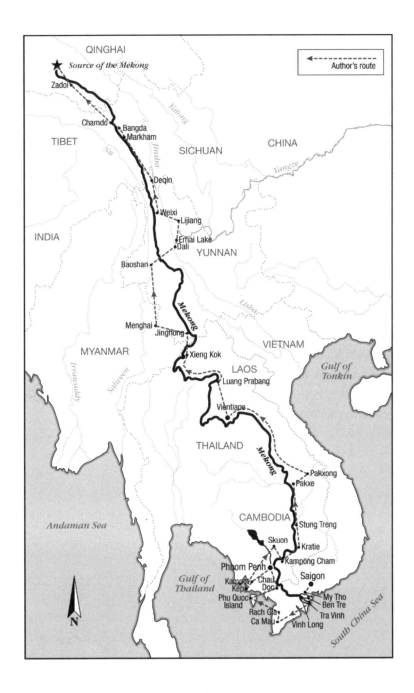

QINGHAI

★ *Source of the Mekong*

Zadoi

Chamdo
• Bangda
• Markham

TIBET

SICHUAN   CHINA

Yalong

Nu

Jinsha

Yangze

• Deqin

INDIA

• Weixi
• Lijiang

• Erhai Lake
• Dali

Baoshan   YUNNAN

Lisha

Menghai
Jinghong

Mekong

MYANMAR   VIETNAM

Xieng Kok

Irrawaddy   *Salween*

LAOS   *Gulf of Tonkin*

Luang Prabang

Vientiane

THAILAND   *Mekong*

→ Pakxong
Pakxe

Andaman Sea

CAMBODIA

Stung Treng

Skuon
Kratie

Phnom Penh   Kampong Cham

Kampot   Chau
Kep   Doc   Saigon

*Gulf of
Thailand*

Phu Quoc
Island   My Tho
Ben Tre

Rach Gia   Tra Vinh
Ca Mau   Vinh Long

South China Sea

N

Acknowledgements

A journey such as this relies heavily on the generosity of many people and I would like to thank everyone who allowed me access to their inner circle. Without their significant contributions this book would not have been possible and it is their collective inspiration to which I owe most gratitude. Heartfelt thanks to all my guides for assisting me and opening the doors of opportunity. To John Pilkington for valuable information relating to the source and subsequent encouragement. To Andrew Sullivan for another inspired book jacket and Barry Walker for naming it. Finally, I would like to thank the Mekong River and its inhabitants for delivering such an inspiring journey of culinary magic.

Introduction

The Mekong is one of the world's great rivers. From the wilderness of the Qinghai Tibetan Plateau it flows from its source at 5224m and travels 4350 km before dumping into the South China Sea. Its dramatic passage takes it through the mysterious land of Tibet, the culturally diverse Yunnan Province in China, into Laos, through Cambodia, before reaching its conclusion in the Vietnamese Delta. A journey following its path was sure to be fascinating and from the moment in October 2006 that I decided to explore its length, it became the object of my fascination.

As a chef, food had to be at the heart of my trip and through it I would explore this mighty river, its inhabitants and hoover up all things culinary. I decided, no matter what, that I would eat what the locals ate and stick to my golden rule of not refusing anything that was put in front of me. Before I left England I expected this fundamental requirement may prove tricky at times but in the countries I would journey through, my powers of acceptance were tested beyond any expected limits and brought about some memorable, if uncomfortable and unpalatable moments.

My original idea was to follow the river from its source but I was forced to rethink my plans when I became aware that severe weather conditions in April would have made this impractical. Temperatures on the plateau can fall to –30ºC during the winter months, so I had been advised to begin my exploration near its mouth and track the river against its flow. Although my mission would predominantly concentrate on food, I had decided, after due consideration, that I must make every effort to actually reach the source of the river. This goal would be the ultimate inspiration to discovering the cuisine and the vital role it plays in the existence of everyday folk.

As the adventure unfolded, my understanding of the river's impact would only enhance my admiration. The bustling, fertile Vietnamese Delta, where old traditions meld with new industry, provided me with a dynamic springboard and brought about my first truly unpalatable moment. In the re-emerging Golden Kingdom of Cambodia, I delve into a gastronomic underworld, which led me to several fascinating encounters. The charming people of Laos, from the lowlands, to the higher grounds of its northern reaches, introduced me to a few of the native delicacies. In Yunnan Province, the unique cultural diversity delivered a melting pot of culinary opportunities and produced dishes that bear little relationship with the country's more famed examples in Eastern China. Tibet, not known for its culinary proficiency, brought only humble offerings. Nonetheless, it still had the capacity to impress, if only for its wild raw produce.

The Mekong River is the least commercial of the world's major waterways, a fact not lost on the French who during their rule sought ways to utilise its position to extend their stronghold in the region. While their imperial ambitions were subsequently thwarted, an undoubted passion for food left its own indelible mark and through Vietnam, Cambodia and Laos many influences remain a part of everyday eating habits.

The trip yielded many highlights, but what struck me most was the sheer depth and variety of food I discovered and the lengths that the inhabitants would go to in order to feed themselves during impoverished times. We must not forget that the Vietnamese,

Cambodian and Lao populace have endured a horrific recent history and in the case of Cambodia, this resulted in a devastating effect on its culinary heritage. During the evil regime of the Khmer Rouge, its embattled citizens had to resort to drastic, unthinkable measures to supply themselves with any sustenance that they could obtain. Indeed, before I left home I had read that the food of Cambodia was so awful that visitors couldn't wait to reach Vietnam where the cuisine had a reputation for excellence. Vietnamese food is rightly lauded but the food of Cambodia was every bit as good, indeed some of its finest examples stood shoulder to shoulder with its more internationally recognised neighbour.

Enjoy the journey...........

Ian Walker

The Delta

Touchdown

Twenty-four hours earlier I was sitting in a lounge at Heathrow airport. It is the beginning of April; spring is slowly arriving in the UK. It is still rather chilly and as usual everyone is moaning about the dank weather. Now, I'm stepping out of a hotel in downtown Saigon. The repressive heat blasts me like a furnace. Punch drunk from the tedious business of long haul jet travel and the delightful pleasures this offers its economy passengers. The smell of cheap coffee and mediocre food still seems to be wafting through my senses. The restrictive, sterile travel experience is blown away in the blink of an eye. It takes but a few strides before I am bombarded with a wide selection of offers. Massage sir, maybe a gold watch, tour mister or would the English gentleman like something a little exotic? If you like motorbikes, you'll love this place. I once read somewhere that if every person who owned a motorbike decided to take to the streets at the same time, there would be total gridlock. Road safety though is not so advanced. The death rates are alarming, the use of crash helmets considered unnecessary and more than one person on a bike mandatory. If there are any traffic rules, these might be considered a little inconvenient. Riding pillion carrying large sheets of glass or clinging to a fridge is normal behaviour. Crossing the road on foot a complete exercise in practicing suicidal strategies. Trust me, the good old Green Cross Code is about as useful as a record player with no needle. Courage is your best friend.

Anyone who has watched one of the big budget Hollywood movies about the Vietnam War, read the Quiet American by Graham Greene or studied the history will all have painted a mental picture of Saigon. The very mention seems to conjure up ill conceived romantic liaisons and high adrenaline pumping adventure. The human reality, cost and enduring spirit of its tenacious people can be observed in many locations. Take the famous noodle bar that played host to American service men – if only they had known that upstairs in that very building, high ranking officials from the North were planning the Tet offensive. The jovial atmosphere would surely have been very different. It is still open serving noodles and offers tourists a powerful reminder of the chaos that reigned here.

There is a spontaneity and infectious energy that grips this city. The economic surge in the east has catapulted Saigon towards a different future. Designer shops, new shopping malls, Western style eateries, the youth's appetite for information and new technology are bringing sweeping changes. The streets are paved with promise. Burger bars and other fast food outlets maybe evident here but the Vietnamese also have an insatiable appetite and deep pride for their national cuisine.

In the early evening nightly food markets spring up all over the city. Canopies are thrown up, plastic chairs and stools surround matching tables. Cooks pick, chop and wash. Inviting smells of intense stocks, fish grilling on barbecues and fragrant bunches of herbs mingle with the sounds of cleavers slamming through meat and locals slurping noodles. Memories of stodgy airline food are wrenched from within me and dumped in the garbage bins of food hell.

The next morning, I check out of the rather plush boutique hotel I had chosen for a first night of luxury. The receptionist interrogates me at length over a missing laundry bag from my room. I feign innocence. She's lucky I didn't leave with the bathroom suite. The sight of this departing on various motorbikes would have lent me legendary status.

After a few false dawns I am finally nestled at the back of a public bus awaiting departure for My Tho. My fellow passengers are busy buying lottery tickets and poring over fake gold watches. The driver is urinating behind the bus and the conductor is on the roof securing luggage. Soon we are clear of the city and hurtling along Highway 1.

There are several lanes in operation, two officially marked out; the third is a complete free for all. Like a game of chicken on a much grander scale, lane three is strictly for the hardcore. The sounds of blaring horns pierce my eardrums as vehicles roar past. For those of a nervous disposition it may ruin you. This is adrenaline junkie heaven.

Seventy kilometres south west of Saigon, My Tho is my gateway to the Mekong Delta. Within minutes of alighting, I'm perched on the back of a motorbike taxi heading for Ben Tre. A short drive brings us to a port and affords me the first view of the mighty Mekong River. Passenger ferries are still a vital transportation in these parts. The complexity of the delta infrastructure is such that their daily operation is a lifeline for this highly populated area. Bikes hum along the jetty with slick efficiency. The ferry is loaded within minutes. The great river's flow is fast as it rushes towards its conclusion and dumps into the South China Sea. I look back against its flow and dream of the journey ahead. This is my guide of the coming months.

Upon disembarking my taxi makes steady progress. The pungent smell of fermenting fish follows us everywhere. Large green, spiky Durians line the road every hundred metres. This unique fruit translates as 'one's sorrow'. Is this justified? Consider a mixture of pigs' muck, turpentine, rotting onions and a pair of old, sweaty gym socks and I'll allow you to draw your own conclusions. Here though, it is revered. I decide to keep my comments to myself. Imagine the punishment for abusing a national favourite? One week in solitary with fifty fruits perhaps, could anyone stand such torture?

Eggs, Eel and Volcanoes

Hung is waiting patiently in front of the lake. Opposite the cold, calculated architecture of my Soviet style hotel, his elbows rest on the front of his motorbike. I met him a few days ago. Twenty-nine years old, he works for the Ben Tre tourism office situated in the main town of the same name. His slight physique, youthful face and shy demeanour shield a thirst for knowledge. The introduction to the cuisine here has plunged me straight to the core of the region. The food, attitude, desire and passion have been force-fed. In my excitement, sleep deprivation has taken hold. The tiredness though is relegated as I'm swept along in a culinary tidal wave of freedom and expression.

The first day, well one hour after meeting him, I'm shopping for food to have dinner with his family. The ease and fluidity of the situation is totally refreshing. The main covered market is well stocked. We arrive on two wheels, shop, buy and negotiate through the aisles without leaving the comfort of our seats. Enthusiastic sellers tout their produce. We purchase fish from ladies crouched on the blood splattered floor. Dark blue fish, the size of roach with distinctive black stripes flap about on aluminium trays. A bowl sits behind her fed by water from a pipe. Half a kilogram is weighed out. A crack of the knife on the head, scales released and guts removed, followed by a thorough rinse, quick drain and dropped into a thin bag. A lady passes laden with sweet goodies and in seconds I'm munching away on a doughnut made from rice flour, peanuts and a heavy sugar coating. People caught in the congested gangways shout, sound horns and rev their engines.

The subsequent dinner was well received. One dish in particular stood out for its aggressive use of cracked black pepper. Hung's sister, Oanh, had prepared two thick steaks from a basa fish. This white-fleshed river specimen sits in a round oval clay pot. Thin slices of garlic, red chilli, onion, fish sauce, salt and a pinch of sugar are added. She then sprinkles over a generous quantity of the pepper and allows this to marinate for about half an hour. Cooked over a medium flame for between twenty and thirty minutes, the resulting dish is a revelation. The dark liquid is intense. It is a long time since I have praised black pepper so much. Have I taken this spice for granted much of my cooking life? This early episode has ignited my appreciation. As cooks, we seem pre-occupied with exploring new ingredients, thus neglecting a basic store cupboard condiment.

Ben Tre is famed for its fierce resistance against the Americans during the war. The province is justifiably proud of this and equally so for its culinary treasure. Coconuts have a huge prominence here. The plantations produce a significant portion of the tropical palm nut. For lunch one day, Hung drives me to a restaurant on the banks of the Ben Tre River. Reached via several narrow streets, the houses open straight into the restricted space. Locals swing in hammocks, sip coffee and chat with neighbours on stools as we drive by. The time is only 11am, that morning's bowl of pho consumed for breakfast is still working its magic. The establishment is devoid of any custom. Still, the Vietnamese eat when they are hungry; the dictation of meal times is an alien concept here. Large swathes of water borne plants called Luc Binh flourish in the water. At certain times of the year they produce a spectacular colourful flower. An old jetty, still intact, is no longer used. Formerly a landing station for boats, the construction of a bridge downriver is a growing trend all over the delta.

The first two dishes delivered contain coconut in some guise. Four enormous plump river prawns, their long red pincers still intact, hit the table. Simmered in coconut water with a hint of salt and sugar, the meaty flesh is sweet and juicy. Tiny dishes of salt, red chilli and lime wedges sit to the side. I happily squeeze the juice, mix them together, dip the pink gems and wallow in the sheer, delightful, simplicity of it all. Something more complex follows. A slight confusion leaves me believing I am just about to tuck into pork meat. I must admit I've never seen a pig that hops, swims and hides out in rice fields. Glimpses of dark green skin leave me utterly perplexed. Hung grabs his small computer device that he is never without. He types in the word '*ech*'. Thanks to the brilliance of modern technology, I now know I am not eating the protein of a rare, water loving leaping pig. Instead, the tiny morsels are very much amphibian. Chopped up pieces of frog, fried with nutty brown garlic and onion is simmered in coconut milk, thickened with a rice flour paste and flavoured with bitter gourd leaves, thickly shredded wood ear mushrooms and topped with chopped crunchy peanuts and spring onions. The bitter leaves are exactly that. Their flavour adds a striking balance with the coconut milk and the already common theme of adding a little sugar to the pot.

On the table behind us, our waiter places a small stove. With its gas canister slotted underneath, it is identical to the convenient appliances that people use when camping. A pan with a lid sits ready for action. I briefly wonder why this is not performed at our own table. The flame is ignited and the cooking commences. Intrigued, I stand up and move to observe. The waiter releases the lid; aromatic steam rises and shoots directly up my nose. He seems a little tense now. Quickly he picks up a plate next to him. Slivery eels writhe as they prepare to enter the boiling mass. In they go. He slams the lid down. The fight to keep it tight and secure as the liquid erupts offers a few anxious moments. The theatre of the spectacle is compelling. My days at catering college preparing Steak Diane and Beef Stroganoff seem like a formal exercise in conservative cookery. This is the stuff of revolutionaries. I know of a legendary cookery writer and TV presenter that would perform naked cartwheels at such a show of exhibitionism. Things have settled down in the pan now and everything is transported to our table. A garnish plate of thick slices of white radish, water celery and lime wedges are delivered along with a bowl of cooked rice noodles in the exact shape of spaghetti. The broth surprisingly omits fish sauce and lemongrass. We add the garnish and heat for a few minutes. The liquid has a delicate, sweet flavour and slightly sour notes. I crunch through the soft, pliable bone of the tiny, earthy eel. These once wriggling creatures now sit digesting in my stomach. All this instantaneous excitement and it is only midday.

I'm sitting in a restaurant about 5 km out of town. Carry on and you end up back at the ferry port. The road is lined with dining establishments. The majority are open-air and many specialise in certain culinary practices. Dog, rabbit, goat, seafood and barbecue restaurants all do battle for your custom. Hung has brought a friend with him tonight. With a fuller face, stocky frame and elaborate quaffed hairstyle, Lamp appears almost obese for these parts. His English tongue is as comprehensive as my guidebook Vietnamese. Direct communication is limited. The bikes are conveniently parked outside. An attendant issues a ticket and marks each seat with white chalk.

At the table, a petite young lady arrives with menus. Dressed in tight fitting jeans and a striking figure hugging T-shirt, her beauty is clearly apparent. Confidence and a slight arrogance suggest she needs no reminding. I nudge Hung and rib him a little. Single at the moment, the need for a wife is fast approaching. He jokes that he needs to earn more money and boost his career prospects before entertaining the admiration of the right woman. 'Is it like this in England?' he asks. 'Not exactly,' I tell him. 'Sometimes, as men we look for a woman with money. Equal rights and opportunities are the buzzwords in the UK.' I'm not sure if he is shocked, puzzled or thinks this prospect is totally absurd.

What she has in beauty though, she lacks in brains. She hands me the menus. I swiftly launch them over to my amused companions. The sky, magnified by a blanket of brilliant stars offers assistance to the dim, feeble lighting.

In food, I believe you don't really know a country until you have eaten everything it has to offer. It can challenge your very perception of the cuisine and its people. Embracing this theory, for me is the minimum requirement. However, I'm just about to test this like never before. It all starts very innocently. A lady appears from a set of white swing doors that separates the kitchen from the seating area. A pan balances on the gas stove she carries. Unlike the eel episode, she places it immediately on the table. I'm not sure if I'm pleased or disappointed. The thought of another thrilling gastronomic encounter rather appeals. A second lady brings a garnish plate of bitter gourd leaves, chunks of cucumber, lettuce and a separate bowl of six white eggs. Hung and Lamp both smile. Their expressions though have a certain smug, unnerving glow to them. I glare at them inquisitively. I study the contents in the pan. All perfectly innocent. A crab based stock, minced white fish balls, button mushrooms and some grains of rice. So, why do I feel so uneasy? Two very different and significant events are about to unfold.

A third lady appears. She lifts the lid. The contents are boiling furiously. She lowers the heat. The eggs remain intact. Many thoughts stream through my brain. Maybe they are hard-boiled. Is she about to peel and slice them into the pot? If raw, she could crack them into a bowl and whisk them. Poaching them whole may also be an option. I settle on the last theory. Soft poached eggs, delicious crab broth and meaty fish balls. I'm so convinced of the result, I ease back in my chair and sip on an ice-cold coke. The moment of truth is upon us. A solitary egg is gently lifted. She hovers over the simmering pan. A gentle crack sounds as she connects with the edge. The slight hollow note blows the hard-boiled theory out of the water. No bowl to hand. The whisked scrambled idea is now not an option. I must be right. I sense the arrival of the thick white albumen and the whole pale yellow yolk as it hits the hot liquid and begins to coagulate. Here it comes. The contents drop easily from the shell. In that microsecond before the contents join the pot a stunning realisation thunders through my every bone. Things are not as they seem.

Am I going completely mad? Is the heat and sleep deprivation clouding my clear judgement? Maybe I'm dehydrated? Someone could have spiked my drink with a mind-altering narcotic. That's it. I must be hallucinating. Whatever state my mind is in, I'm convinced I saw a black object drop from the shell. She quickly repeats the process with two further eggs. Hung and Lamp study me carefully. A look of disturbing amusement is etched across their faces. They had promised me something special tonight and delivery in their eyes is close to fruition. The lid is secured once more.

Already reeling from this episode, my mind in meltdown and alarmed at what I might be about to eat, another event is unfolding. A heated commotion has broken out. In the entrance two ladies have got each other by the hair. Their aggressive screams resonate, breaking the still night air. Hatred swells in their pierced eyes. The dispute spills into the restaurant. Members of the staff rush over to intervene. Their attempts have little impact. The ferocity intensifies. The smaller of the women releases her hand from the tight grip of the older ladies long, straight hair. Her right hand plants a stupendous swinging punch to the jaw of her opponent. She reels away briefly, the impact of the blow causing her to stumble. Quickly though, she turns and lands and almighty riposte. A cracking straight right connects with the side of her wild rival. These two feel no pain though. Further vicious blows are exchanged. Little notice is taken of a tall, wiry young man who has just burst into the restaurant. Without breaking stride his propelling right arm is unleashed. He lands a massive, crunching right hand uppercut to the unsuspecting older lady. The brutal assault leaves me in a rage. I force myself to stay seated though. Domestic violence is best left to the locals and not some well meaning European stranger. In any case, having witnessed the ferocity of these hardcore women my seat seems like a safe haven. They scare me more than the solitary man. Hung though has other ideas. He leaps to his feet, outraged and embarrassed at this awful spectacle. He is almost upon the action when a man appears from behind the swing doors. Maybe he is the owner. He certainly approaches with confidence and authority. Words are spoken and gradually the situation seems to calm a little. The separation is complete when he guides the older woman to the safety of the kitchen. Hung returns, his brave conciliatory services no longer required.

That battle seems to have reached its conclusion. Mine though is just about to begin. During the Ben Tre mixed world boxing bout, the mystery of the egg has been concealed under the tight fitting lid. Lamp removes it and stirs the contents. My eyes are fixed firmly on the pan. All other thoughts are erased; my concentration zooms in on just one thing. He lifts out the object of my fascination. Intrigue turns to horror. For maybe one of the first times in my life I'm totally speechless. Getting me to shut up is akin to asking a politician to give you a straight answer. A nauseating feeling sends shockwaves through my shaking body. This is no normal egg. The speciality of the house is the fertilised embryo of a duck. It is matured until it is not quite a foetus. Bloody hell, I'm just about to eat an abortion. S**t! My trauma is abruptly interrupted when, having spotted the old lady being released from the safety of the kitchen, the wiry chap runs back in and inflicts another savage blow. This is all getting a bit much. This guy is seriously stretching my patience. How rude can you get? Can't he see that I'm suffering serious turmoil here! I'm just about to eat an aborted duck and he thinks it is acceptable to disturb my moment of moral dilemma. The agony of contemplating eating it leaves me in a difficult cultural situation. I have never before turned down anything on my travels. Dog, monkey, small bush animals, fermented camel's milk and unusual reptiles have all been consumed with no guilt. Is this any different? Nothing makes you think as much as when the reality is so clear. This embryo was maybe days from becoming a duckling. That thought sends a sharp pain to my conscience. I try to think clearly, rationally and with little emotion. I promised myself that I would eat anything the locals would eat. I take a deep breath. I have to eat it.

As one is placed in my bowl, I study it more closely. The minuscule eyes seem to come alive as they glare deep inside my soul. I'm sure the others are showing equal solidarity. A little broth and garnish is served. I pick up my chopsticks and clamp it gingerly. A mass of blood vessels is attached to the minute body. I draw it slowly to my mouth and take a hesitant bite. I crunch down on the bones that disintegrate readily. A few tiny feathers tickle my tongue. The grainy pudding texture of the blood sac follows quickly. Eating food like this offers an immense psychological battle. Once this is overcome, the taste and experience seem to become easier. The body is far from offensive and I even take some pleasure from eating it. The blood vessels though are quite revolting and cause me to choke in the anticipation of a trip to the lavatory facilities. The broth flavoured with pounded crab shells is delicious. Light, sweet and packed with flavour. The fish balls slightly rubbery, meaty texture is a welcome return to familiarity. It has been quite a day.

Soul Food

Identifying a nation's cuisine with one dish could, on the surface, seem a little naive. Indeed which dish would you select for France? Coq au Vin, Bouillabaisse, Cassoulet, Pot au Feu? In Italy, how do you choose between Osso Bucco in the north and Pizza Napoletana in the south? Would you choose roast beef and Yorkshire pudding in England, Haggis in Scotland, Irish stew in Ireland and Laver bread in Wales? You can't say hamburger and fries in the USA can you? Mole in Mexico, Fejioda in Brazil, Moussaka in Greece or Chicken Bhuna in India? The answer to this is an emphatic no. However, just occasionally you discover one such dish that binds its people and demonstrates that food has a celestial and spiritual power beyond its simplicity. Even if you can't quite call it the national dish, it could easily be considered an addictive obsession.

Every morning I would stroll along to Hung's office on the corner of the main drag. My slight time keeping problem would mean missing our 7.30am meeting and arriving nearer 8am. Hung would always hop on the bike for a journey that took less than thirty seconds. The first time he did this I had assumed the journey would be a little longer. 'Why don't you walk such a short distance?' I ask. You'd have thought I'd just asked him to run a marathon. Walk? You English people have some funny ideas, might have been his response. Instead he entertains my comments with silence and a simple shrug of the shoulders.

Anh Hong is not a unique restaurant. Like thousands of similar establishments up and down the length of this country it serves just one dish. It doesn't have a menu; well, with no choice it would seem rather foolish. What a great concept. You don't even have to engage your brain. Here they open for business at 6am and wind things up about four hours later. With its high ceiling, whitewashed distressed walls and sparse simple furnishings it continues the trend of simplicity.

Originating in Hanoi, the ubiquitous *pho*, pronounced *fur* or *fuh* is entrenched in the psyche of the Vietnamese. Traditionally served in the north for breakfast, this sublime bowl of food fuels its people for the coming day. I've eaten other things for breakfast here. I enjoyed *com tam* one morning. Three thin slices of grilled belly pork marinated in chilli, sugar and oil was very acceptable. The plate of fluffy steamed rice used cracked grain the size of couscous. A sauce of coconut water, chilli and sugar is used to spoon over the rice and the grated cucumber that is heaped to the side of the sticky meat. As a palate cleanser a small bowl of broth with minced pork, carrot and white radish slices is a fine touch.

The history of pho has been much debated by literary scholars. Influences of a thousand years of Chinese rule and almost one hundred years of French occupation are incredibly significant. There can be no doubt that many of the ingredients including rice noodles and spices were imported from China. The real credit though is almost certainly attributed to the foundations of French European cookery. It has long been thought that the popular classic *pot au feu* was the catalyst in the creation of pho. There are many things that can easily quantify this theory. The French certainly popularised the use of red meat. Prior to this, the Vietnamese had rarely contemplated eating cows and buffaloes. These were highly valued and considered as indispensable beasts of burden. At this time, their preferred choice was pork, chicken and seafood. French cooks used bones and meat trimmings to produce wonderfully rich stocks that caught the native imagination. The Vietnamese cooks of the mid-1880s seized on this foundation and began to introduce their own flavours. The impact was immediate and soon word spread of this new phenomenon. Originally the recipe was a simple affair and relied on very few ingredients. For many years it remained a dish enjoyed only by those lucky enough to live in the north. However, in 1954 pho was about to experience a different, more indulgent attitude. The communist north was now divided from the south. Over one million inhabitants fled south during the fighting. This single episode catapulted pho to a wider audience. In the cafes of Saigon people who were used to eating *hu tieu*, a bowl of noodles with a broth made from pork bones and meat, were beating a hasty retreat. The stampede and excitement that greeted its arrival is perhaps one of the most notable culinary social shifts in the country's long history. Innovative cooks grabbed the opportunity to introduce more complexity to its preparation. Different garnishes were added, sauces made to accompany, and herbs became more important. Meat was also in more abundance and the introduction of a greater quantity to the finished dish can be accredited to this. The story of pho though has far more significance than just food for the Vietnamese. Many consider it a symbol of freedom, a product of self-determination and the single most important sign of unification among its people. It is this that makes it so uniquely Vietnamese and without it the country would be indelibly poorer.

The preparation begins the previous day. Great pho needs an exceptional stock. The recipe at Anh Hong has been passed down through the generations of this family restaurant. In a large, solid boiling pot they put shinbones, oxtail, a piece of meat like brisket and any other scraps that are available. Cold water is added to cover. It is then bought to the boil and simmered for a total of eighteen hours. Towards the end of cooking a mixture of spices is added. Regional differences exist in this area. Root ginger, star anise and cinnamon bark is the favoured combination of this establishment. To the side of the pot a bowl of orange fat is evident. This contains the carefully skimmed impurities that are released from the bones. It is this meticulous care and attention that produces the clarity required for any master stock. My days of tending and nurturing veal and beef stocks in the many restaurants I worked in, come flooding back to me. The simple, pure pleasure of creating an outstanding liquid from such basic ingredients is a highly satisfying reward for the diligent cook.

A container of chopsticks, metal spoons and a tissue box furnish the simple table. A bottle of chilli and tomato sauce stands next to a peanut concoction. The compact busy cooking and preparation area is a well-marshalled slick operation. A lady washes herbs and bean sprouts. She arranges them neatly on plates and consistently replenishes as staff members whisk them over to customers. Behind, another sits on a stool and skilfully slices wafer thin pieces from a slab of beef. Using an enormous cleaver, her proficiency with such a large tool is readily admired. Raw fine rice noodles like vermicelli sit positioned next to a pot of boiling water. A lady with a long armed sieve constantly blanches these ready for the bowls at the front. Two cooks are responsible for building the ingredients in to the finished dish. First, the noodles are deposited. The glorious clear steaming stock is ladled over and the slices of raw beef placed on the top. A liberal sprinkling of chopped herbs, spring onions and slivers of raw garlic come next. The orange fat is not completely wasted. A few drops are added at the last moment before the bowls are whisked away to more eager waiting patrons. At Anh Hong a small bowl of additional stock containing the slowly braised meat from the pot is served in conjunction with the main attraction.

On a table opposite, four animated men chat enthusiastically. They seem to pause and fall silent to pay homage to the heavenly bowls placed before them. A waitress appears with a metal bowl containing bones from the stockpot. She dumps them ceremonially in the centre of the table and places a sharp knife to the side. Without delay they are being picked apart for any scraps of gelatinous meat. Seemingly a little impatient, one man grabs a bone with two hands and begins sucking flesh with the determination of a hyena gorging on a wildebeest.

The tantalising aroma that fills the room reaches its peak when the pho is placed before you. I watch Hung as he educates me on the etiquette that, at this very moment, millions of people all over the country will be instinctively performing. He squeezes some tomato and chilli sauce onto a tiny plate. From the garnish plate, sparklingly fresh mint and basil are torn and added to the bowl. Crunchy, juicy bean sprouts and a good squeeze of lime juice are the final addition. He lifts the noodles high from the bowl as he grasps them with his chopsticks. They plunge back into the steaming liquid and combine with the other ingredients. I shadow his every move. I watch as the slices of red meat gradually change colour. The intoxicating aroma from the beef stock begins to cast its addictive spell. I suck up the noodles, slurp the broth and dip meat into the chilli sauce.

The stock is deep and rich. Subtle notes of cinnamon, star anise and ginger sing on my palate. Hits of fresh herbs enliven. Any thoughts that the complexity of flavours would overwhelm me vanish in a nanosecond. Right now, this humble establishment feels like a gastronomic paradise. No matter that the floor is covered with scraps of meat, escaping noodles, cigarette butts and discarded tissues. A military coup could be happening outside and I wouldn't notice. The combination of fluids, protein and carbohydrate are the perfect nutritious start to the heat of another day. It leaves you completely satisfied without bloating your stomach. This is food that is socially cohesive. Rarely prepared in the home, this tour de force can be enjoyed by rich and poor alike. It makes no distinction of rank and file. It spreads wealth throughout its people and costs very little. It is quite simply a national institution.

Lau Mam

Since my arrival Hung has been waxing lyrical about a Mekong speciality he insists I must try before I leave. The food in Ben Tre has been constantly intriguing. I've enjoyed delicious grilled goat meat marinated in chilli, sugar, salt and garlic. You cook the meat yourself on a dome shaped vessel fired with charcoal. Using small sheets of rice paper you construct a delicious mini roll using grilled okra, basil leaves, cucumber and thin slices of green banana. This is then dipped in a sauce made from soy cream, red chilli, peanuts and soy sauce.

Steamed river clams with fine shavings of ginger, dipped in salt, black pepper and lime juice. Stir-fried baby squid with florets of cauliflower, strips of carrot, celery root, coriander leaves and flowering chives is an honest use of ingredients. Finally, fried rabbit cooked in coconut water, finished with local honey and crunchy peanuts is extremely moreish.

Lau Mam, though, fails to excite any passion among the already splendid array of food I've been feasting on. Essentially it is a fish stew with pork. The first step is to simmer some salted fish in water. The resulting liquor is then strained. Thin slices of belly pork, lemongrass and garlic are then braised until the pork is soft. Chopped eggplant, bitter gourd and sliced red chilli enter the pan. Next comes an assortment of fresh fish and shellfish. Here the selection included basa, shrimp, squid, eel, skate and minced fish balls. Covered with a lid, this is all then simmered until the fish is cooked.

The proprietor, a jovial lady, was most interested to hear my verdict. Not wishing to offend I feign a smile and offer many congratulations. It all started to go wrong when the lid was released at the table. A fowl pungent stench almost knocked me clean from my rickety chair. An instant nausea grips me. Early memories of cheap, dried Parmesan cheese, mixed with a powerful British cheese called Stinking Bishop and sweaty underwear do little to inspire me. All the fish is drowned by the intensity of the powerful salt base. I struggle to identify any single distinguishing flavour as I dutifully force a few servings down my neck and apologise to my unfortunate stomach.

Market Mice

After a final bowl of pho at Anh Hong, I bid farewell to the owner and her staff. Hung is busy negotiating transport for my onward journey. Upon his insistence I am travelling the more interesting route through the countryside. He hands me a CD of traditional Vietnamese music, a piece of paper with useful information and advises me to eat snake if I visit Sa Dec.

The passage to Vinh Long takes me through many small towns and villages. The wind is lively today and the stiff hot breeze blasts across my face, drying my skin. At first my driver makes swift progress on the smooth tarmac road. The motorbike zips along, its tiny engine responding willingly. Around 11am the schools turn out. Waves of elegant girls dressed immaculately in flowing white silk gowns flood the streets. Poised with exacting posture, they sit bolt upright with perfect straight backs, as they cycle home, chatting happily with their friends. A young boy careers along on a bike that is much too big for him. He laughs infectiously as he struggles to gain any control while he hurtles downhill. He employs his feet as he attempts to slow the bike. His carefree attitude brings a grin to my face. The smell of grilling chicken and pork do battle with burning incense for the predominant aroma. Farmers with large sticks herd solitary cows; water buffalo can be seen penned into enclosures and pigs caged in bamboo crates are towed by bikes.

We turn off the main road and the flawless tarmac gives way to a dusty, bumpy, red brick rabble. Our speed slows considerably. Buses pay little attention to the quality of the track, surging past, throwing up clouds of red earth that shower our bodies, blur our vision and physically choke us. I admire the extensive fruit orchards, with row upon row of orderly formed trees irrigated by efficient neat canals that run through them sustaining the roots and developing the fruit. Banana trees, leaves yellow in places, patiently wait for the expected deluge of precipitation that announces the rainy season. Mangoes, longons, papaya, tamarind, jackfruit, durian, custard apples and plums will flourish and ripen quickly when the rains come. This is a critical time for all of the farmers here, whose very existence depends on a decent harvest.

We make a number of ferry crossings as we criss-cross the extensive network of waterways that form this unique landscape. Occasional colourful, elaborate pagodas break up the mass of fruit trees. Reminders of the river's importance are numerous. Men who heave crates ashore unload large barges stacked with spiky green durians. A multitude of coconut processing factories are conveniently positioned. Huge piles of shells create little mountains. The smell of the creamy flesh lingers in the warm air. I stop by the roadside and buy the first of the seasons rambutans. A series of stalls advertise bunches of the red spiky skinned fruit. A man dozes in his hammock sheltered from the midday sun. The young lady serving delights in practising her English. For the equivalent of twelve pence I purchase an enormous bunch. In the UK a packet of just six fruits may cost around £2.00. I pierce the leathery surface to reveal the white gleaming flesh inside and suck on the fragrant fruit. Its sweet and slightly acidic taste is a joy. I spit out the soft cushioned stone and allow the fresh, perfumed flavour to loiter in my delighted mouth. The excitement of eating fruit at source should never be underestimated. The wide expanse of the Song Co Chien River is the final crossing before you reach Vinh Long.

The previous day's journey has left me nursing some trademark British scars. The lower parts of my arms are beetroot red, my tingling hands are burnt and uncomfortable. I only remembered that I had packed a bottle of factor 15 sun lotion when it tumbled onto the floor of my hotel room. Dressed in a cool, long sleeved cotton shirt I embark on another day.

Vinh Long is a place in transition. Extensive building work is underway in preparation for an upgrade from town to city status. The town planners have ambitious projects to develop this area into the jewel of the region by 2010. Some bright spark has even managed to convince the marketing department to describe it as a Riviera destination. Maybe they should check the exact translation of the term first. It is true that the climate and vegetation are subtropical. Even the most accomplished exponents of public relations though, would struggle to convince that it is a coastal region. My mind wanders briefly to the chic destinations in southern France and northern Italy that one uses as a benchmark.

The bowl of pho in my hotel's restaurant represented a

humiliation to the art. No doubt the six young American blondes screaming for french fries didn't care. The undistinguished broth was served with egg noodles and a plate of herbs that looked like they had been dragged out of the refuse. I register my disgust silently and leave rapidly after only a spoonful. The morning streets are thronging with activity. Stallholders spray water to refresh produce and labourers busy themselves digging.

I've arranged to meet Van at the small agency that she owns. She arrives punctually at 7am riding pillion on the back of her husband's motorbike. She has agreed to show me around the main food market that is situated about 400m up the road. The floor is wet, muddy and uneven as we ease our way into the covered, ramshackle area. Immediately I am hit with the delightful morning sight of tripe, significant blocks of dark congealed blood, bowls of beef kidneys and every other element of an animals anatomy. A seller pulls out a long singular white veined trail of intestines as an eager customer moves in for a closer examination. For me this represents a mind mangling alteration in food attitude. The direct, open honesty is enough to alarm your average British supermarket shopper into abandoning meat consumption completely. In the UK, eating liver, kidneys or any offal is considered only for the brave hardcore who recognise the benefits of these tasty delights. Here, the appreciation of the whole beast reminds me of how far removed we have become from the animals we eat. This is no freak show, but the direct reality of everyday life to the humble cooks of this area. Every last scrap is utilised, the possibilities for cooks hold no boundaries.

The putrid smells that violated my airway a few seconds ago seem to quickly disappear as I become engrossed in the environment. A slightly familiar display grabs my attention. An abundance of orange flowers with bees hovering in and out remind me of courgette flowers so loved by the Italians. However, these are the flowers of the pumpkin. Van tells me they are delicious stuffed with minced pork and fish. Seasoned with a little black pepper, sugar and salt, they are then dusted in rice flour and deep-fried until crisp. Dipped in a little fish sauce before eating, I find it impossible to disagree.

We make our way to the rear of the market. Buckets of salted Mekong crabs sit on the ground. These small crustaceans live in the water coconut palms that are a feature of the region. If you have made it this far, the next tourist attractions are spatchcocked mice, their larger cousins the rats and bound up frogs that freak out when the flash illuminates from my camera. A lady squats on a stool surrounded by some unflattering headless shrimps that attract a mass of flies picking at the dead flesh. She is eating a bowl of shrimp soup completely unperturbed by the insects, occasionally glancing up in the hope of some customers that I fear may never appear. I hope she is enjoying the soup, for I guess she may be resigned to cooking these sorry specimens herself tomorrow.

The action is unrelenting, a multitude of tasks being performed at every juncture. Women deftly slice banana flowers with lightening efficiency into wide blue bowls, the fine heap of shreds the epitome of exacting perfection. Some waterfowl intrigues me. The skinned birds with their beaks intact and skins removed are the size of small quails, although I don't find out their name. Equally fascinating, are a group of headless, skinned frog, these creatures are still very much alive and in the cruellest of ironies share a tray with some fully intact frogs that I'm sure must be taunting their naked brethrens.

The back of the market leads straight to the river. The striking blue vessels sit docked, their crew resting, unloading or carrying out essential maintenance. All the fish on display here are alive. Amusingly one leaps out of a bowl. A small catfish slivers and slides on the muddy surface. It is only a few feet away from me so in a show of solidarity to the traders I decide to retrieve it. I lunge at it quickly and attempt to grab its tail. Although I make contact it slips easily away. I try again; this time aiming further up the body, although alas with the same success. My comical efforts though seem to have endeared me to the traders. Ripples of laughter turn into roars of hysteria as I almost dive in my final attempt. Three strikes and I am officially out as young man appears, still in the throes of hilarity and spares me any further embarrassment. The variety of fresh water species is astounding. Van ushers me over to show me her favourite. Sporting a distinctive yellow tail, this wild fish from the Mekong is a victim of its own culinary success. Over fishing has been cruel to it and she fears for its survival. Farmed fish is providing the solution to this and many other species that have been hunted to near extinction in these vast waters. The desire for fish is such that the boom in farming is fuelling a most unique situation in the region. Vietnam and in particular the fertile, rich land of the delta is the second largest exporter of rice in the world. However, such is the demand and possible lucrative rewards for fish that, many people are destroying their rice fields to build ponds and lakes to exploit the potentially higher returns and boost their standard of living. With both the domestic and export markets rampant and showing no signs of slowing in the near future, it is difficult to argue. A surplus of fish though, may lead to a huge deficit in the production of rice. This represents an astonishing twist that is littered with much irony.

Moving on, we pass big tanks that are packed solid with writhing black and white striped water snakes. A stout lady quickly lifts the lid and proficiently hooks one of the thin creatures. Without delay she slams the cover shut. I imagine the chaos if they were all to escape. On the floor a pink bowl rests. The lady, who is wearing bright yellow sandals adorned with huge blue bows, grabs a sharp knife. She runs the blade the length of the snake's body.

Blood splatters the floor as it is swiftly cleaned with water and thrown in with a group that are already prepared. Having never eaten snake I'm fascinated and incredibly curious to discover the merits of eating these reptiles. Hung had told me to eat snake in Sa Dec and now Van advises me that Ca Mau is the true destination to enjoy the experience. As in any area of the world, people's culinary views are subject to their own personal experience. I decide to investigate a little more before I make my decision. A few feet away I spot six tiny turtles swimming in a tank. The selling of these is totally illegal in Vietnam. Traders, buyers and the authorities though treat the law with much disdain. No attempt is made at concealing the animals. This is not some under the counter transaction but an openly traded commodity that is sold like all other food items.

Shrills, squeaks and snorts reverberate with the familiar sound of pigs. In an area designated exclusively for traders of these young livestock a group of buyers peer into strong steel open top cages. The majority of animals are afforded little space. Packed in very tightly, they lay motionless. The lucky ones who have room to manoeuvre brush against each other as they stand. Buying pigs to rear personally in the home is very popular here. It makes both practical and economical sense. Firstly, you can feed the animals what you choose and thus decide the quality of their diet. Secondly, the cost of buying a pig, rearing and slaughtering for the table is a fraction of the price of purchasing from the market. Unlike in the British Isles, it is considered perfectly acceptable to slaughter your own stock. Having made his choice, a man points to the pig he wishes to buy. The decibels are raised immediately. Wild hysteria greets a man as he is sent into the pen. A blue five is blazoned on the smooth, arched back of the animal. He grabs it firmly with both hands under the belly. It lets out a piercing high-pitched noise that penetrates my eardrums. A smaller single cage is standing by and the pink beast is stood in. The pen is lifted onto the waiting scales and the participants agree the weight and price. The cost is recorded in a black book and the sale is complete. With only a solitary pig to transport the buyer secures the animal in a cylindrical bamboo basket that he will attach to his waiting motorbike.

Leaving the market, we walk past plentiful sacks of rice and neat piles of dried shrimp. An impressive display of neatly stacked whole dried fish is a reminder of the techniques employed centuries ago to preserve the abundance of wild fish that these waters used to produce. These would more likely all come from farmed sources now. A lady chewing beetle nuts sits quietly in a chair. Her dark purple stained teeth a common sight amongst the elderly. The practice is said to strengthen their teeth and was once believed to help in the prevention of malaria. Van, a well-educated, knowledgeable individual assures me that malaria is no longer prevalent in this area. The practice is principally ignored by the youth who prefer not to have such a visual display on their teeth.

Opposite the market entrance is a covered walkway of inviting food stalls. Two men haul huge bundles of water hyacinth plants from the back of a tricycle and a frail, elderly woman crouches on the floor surrounded by a constant huddle of people. Concealed by her wooden conical hat, she dishes out bags of boiled water chestnuts from a deep wicker basket. With the sounds of the melodic singing of prices fading, we begin heading to the main meat market.

As we walk into the mass of hanging flesh on display, Van informs me that meat is not a popular choice for her or many younger Vietnamese. She, like them, is concerned with animal welfare and the quality of product that this produces. I don't know why, but this was the last thing I had expected to hear. She deplores the modern practices of intensive farming. The animals are pumped full of chemicals, fed a poor diet and raised with inhumane speed that basically cripples the animals. 'Is it the same in your country?' she asks. 'In many ways, sadly it is,' I tell her. Like her, I like to know where my meat has come from. Our shared beliefs cross a universal divide and I empathise with her views.

I look closely at some pork meat. The unimpressive flesh is flaccid. The white skin is loose and wet looking. This animal has clearly been reared aggressively resulting in a high yielding carcass that has sacrificed quality for quantity. The stench of blood, rancid fat and putrid entrails cling to the stale air. Flies land and settle grabbing what they can before being instinctively ushered away by a wafting hand. A woman, her legs tucked together to one side sits beneath a plump liver that hangs from a rusting hook. She brings a heavy cleaver down on some beef bones while a neighbouring trader slurps on a bowl of steaming broth. What I can't understand here is the lack of variety. I've only seen cow and pig meat for sale. I had expected a vast array of different kinds of fleshy protein. This leaves me a little bemused and I'll confess a little disappointed. I do love the raw intensity that these markets offer, as places where your imagination is ignited instantaneously and inspiration is rammed down your throat with brutal but mouth-watering force.

Street Food

The time is about 5pm as I step off the bus from Can Tho. I have just paid a visit to the city's sprawling university campus, where I met with several professors to discover a little specialist agricultural and aquacultural knowledge. Due to various factors, my stomach had been cruelly denied any food at lunch and was thus begging for grub to enter its grumbling domain. I begin the short walk back to the hotel from the main bus station. Across the road I see a plume of light smoke rising to the sky. Usually your brain issues instructions, although here my stomach overrules and almost jumps out and is there before my head has registered the word food. The tantalising smell of grilling meat sends my belly into a nervous frenzy. The smoky charcoal aroma wafts slowly through the air leaving me salivating. A man stands over the small mobile unit. Positioned slightly off the pavement, it rests against the irregular kerb. An electrical store, its contents spilling onto the street, provides the backdrop. The elderly owner, a wise looking fellow, stands chatting to the cook.

The compact unit is arranged with all the necessary components for a yummy snack. Pounded pork meat is threaded onto skewers and marinated in a sticky, chilli glaze. A pile of mini baguettes, bowls of shredded carrot, white radish, lettuce leaves and fresh whole leaf herbs are readily to hand. He has a jar filled with fish sauce that contains shredded pork rind. All his meat is cooked to order. Maybe the lack of refrigeration should be a concern. The hot air temperature and festering meat would be enough for the good old environmental health officers back home to haemorrhage into orgasm and head to the high court screaming blue murder. Having placed my order, I watch as the meat hits the smouldering heat of the charcoal-fuelled fire. This is essential for the spirit and taste of the cooked meat. Gas grills just don't cut it and add nothing to the finished flavour. The sticky glaze chars the meat as he quickly grills them on both sides. Within minutes he is assembling my snack. He grabs a baguette and splits it lengthways in half. The small kofta like grilled meat is deposited and quickly followed by the shredded carrot, juicy white radish, lettuce leaves, mint and basil leaves. A splash of chilli sauce follows and then he removes the lid from the large plastic jar. With a metal ladle he flicks a generous amount of the fish sauce and allows a few pieces of the pork rind to fall into the sandwich. Wrapped in a piece of newspaper; didn't we use to have fish and chips like that? Secured with an elastic band and in the time it takes to order a fast food meal deal you are presented with a quite superb, inexpensive treat.

Walking on, I turn right to the road that leads you to the waterfront. After a few minutes I approach a lady busying herself behind a mobile glass counter. Tiny inviting pots of what I instantly recognise as related to that French classic, crème caramel, are arranged neatly in the unit. There are also some triangular looking sponge cakes. I order both. She inserts a small wooden skewer through the sponge and places them in a tiny plastic sack.

Back at the hotel, my stomach's anguish is seconds from being appeased. I bite into the sandwich. The baguette, which has far outlasted its colonial rulers, is immensely enjoyable. The sweet sticky charred meat, the juicy root vegetables, and hit of fish sauce, chilli spice and perfumed herbs combine to produce a superlative piece of fast food. The chewy pieces of rind once more demonstrate the ingenuity of the cooks here. With the savoury element triumphantly digesting, I move onto the sponge. Filled with creamy banana custard flavoured with coconut, it fails to ignite any enthusiasm in me. The heavily manufactured cake has the texture of an inferior Victoria sponge and the highly processed sponge fingers that appear in trifles back home. The only thing it satisfies is the need for a sugar hit. The crème caramel though is much better. The dark liquid sugar is the correct colour. The slight acrid notes balance with the soft, baked custard and the local addition of creamy coconut is a praiseworthy touch.

The convenience of street food is undeniable. I love the interaction and total spontaneity that it offers. The colourful displays of food, the simple seating and dining arrangements that offer a communal atmosphere. The rows of covered food stalls I mentioned briefly earlier are an excellent example of this. Displaying food openly in this manner does leave you with one major issue though. When you are confronted with a blanket of lip-smacking food, how do you choose what not to eat? Four stalls in, I'm drawn to some light, crispy looking spring rolls. Managing to secure the last red plastic stool, I squeeze into a cramped space between two ladies. I allow my elbows to rest on the counter. I smile at the lady, and utter a few words in Vietnamese. Unsurprisingly I receive a bewildered blank look in return for my incompetent grasp of the language. I gesture towards the crispy rolls. She places six in a plastic bag and hands them to me. I motion for some dipping sauce like the woman is enjoying next to me. A tiny pot of fish sauce with a little coconut water contains slithers of white onion and sliced red chilli. Biting through the crispy exterior reveals the meaty texture of pounded pork and the addition of taro root. When I have finished I don't linger and stroll off to find something sweet. The very last stall on the corner delivers a quick, fascinating solution. A lady grills bananas that are encased in a paste made from sticky rice and the flesh of coconut. To begin the cooking process they are first wrapped in banana leaves to protect them from the fierce direct heat. This initial procedure allows moisture to build up inside and help the sticky rice to set. Once removed, they are placed on the charcoal grill and cooked until lightly charred and slightly smoky. To serve, the encrusted banana is placed in a deep plastic bowl and covered with sweet, silky coconut custard. The crust is delightfully chewy. Inside, the steamy fruit is soft, mellow and creamy. The thick custard is a little reminiscent of some packet varieties I know but the whole concept is pure comforting genius.

Scottish Delta

In these subtropical climes thousands of miles from home, the last thing I should be having thoughts about is a place that lies on the east coast of Scotland. Why am I having these feelings of nostalgia for a town that hugs the wild shores of the North Sea? Maybe the malarial medication is kicking in, causing me to lose all sense of reality and perspective. The restaurant I'm sitting in, although themed, is certainly not of Highland ancestry and the employees are not prancing about in kilts and playing bagpipes. I'm on this trip to discover the wild exotic foods of Indo-China not the benefit of deep-fried chocolate bars (ok, a little harsh, apologies) or haggis.

In front of me is a creation of such astounding simplicity and splendour that for a moment I'm frozen in a sea of admiration. I'm not sure what I was expecting when I spied the efficient waiter sauntering towards our round table carrying a charred piece of wood. The entire restaurant is filled with hexagonal, bamboo structures that allow you to eat in a degree of privacy. The tables seat at least eight people comfortably. Three young ladies accompany me this evening. Each one works at the Cu Long hotel in Vinh Long and after a little gentle persuasion they agreed to reveal their favourite food destination. Oanh is the most animated of the girls. Her bubbly personality exudes confidence as she discusses the menu with her friends. She asks me if I like mice. Her friend squirms at the mere suggestion while I ponder the question. In the UK, mice are considered pests. The many London kitchens I have worked in specialise in these small creatures. The urban city squalor is ideal breeding grounds for these rodents and restaurants employ varying tactics to catch them. Early morning inspections in the cities thousands of dining establishments are routine practice. The sight of dead mice caught in traps is as much a daily occurrence as a wet fish delivery. The fundamental difference though, is that while you drool over a slimy firm whole turbot ready for the day's special, the freshly caught mouse is discarded without any thought. The nearest we come to digesting one is the legendary white chocolate variety that I used to eat as a kid. Can it be true that she enjoys the flesh of this tiny intruder that my sister once stood on while stepping from her bed one morning in South London? It is another astonishing revelation of a cuisine that allows nothing to escape its attention.

Food comes to the table here in no particular order. Our own regimented style of serving appetiser, starter, main course and dessert is catapulted into the depths of the mighty Mekong. The freedom of expression is refreshing as dishes are delivered immediately upon completion. A simple plate of deep fried tofu is accompanied by a pot of sweet chilli sauce. Another has silky diced tofu suspended in fish sauce and chilli, which we mash up. The uniformed chunks have a light golden crisp exterior, while the centre is creamy and soft. I have a bit of a love-hate relationship with tofu; here though I enjoy its attributes and the salty, rich, creamy supplementary tofu dip is pure innovation. Stir fried green flowers arrived simultaneously. From a distance they remind me of the salty, marsh loving samphire that grows wild in many area of the British Isles. Whole cloves of caramelised garlic that retain a distinctive bite bolster the flowers delicate flavour. My Scottish connection comes next. In front of me is a length of charred, circular bamboo bark. My mind races as to guess what could possibly be concealed inside. The waiter carefully splits the bamboo down the centre and an alluring steamy smoke escapes as a whole fish is revealed. The agreeable smell of fish mixes with the scented bark and sends my mind racing thousands of miles away. Arbroath Smoky, I excitedly shout. The girls flash me a quizzical look. What on earth is this daft Englishman getting so keyed up about? It seems impossible but at this very moment, I'm struggling to look beyond the very qualities of a revered Scottish gastronomic delight. The similarities are certainly uncanny. Arbroath Smokies are made with haddock or even whiting. Having been beheaded, cleaned and dry salted they are then tied by their tails in pairs and hot smoked. Coppery brown on the outside with a creamy white flesh inside and a taste, best enjoyed while hot, that has a mellow, salty, smoky flavour. The Scots call this eating 'hot off the barrel'. Originally smoked over domestic fires, this gave way to numerous smoke pits, set up using half whiskey barrels that rested on ledges in the cliff face. The cliff top fishing village of Auchmithie is widely credited with the original process and only when families from here settled in Arbroath was the name changed. A traditionally prepared smoky is one of life's truly exceptional eating experiences. Here a river fish is used. First a skewer is fed through from head to tail and then placed in the bamboo. It is sealed and put on a fire of glowing charcoal where it steams and smokes while protected by the natural casing. The ingenuity of utilising the bamboo is practical, cheap and wholly beneficial to the end texture and flavour. The simple, pure method of cooking strips away the need for any elaborate flavours and thus would find favour with any fish loving soul.

Another such dish is a whole spatchcocked chicken (split from the back and flattened) covered with a mixture of wet clay. After this has set sufficiently, the cook bakes it for fifty minutes in an extreme heat. The bird is kept brilliantly moist and again the natural style of cooking is a triumph. Dipped in a little salt, black pepper and lime juice it is devoured with equal delight. During this period, the cooked mice have been delivered and sit unimpressively on the table. Once again they are spatchcocked. The scrawny rodents have been roasted in a fierce oven and glazed with honey. My moral experience with the duck foetus in Ben Tre has left me suitably prepared for such an occasion. They have been chopped in half, so I grab a piece and take a bite. Blindfolded, I would challenge any carnivore to find fault with the taste. Mind over matter rules here. The flesh is darker than chicken, offers a similar flavour with distinct light gamy attributes and I suck every last piece from its body. I stare at the naked carcass next to me and promise to never look at a mouse in the same way again.

Famous Tra Vinh

Seventy kilometres south east of Vinh Long is the serene town of Tra Vinh. The journey here was a little stop-start, accentuated by the fact that unlike buses back home, many only depart for their destination when full. The majority of the small to medium size vehicles are privately owned, so it is paramount to capitalise on every spare millimetre of space. Timetables for these do not exist. I spent four long hours in the dusty terminus while the driver and his wife slowly filled their humble vehicle. Food selling hawkers entertain me with an assortment of light snacks, drinks and ice creams. The competition is fierce, although there seems to be a calm equilibrium and respectful understanding between the ladies. On route, parched fields and huge mounds of conical shaped rice cuttings dominate the landscape. Turned a camel colour by the dry and sunny conditions, it is a sure sign that the rice season is at a close. Workers are now preparing the ground for next year's harvest. The void in proceedings makes the surrounding area feel curiously redundant of any life.

A commanding statue announces your arrival to the town. The powerful image of men bearing arms is a memorial to all those that fought in the American war. Just prior to this, shielded from view, is an impressive pagoda. There are said to be over 140 spread over this region, a direct result of the many Khmer people that were believed to have settled here first. Today they still account for thirty per cent of its population. Buddhism flourishes here and adds a tranquillity that has yet to touch me. By pure chance, my arrival coincides with their most important celebrations of the year. This weekend delivers Khmer New Year and with it a feast of colourful festivities.

The streets are less crowded here, the volume of bikes has decreased significantly and the general vibe is altogether more sedate. Impressive tall Sau Dau trees tower over the well-planned roads and offer a natural blanket of shade. Bright, colourful, blossoming flowers ignite a magical passion that seems ingrained in a community that glows with pride. The crumbling exteriors of old French colonial villas and houses are interspersed with sympathetically designed updated versions. The tired painted window shutters and washed out external walls are now quite distressed. Their obvious architectural charm still offers fading glimpses of the French designers' belief in building dwellings that oozed charm and integrated both practically and aesthetically in this subtropical environment. I sit and enjoy a coffee in a rather shabby establishment that neither appears to be a café nor a home. Two men play chess in the corner as I relax and watch life float dreamily by. The enduring benefits of this town seem to spread swiftly and wrap me comfortably in its enchanting spell.

Van arrives sharp at 8am the following morning. She sits quietly in the expansive foyer of the three stars Cu Long hotel. The personnel here are incredibly charming, very efficient and the well-kept large rooms are an absolute bargain. Her long black silky hair, high cheekbones and shy demeanour are sparked by a warm endearing smile. Long flared black trousers cover her dainty black-heeled shoes. She is far more curvaceous than many women of her age that I have seen since arriving in Vietnam. Last night she introduced me to a quite unique speciality of the region. Following on from some delicious rice paper spring rolls that we filled with grilled minced pork, shaved slices of green mango and banana, herbs, lettuce and cooked rice noodles, she drives us to a favourite spot of hers. Hordes of young students enjoying the cool evening sit by the side of the road. Only the twinkling stars and a few dim lights from nearby dwellings offer any illumination. Small china bowls, the size of a teacup are delivered to our low-slung table. A highly sweetened thick coconut liquid contains a symphony of surprising ingredients. Diced sweet potato, tapioca, jackfruit, pumpkin, tiny cubes and ravioli shaped gum stuffed with green bean paste. While Van eats hers enthusiastically, I'm quickly attempting to grasp the complexity of such a creation. The gum is comforting, just like eating sweet flavourless fruit pastilles. I like the tapioca too; the translucent by-product of the cassava offers respite from what is otherwise an overtly sickly concept that I struggle to finish. I am certainly in an exclusive club of one though, for it seems to be much loved here.

Van drives her motorbike in tune with the pace of Tra Vinh. Rarely exceeding a very unhurried 20 km per hour, it gives me time to appreciate my surroundings. The Hang Pagoda is 5km out of town. A curious, fading arch that slants acutely, dates back to 1673 and is the only original structure left of this prominent place of worship. Carpet-bombing American B52s in the war heavily ravaged this area and inside there are many poignant reminders of the damage that occurred here. The peaceful grounds occupy very few visitors today, except for the trigger-happy Ho Chi Minh photography club. Prayers, speeches and regular chanting resonate from within a building. Inquisitively, I approach the entrance and stand in curious silence for a few minutes, before an elderly gentleman ushers us inside. Having removed our footwear we are invited to join a group of six men. Tea is offered as elderly Khmer women study me from a distance. Dressed in traditional attire of white tunics and dark blue trousers their diminutive faces appear etched in wisdom. In this culture, the elderly are treated with the utmost respect and their social status is assured at all times. I am in privileged surroundings. To my left, lines of monks are seated on a slightly raised area. Sharing their food, they eat with vigour but dine in total silence. Monks offer speeches and prayers. The worshippers, their feet turned behind them as a sign of respect to Buddha, reciprocate by a simple joining of both hands. Palms faced inward, raised and stretched out in front of them, they respond with frequent bows and gentle chants that are performed in calm unison. We sit for an hour. My back aches terribly and I bemoan my appalling posture.

Mid-morning we drive north and ride parallel to the Song Co Chien River. If we had kept going we would have eventually reached the Ho Chi Minh museum. Instead, a few spontaneous moments later, I am jumping from the back of the bike and standing beneath a red banner that advertises Khmer New Year. A man carrying a young child appears at the entrance. He speaks a little English and suggests that I might like to join in the local festivities. Rare offers such as this take little thinking and I ponder for the few seconds it takes me to step into the party. Two young boys have just competed in a sack race that is conducted in a shrill of hysterical cheering. I'm overwhelmed with offers of rice wine. Six tables are divided with an equal amount of guests. Separation by age, sex and hierarchy is clearly evident. A small sound system with tall black speakers seem incapable of coping with the output, blast out hypnotic Cambodian rhythms. The tables are spread with food, water, eating equipment and the odd bottle of stray home brew. The men, many of whom seem just a little inebriated, pour me glass after glass of their potent brews. Their generosity flows effortlessly, although if I carry on at this pace I'll be having my stomach pumped in the local hospital before lunch is served. The problem I face here is that once you drain your glass tradition dictates that it is refilled without delay. Delicate control, that's what is required. Smart words are so gratifying. Executing them may prove a touch problematic.

After a solid twenty minutes of downright suicidal drinking, I can barely believe that the time is only 11.30am. The little control I have exercised by sharing each glass with the server has proved about as useful as a one legged man attempting to kick open a door. The brew rushes to my head. I begin to sweat profusely, as the fierce midday sun streams down. The sensible option now would be to sit down. Foolishly though, although much to the delight of the people, I enter myself into a sack race. I feel I should do my bit for international sporting relations and I've always had this natural competitive streak within me. The elders nod their approval. I kind of wished that foreigners were banned from entering at this stage. The woven khaki sacks are strong and large enough to swallow a child. I remove my decrepit brown sandals and place my green hat on the ground. I gingerly step into the bag and drag it up to my waist. I grab both sides with each hand and prepare for the action. My opponent who looks confident is very youthful and probably not under the enormous burden of alcohol. The nominated starter holds up three fingers suggesting we complete three lengths of the short fifteen metre course. Bloody hell is this guy trying to eradicate me from this earth. I offer one finger in return. It is accepted. With a short, sharp blast of a red plastic whistle and screams from the eager crowd the race begins. My rival's start is electric. He bounds off up the course as I stumble and try to remember how to manoeuvre successfully. I'm laughing so much at my own idiocy that by the time I develop any rhythm, I've been comprehensively defeated. The exuberant crowd insists on a rematch. Once again we line up. This time my start is a little more polished. I propel my sweat dripping body with every ounce of my alcohol-induced determination. There seems little to choose between us as we launch ourselves dramatically over the line. My exhausted body is trembling and struck with acute nausea. My efforts though are rewarded with a victory by the finest of margins. A sporting draw is announced.

Since my arrival the women have been busy preparing the lunch feast and the now finished dishes are delivered to the table. Tubes of squid with tomato and pineapple and thin strips of tripe are mixed with shaved green banana and slices of watery cucumber. A pan of lightly thickened rice broth with steaks of fish whose texture is a little oily and although the flesh is white its flavour is similar to the wild salmon from British waters. Large chunks of juicy, refreshing watermelon offer a wonderful palate-cleansing finale. The rice wine though is still being served with equal relish. I settle in my chair as a scattering of men begin dancing. The relentless beats blare from the speakers as my feet gently tap along. A bulky red-faced man gleefully insists I join in. The dancing is fluid as their bodies gyrate. There is much laughter as I attempt to replicate the exaggerated movements. The next thirty minutes is a joyous, frenetic scene of wild dancing. All the hectic activity has left my body severely dehydrated and I'm indebted to Van for exacting a controlled exit. My head is throbbing uncontrollably as I clamber onto the bike. Back at the hotel I collapse onto the bed and pass out for a much needed self induced afternoon siesta.

In the evening Van gently teases me about my exploits of earlier and thankfully assures me that I was well received at the party. We drive to a splendid gem of a restaurant that we reach through a series of narrow alleys. Surrounded with mango, bonsai trees and a prominent coconut tree that remains unruffled in the perfect still of the cool night air. Phuc, meaning happy, offers a relaxing atmosphere. We enjoy only a solitary dish tonight. Half a chicken is steamed in its own juices until just cooked. Whole cloves of garlic, oblong chunks of zucchini, okra and tiny mushrooms are added. A good sprinkle of shredded spring onions and nutty toasted garlic slithers garnish the ensemble as it is presented on a metal platter. The well-flavoured bird includes part of its beak, eye, neck and feet. The juicy pieces of zucchini combine with the slimy qualities of the okra. The blend of whole and toasted garlic offers an interesting perspective of this bulb's culinary uses. The fowl though would have benefited from a more sympathetic slow cooking process. The only successful formula to eat its flesh is to gorge on it like a cave man. The flavour delivers a deep rich taste though and with its dip of lime juice, salt and red chilli it is another fascinating, unexpected concoction. I arrive back at the hotel and tune my radio to the BBC World Service and listen to Silver Birch win the Grand National at odds of 33-1. Unsurprisingly, Manchester United destroy Watford by four goals to one in the FA cup semi-final.

The next day we tour the pagodas and enjoy the many local celebrations for Khmer New Year. The obvious spirituality of this important time of the calendar is supplemented with pure fun and games. One I found highly amusing starts with a contestant being blindfolded. Hanging from a tight supported length of rope is a clay pot containing money, sweets and other gifts. Beneath this, a large circle is drawn with white chalk. Starting from a distance of about fifty metres, the contender is spun around three to four times to aid in disorientating them. An elderly gentleman hands them a long wooden pole. He has a shallow round drum made from stretched cowhide, that, after a whistle commences proceedings he begins to beat. The person begins to stagger towards where they consider the target to be. The animated crowd scream instructions at the wandering participant. The furious beating of the drum intensifies gradually throughout. If you eventually get near the target, the pole is drawn up high above your head and swiftly brought back down to hit the target. I stand watching for thirty minutes and not one person is successful. The spectacle of watching bumbling humans, acting like complete fools, is always indelibly humorous.

The urge to linger in Tra Vinh is difficult to resist. The food here has been a revelation. Although not all to my taste, the diversity and freedom of expression is hard to fault. There's the peculiar blend of a coffee, coconut and green bean jelly that sits on a bed of crushed ice. Coconut milk, sugar and water are added to the glass and topped with chopped jackfruit. The many bakery kiosks that offer pastries and cakes that I could never walk past without buying a slab of dense moist chocolate cake filled with peanuts. A cake produced with grated fresh coconut, rice flour, eggs and sugar also became a firm favourite and choux buns filled with thick pastry cream cement the French influence with concrete conviction. I've enjoyed soups with chopped liver, heart and any other imaginable offal. My final evening I order up eight magnificent large river prawns. Brought to the table raw, they are set on a bed of thinly sliced onions, slivers of garlic and a scattering of fresh herbs. The metal platter is placed on the stove and a liberal amount of Saigon beer is added. The sweet plump prawns react surprisingly well to the fermented, tangy liquor. A clay pot of a whole chopped duck swims in a fat filmed broth. The liquid beneath unaffected reveal slabs of congealed blood, gizzards and all known parts of the bird. Chunks of sweet potato, tomato, spring onions and coriander leaves combine in the final dish of my four days here. In the words of Van 'this place is very famous.'

Off-Target

Moving on from a place that so vividly captures your imagination is always touched with poignancy. The expectation of what lies ahead however can usually compensate for the slight disappointment you feel as you depart. Today the issue and romance of travel are sternly tested. The bus I'm on (and I use the term loosely) as we head away from Tra Vinh appears to have been hastily dragged out of retirement. Van had confidently informed me that this was an express bus. Maybe it was in 1938 when the average motor vehicle managed to reach the dizzying speeds of 30 km per hour. Now though it is a relic from a bygone era. I'm sure I've just witnessed a cow racing past us. Maybe if we tied the animal to the front it might accelerate our speed. The journey is slow and tedious. My feet spend the entire trip dangling over a cage of rats and mice. The pale-faced man next to me spends the first four hours throwing his guts up. That's bad enough but when a lull in his sickness mercifully arrives, he decides it is funny for his stomach to accept more food. The lady conductor, who otherwise rules with an iron rod, pays little attention and generally ignores the display. Nine painful hours later, having covered the paltry distance of 230 km, we trundle into Cau Mau.

The colourful, vibrant streets of Tra Vinh are ripped brutally from my heart. The noisy, hectic streets are dirty and the architecture sends me into an immediate depression. Grey and drab, I feel like I've entered a communist time warp. The hotel I check into employs staff straight off the Stalinist conveyor belt. My grubby room is noisy and offers unflattering views of rodent infested rubbish piles. I'm tired and irritable already. Outside, the night sky illuminates with brilliant flashes of lightning. Thudding cracks of thunder are followed by torrential rain that beats down with immense ferocity. I loathe this place already.

Tomorrow I will leave early, but first I must investigate the reason I have come here.

The many restaurants that I have frequented until now have been humble eateries. The building before me suggests that I'm stepping up a class. The fact that I am sopping wet and a little underdressed is not good start. The lady who had shown me around the market in Vinh Long suggested I hook up with two of her friends here. Expecting them to exude a similar confidence to her I am immediately disappointed. They seem ill at ease in this environment. It is packed with surly businessmen who ogle the intimidated pretty girls that advertise Chivas Regal. The smart waiters wear red waistcoats, bow ties and neatly pressed black trousers. We walk up one flight of stairs. My feeble companions accept a solitary table positioned on the landing. I gently protest and request that we are offered another option. This is the only available table in the restaurant replies the waiter. With nonchalant haste, I march up another flight of stairs. Three gloriously redundant tables bring a wry smile to my face. I'm not impressed. His dismissive attitude and low opinion of us bring my blood to an injurious boil. How I long for the hospitality of Tra Vinh.

A change to a more positive manner is only minutes away. Snake is a luxury item, so the slightest hint that we are interested in eating one brings about a sudden reversal. An unexpected burst of enthusiasm sweeps over our rude waiter. His personality change defies medical science. Menus are rushed to our table as a rather undistinguished headwaiter appears. He lists the options available and suggests we could choose the animal from downstairs. Expecting to see a mass of writhing activity, I'm disappointed at the paltry sum of reptiles displayed. I'm staring through a glass enclosure at two considerable and six small snakes. The forced charm is oozing from him, as he begins a theatrical sales pitch. He lifts the lid. Holding a long pole, complete with a metal hook, he begins to tease them by poking and prodding. He lets out roars of laughter. I'm sure he thinks he impresses me with his showboating. Far from it, the guy is a first class joke. His undignified style has just lost him a sale. I've no intention of paying $70 to pamper his ego. I do though decide to humour him and pretend I am still interested. My mission to consume snake will have to wait. As we head back upstairs he continues his tiresome spiel.

Eventually I put him out of his misery. His face looks full of disgust for me. He stomps off, no doubt murmuring expletives under his breath. The possibility of escaping without eating is highly attractive. The hour is late though, so I decide to stick with it. I'm glad I did. An otherwise tiresome day reaches its climax with food of the highest quality. Grilled tubes of squid receive timing that serves them at their peak. The now familiar dips that accompany such fare are represented by salt, red chilli and lime juice. I suck delicate soft meat from the bodies of crabs baked in salt. The soft-shelled crustacean allow you to extract every last morsel without fear of damaging any part of your mouth. The final dish is a champion of style. The undeserving waiters present a tour de force of eye-catching, theatrical gastronomy. A decorative, blue and white china pot complete with a matching under plate is placed on the centre of the table. Oblong white firelighters surrounding the base are promptly ignited. The flames roar up and totally engulf the vessel. Inside thin strips of beef bubble away with chopped onions, garlic, lemongrass, chilli, shredded young ginger and chopped peanuts. WOW! In the blink of an eye the restaurant has found its redemption. I temporarily cast aside my contempt for the diabolical service and laud a moment of true excellence. The frustrations of the day ebb away and bring total justification for such a long excursion.

Liquid Gold

The 7.30am express boat blasts its piercing horn. A few final passengers scramble aboard and urgently duck their heads to avoid the doll's house sized entrance. I'm already seated on the blue wooden backed benches aboard the long, narrow, vessel. Shabby thin green curtains provide a negligible barrier from the early morning sun. Stacks of orange lifejackets are situated to the front and rear. Huge waves of debris are disturbed as the driver reverses carefully away from the bay. Today I'm excited. My physical contact with the river has previously been limited to short necessary crossings, so I'm thrilled at the opportunity to experience an extended journey up to my next destination. This form of public transport is sadly in rapid decline. The people now much prefer the convenience of travelling by bus. The rapidly improving road infrastructure combined with aggressive bridge building projects may eventually make this form of transport redundant. The less than half-full boat is tangible evidence of its fall in popularity.

Rickety stilted structures line the waters edge. The intricate, clever canal systems support a wealth of business enterprises. A man smokes his pipe in the entrance to his hardware shop and contemplates the day ahead. Customers pull alongside to make enquiries. Many still pilot traditional crafts that require a great deal of experience in the choppy waters. Transactions are not just confined to stationary situations though. We are now in a wider channel. Mid stream our pace is gentle in the congested waters. Speed restrictions assist in preventing near certain carnage if not strictly adhered to. The discipline on the water certainly seems to contrast with the hazardous highways on dry land. Our skipper sounds his horn at regular intervals. A middle-aged woman proficiently pulls alongside. She stands deftly at the rear of her elongated, slender rowing boat. Long wooden oars held high, cross at the top and strike the water simultaneously but in alternative directions. Her balance is impressive. She is a picture of composure as the swell from our engine creates mid-water bedlam and her balance remains supreme as a man hauls up a huge box that comes to rest at our stern. How she doesn't fall in I've no idea. The ease and fluidity of the transaction will no doubt have been performed on a daily basis for generations. Robust barges stacked to the rafters with bananas lie motionless. The crew relax in hammocks, smoke cigarettes and play cards on the deck until the time comes to depart.

Just ahead lies the open water of a more significant channel. The engine bursts into life creating an ear-shattering crescendo that has me plugging my ears with my fingers. Our speed dramatically increases. Behind, I can just see rowers turning the bow inwards to cut through the series of waves that are produced. They bob furiously up and down and only patience will deliver them to more settled conditions. The murky brown canals are substituted with a greener, purer outlook. Lush green water coconut trees, their roots evident above the water line, flank us on either side. An open top speedboat roars through. The crouched passengers each wear white crash hats that wouldn't look out of place on a building site. We dock briefly at numerous zones on the way. We pick up and deposit passengers with equal regularity. At one stage, I find myself sitting next to a kid with such severe acne that any other distinguishing features are fighting for their very survival.

I scramble around in the depths of my satchel and produce a solitary pair of earplugs that dull the sound sufficiently for me to attempt a brief snooze. I'm abruptly shuddered out of my semi-comatosed state as the boat produces some erratic movements. I've been dozing for about thirty minutes and in that short space of time our skipper seems to have turned into a crazed lunatic. His docile style is dangerously substituted with driving that wouldn't look out of place in a high action adventure movie. If this isn't an attempt at taking his life and ours, it sure as hell feels like a cracking rehearsal. We are back in a minor waterway, the channel is heaving with boats of all shapes and sizes and there seems little room to manoeuvre even at a conservative pace as he recklessly blasts through gaps that allow no scope for error. Our irrational proximity to other boats at such hair-raising pace make a mockery of the speed limitations so strictly adhered to previously. My pounding heart relaxes only when the engine is suddenly cut. I exhale with a huge sigh of relief. The skipper sits back and nonchalantly lights a cigarette. We have arrived at Rach Gia.

Sixty-two nautical miles from Rach Gia and located in the Gulf of Thailand is the island of Phu Quoc. It covers an area of 567 sq km and is about 62 km long and 3-28 km wide. In the early seventeenth century, the island was a deserted area where Vietnamese and Chinese immigrants earned their living from harvesting sea cucumbers. For a four year period between 1782 and 1786 it became the stronghold of Lord Nguyen, later recognised as Emperor Gia Long in his confrontation with Tay Son forces. French rule began here in 1869 and their occupation exploited its landmass for rubber and coconut plantations. Though to many, its most recent history aligns with mainland Vietnam. From 1967 to 1972 a POW detention camp held over 40,000 inmates, at a site measuring 400 hectares built in An Thoi. To this day there is still a significant military presence here. Since being liberated on 30 April 1975, Phu Quoc has slowly been developed into a tourist destination and the completion of the airport brought a wave of rapid investment. The many sandstone chains that gradually descend from the north to the south lend this island the local name of '99 mountains'. The longest one is Nam Ninh, which stretches for 30 km along the eastern edge with its highest peak scaling 603m, called Mt Chua.

The island though holds a famous secret that I have been longing to discover since my journey began. The diversion from the freshwater tributaries of the Mekong is a crucial ingredient in understanding a national treasure that influences the tables of an entire nation. If pho is considered the national dish, then fish sauce or *nuoc mam* can justifiably be described as the sole ingredient that is a revered staple of every Vietnamese.

Documenting the history of fish sauce with any certain accuracy is exceptionally difficult. Many of the secrets of making it are linked with families unwritten accounts. Phu Quoc's known records date back only two hundred years, although when you discuss the subject with local people the heritage appears to extend at least another century. The abundance of fish in the rich waters produced a surplus that required an innovative solution. People fermented small quantities in their homes to preserve any excess catch. It would be extremely rare to find anyone brave enough to withstand the putrid smell of producing at home nowadays. In the UK, the most widely used fish sauce is imported from Thailand. Vietnam stopped selling to the European market after 1975 and the Thais seized the initiative to enter the arena. Phu Quoc fish sauce was widely available until the Americans pulled out of Vietnam and placed crushing embargoes on exportation of Vietnamese products. The only route to market was by emblazoning bottles of the sauce as Thai in origin. It was to have a damaging long-term effect and when it returned in the mid-1990s, it was commercially overlooked for the familiar Thai version that even the Vietnamese had become used to. Its recent surge in popularity is a source of huge pride to the country's people. The French, who know a thing or two about protecting the origins of specific geographical foods, acted to bolster its reputation in May 2002, by slapping a ban on any imitations. The production of fish sauce on this tear shaped island is now an important industry and contributes significantly to the economy. The estimated annual output is now in excess of ten million litres.

Fish sauce is manufactured throughout South East Asia and other areas may produce more prolific quantities than Phu Quoc. What distinguishes the quality of production here is the island's beneficial and crucial location. The fishermen have access to shoals of the highly prized schooling fish, the anchovy. The tiny specimens, traditionally abundant in these waters, are widely regarded as the fish of choice to produce the finest liquid. Other fish may be used, including larger varieties such as mackerel and sardines that also produce excellent results. The delicate flavour and high protein content (forty per cent) of anchovies however produce the best and most distinctive version.

At the Luan Dien factory in Duong Dong the owner slides back the corrugated steel door. The light lingering smell of fermenting fish that is ever present all over the island increases to a nauseating, potent force that clears your sinuses in an instant. Before me are lines of formidable circular wooden vats made from local Boi Loi trees. They slope gently upwards to the top and have wood that twists like rope around their circumference for additional exterior support. The business has been in her family for over one hundred years and now produces in excess of 270,000 litres a year. The scale of manufacture may be on far larger scale than the olden days but the method of production mirrors the actions of their forefathers. I climb one of the ladders used to monitor the progress of the fermentation procedure. Inside each vat are ten tonnes of fish, four tonnes of salt and fresh water that is poured in to cover at the beginning. They use none of the artificial additives that are common in many inferior products. The addition of these rapidly increases the fermentation but takes the purity away from the sauce. Truly authentic nuoc mam must only contain fish, salt and water. Many mediocre sauces can be ready in a matter of months but the pure, natural liquids reach their peak after one year. The large shed that houses the production area has a river that runs behind it. The fishing boats dock here and land the fish immediately, delivering their top class catch directly to the back door of the factory. The warm seas that surround the island contribute to the particularly high protein content that is fundamental to high-grade production. The owner though is beginning to worry about her business. While her production increases year on year, the effects on the fish stocks has been catastrophic. The pressure from over fishing is contributing to panic among the community. Prices have risen dramatically from 3500 VND per kilo three years ago to 4700 VND now. The premium attached to the fish sauce has until now fended off a significant drop in profit levels. How the situation plays out is her chief concern and without strict fishing quotas, some businesses like hers face an uncertain future.

When the liquid is mature enough to be decanted, I am fascinated to learn that this is not carried out all at once. Interestingly, there are three stages that dictate the quality of each batch. The best, most prized liquid is removed first and contains the highest protein content. Three thousand litres of the deep golden, clear fluid flows from the bottom of the vat through a simple clear hosepipe. I watch and marvel as the liquid gold strains through a fine mesh and pours into the large plastic drum that sits on the concrete floor. The second batch is filtered ten days later and a further ten days elapse before the final consignment is removed. The finest fish sauce commands a wholesale price of 45,000 VND per litre, while the second and third achieve more modest premiums of 20,000 and 1015,000 VND respectively. I stand and admire the intensely flavoured, clear pungent sauce that has brought culinary fame to this beautiful monsoon sub-equatorial island. Its recognition and distribution so sadly neglected during the trade embargo is now proudly stamped with the quality assurance of Phu Quoc.

Three Ways with Fish Sauce

Fish sauce is one of the truly great seasonings of the world. A table without it in Vietnam is a traitor to its heritage and taste. During my brief four-day stay on Phu Quoc I sampled some fine examples of its cuisine. Seafood is the big draw here. I would wander down to the harbour and watch as the fishermen unloaded the day's catch. Squid is plentiful in these waters and the restaurants serve it in a variety of ways. *Muc um* stood out one evening when I had dinner with the husband and wife of a small agency in Duong Dong.

Tubes of squid are cleaned and stuffed with a filling of finely minced pork, onion, mushrooms, garlic, shrimps and blanched rice vermicelli strips. First, they are fried in a hot pan to introduce a little colour and develop the sweetness. Next, some fish sauce, tamarind pulp and a splash of water are added along with a pinch of sugar. The pan is covered and allowed to simmer gently. It is brought to the table in neat slices accompanied by the rich liquor. I love the tender squid and soft meaty filling. The sharp tamarind compliments the salty fish sauce to deliver a dish of exceptional flavours.

There is a restaurant in Duong Dong situated on the sweeping bend of the river of the same name. In the evening diners can admire the shimmering waters and backdrop of local fishing boats that are lit up by tall lanterns. On the first occasion I visited, I dined alone. This is an exceptionally large establishment and I had a few problems getting a table. Eventually the kind waiters courteously arranged a suitable solution and I enjoyed two dishes of clean fresh simplicity. Both of them were completed on a small gas stove at the table. The first involved slices of flesh taken from giant elephant snails that I had seen in abundance in the market here. The dark edged, creamy coffee colour morsels are scattered with generous whole stalks of lemongrass, chopped garlic and a pinch of sugar. As they start to cook on the flat dish, I'm instructed to sprinkle over some fish sauce. A few minutes cooking is all that is required. I soak the dense, soft meat in a dip of lime, salt and black pepper. The penetrating flavour of the citrus lemongrass is wonderful and the resulting light stock is thoroughly appreciated.

Along with fish sauce, another of the island's traditional products is pepper. The next dish demonstrates the qualities of each admirably. Chopped up cooked chicken pieces along with a little of the fowl's offal is cooked with whole mustard leaves, batons of spring onions and slivers of garlic. During cooking I sprinkle over a generous amount of coarse black pepper and fish sauce to bolster the flavour delivery. I don't know why but I'm both surprised at the moderation and delighted with the restraint shown with the cooking sometimes. A few quality ingredients carefully prepared is often more a show of the cooks confidence than the temptation to add one component too many that may destroy the balance. This has been stunningly reinforced here.

Bitter Sweet

The bustling border town of Chau Doc nestles on the west bank of the Bassac River which flows north into Cambodia. It has possibly the most colourful, instructive religious environment of anywhere in the delta. The Cham dominated district of Chau Giang where practising Muslims live in among mosques align with Buddhism,

Christianity and the more recent introduction of the complex Cao Dai faith. The latter is a beguiling combination of Christianity, Buddhism, Islam, Confucianism, Hinduism, Geniisim and Taoism. It is about as complex a religion that I ever witnessed and leaves me in a state of permanent bewilderment. Their temples offer a master class in elaborate colourful design, whose bold fusion of style mirrors the diversity of the faith.

I'm sitting cross-legged in a traditional dugout canoe on the wide expanse of this major tributary of the Mekong. If you venture south from here, the traffic-choked city of Long Xuyen greets you after about 50 km. A much shorter journey in the opposite direction and you arrive at the Cambodian border. This important juncture is a critical trading post and the Khmer influence of its neighbour permeates daily life through the activity on the water and the bustle of the friendly city. Until the mid-eighteenth century this area was controlled under Cambodian rule. During the reign of Pol Pot's evil genocidal regime, the area was the scene of much conflict. Regular forays by the Khmer Rouge into this corner of the delta inflicted much pain and brutality on its people. As I sit and gaze at the peaceful outlook that surrounds me now, it is difficult to comprehend the bravery of mercenary sailors who battled through rocket propelled attacks to deliver much needed supplies to a tormented population. The Vietnamese invasion in 1978 of its neighbour eventually brought to an end a period of sustained uncertainty and began the healing process that swept away any fear.

The activity on the water is a fascinating mix of trade and the routine of people who eat, live and sleep on the busy channel. The many floating fish farms that remain a constant feature, mix with barges, canoes and more tourist friendly vessels that allow visitors to sample the reality of daily life. Rickety stilted structures hover over the water in a show of defiance that sometimes beggars belief. Women peer from the open windows of a sturdy barge and signal to a lone female trader. She saunters across and manoeuvres alongside. Her café on the water is laden with goodies. Spring rolls, noodle soups, grilled fish and coffee are just a few things on her mobile menu. Others trade in toiletries, pharmaceutical items and indispensable living requirements. All transactions are conducted on the water, making the need to go ashore a trifle inconvenient and unnecessary. Traders from the central market negotiate on board for bananas, durian and sacks of rice. When the bargaining is complete the goods are dispatched to the shore where a waiting representative delivers them to the purchaser. Being a border area, the waters are rife with smugglers whose main activity is shifting cigarettes. Hidden in the shade beneath stilted houses, wooden boats are readily loaded with black bin liners full of packets. They pole quickly to seek refuge under Vietnamese homes. Middle-aged women, who apparently receive less severe sentences if caught, are the main protagonists. Corrupt customs officials stand sidebyside with the husbands of the women to warn of any raid. The intricate waterways of the delta still remain a powerful symbol and even with an improving road infrastructure play a crucial role in bringing vitality that would be scandalous to neglect.

I spend my days here gathering my thoughts while involving myself in the daily delights of gorging on the local food and wiling away hours in a particular coffee shop. Minutes from my spotless micro hotel that affords me views of the central market and decaying French architecture stands a slice of Vietnamese culture that at various times has offered me a haven of therapeutic distance from the incessant flow of delta life. At the corner of Duong Phan and Anh Phung is a distressed colonial building. Where once the light gold interior paintwork sparkled it is now dull and peeling. The exterior blue shutters, battered and faded by years of neglect, hang above wide hanging canopies that reflect the sunlight. A lady sells filled baguettes from her mobile unit conveniently positioned outside. Pots of pâté and cooked pork sausage line up next to cucumber, radishes and carrot. Displayed in the front, a popular obsession for Laughing Cow cheese echoes a million travellers' comfort food all over the world. The triangular, soft processed creamy spread could never be accused of making strides in dominating world cuisine but if familiarity is what flicks your switch, then these are readily available in a world store near you. I decline the cheese and settle on the pâté. Speedily filled and finished with a splash of fish sauce, the newspaper wrapped package is secured with an elastic band and I amble to a table tucked round the corner. I ease into my maroon plastic chair that bends as I sit and look admirably at a solid wooden chair that a man enjoys in the corner. Inside a group of men smoke and play chess. I order a white coffee, light a cigarette and allow my mind to drift into a state of pleasuring numbness. A glass adorned with an individual lidded tin, filters coffee that drips steadily and settles on the top of sweet condensed milk. Here the glass rests in a bowl of hot water that has a metal spoon for you to stir the thick liquid. This should always be accompanied by a pot of tea that invites you to refresh your palate and hydrate your body. I stir my coffee and watch as the condensed milk struggles to blend with the dark liquid. White streaks appear at the bottom as it gradually incorporates. I remove the filter lid and flip it to allow any excess coffee to be caught in the main body. Although I wax lyrical about these establishments, it is not necessarily about the quality of the coffee served. It is invariably very bitter and the thick, acrid and overly sweet liquid often leaves me screaming for a decent, well-balanced cappuccino. Sometimes I would thin it down with some boiling water to make it more palatable or try the immensely popular iced version that comes in white or black handled glasses with a straw that compounds a mass of crushed ice. The Vietnamese are obsessed with these venues. You may find them at busy road junctions, ferry ports, bustling markets, around lakes and in appealing garden environs, the likes of which I frequently visited in Ben Tre and Tra Vinh respectively. Their concentration is as thick as teahouses in Burma and housed in equally diverse surroundings. These are places for gentle, sobering debates not for loud animation. They promote fleeting, mindful and intelligent thoughts that inspire a calming reflection. Tomorrow I am destined to travel into Cambodia and continue my quest of following the Mekong River's immense path. I will leave behind the vast network of waterways that inspire this unique landscape. Its wonderful cooks that live with a bounty of tremendous produce and create a myriad of culinary magic that occasionally made me gasp with admiration or left me morally confused. Its approach to food is as extraordinary as the complexity of water that feeds it. It has been a compelling, fruitful start to a journey that is still in its infancy. The tantalising anticipation of what may lie ahead is all the incentive that I require at this stage.

Cambodia

The Golden Kingdom

A mighty, booming crack of thunder shatters the silence of the previous thirty peaceful minutes. The grey, gloomy skies light up impressively as nature unleashes an unexpected violent storm that roars across the open, flat fields and sends an avalanche of dust swirling into the air. The border with Cambodia is just a short distance ahead as I tuck my head into my chest to minimise the impact as I hold tight on the back of the motorbike. Seconds later a deluge of water hammers down with such ferocity, which, coupled with other contributing factors, leaves our vision on a par with that of an elephant's in the dark of an African night. The sudden shift in the weather pattern delivers a sign of the changing season. It is now early May and this brief flurry introduces the beginning of the rainy season that will transform the landscape into a flourishing green mass and swell the Mekong's waters as both its depth and breadth increase.

It is mid afternoon as I arrive at the Vietnamese customs post. I scour the encampment that appears devoid of any personnel. At this moment, many thousands of people across the world will be stepping from one country to the next. Borders are usually little more than an opportunity to check a passport is valid and, if required, the correct visa has been sought. In reality, the state of international and domestic political landscape determines your fate in our ever-changing world. Here the situation is stable and inviting, so I envisage few problems except the obvious language barrier. During my travels in West and Central Africa in 1996, I was introduced to the much harsher realities of transition. In Democratic Republic of Congo, or Zaire as it was known then, I have never felt so intimidated or out of my depth as when I crossed the jungle border from Central African Republic. A valid passport and visa offers you much the same guarantee as a traveller's cheque in one of its penniless banks. I spent three days negotiating and arguing that my visa was valid, pleading poverty, denying links to any European spy network and even defending the photographic image in my passport. Eventually they confiscated my passport and gave me fifteen days to retrieve it in Kisangani. The journey by bicycle and finally by pick-up truck through the unrelenting jungles of banditry, to this day, remains the most vivid emotional examination of my mental capacity in one of the world's most hostile environments. As a young, eager twenty-four-year-old, its impact was profound and thus any incidents are measured by the enormity of this situation. Here, a lone figure appears from the confines of a room. Wiping his eyes, he tucks his shirt into his dark green trousers and wearily glances at my open passport. He directs me to another building and staggers back to continue the sleep that I had jolted him from. His interest in my possessions is such that the state of the art x-ray machine that I pass is considered a mighty hassle compared to the virtues of an afternoon snooze. The Cambodian officials are much more alert. Impeccably dressed in dark green uniforms they greet me with genuine warmth and as the stamp connects with my passport, wish me a pleasant stay in their country. I'm officially in Cambodia.

Cambodia has endured the most horrific of recent histories. Its people share the scars and wounds inflicted on them by the brutal, inhumane regime that was the Khmer Rouge. Over a four-year period from 1975 until the Vietnamese army overthrew it in 1979, their despotic leader Pol Pot orchestrated a cold, calculated massacre that slaughtered millions in a reign of terror that is difficult to quantify. It ranks with Rwanda, Kosovo and the more recent atrocities in the Sudanese region of Darfur, as the most sickening acts of sectarian violence among citizens of a nation that has occurred in my lifetime. Pol Pot's death in 1998 finally freed Cambodia's population and mercifully brought about the demise of the Khmer Rouge, who after 1979 fled to the dense jungles bordering Thailand, where they continued to wage war on successive governments in Phnom Penh and helped instil fear and paranoia in its people. The long, proud history of this kingdom now has the opportunity to move forward. Distant memories of the glory days in the ninth century, when its empire incorporated the east of Vietnam, north of China and Burma in the west may once again herald a period of positive influence in the region. As I was to discover, the country's recent past has left an indelible mark on its people and the rich, culinary food heritage that is chiefly ignored and overshadowed by the more familiar cuisines of neighbouring Thailand and Vietnam. This was an oversight I was determined to prove wrong as a culpable injustice, which Cambodia's proud heritage neither deserves nor warrants.

Having thought I had secured an individual to drive me through to Neak Luong, I take shelter under a rusting tin roof as further rain falls. As the weather improves, another guy pulls up on a grittier looking dirt bike. Wearing a bright sturdy full-faced crash helmet and sporting a not so macho threadbare pink mackintosh, he looks like Barry Sheen in drag. A thick plastic fifty-litre drum full to the brim with gasoline rests precariously on the platform of his bike. The smooth tarmac roads have disappeared and before us are bumpy dirt tracks that have become slippery with the rain. Not surprisingly, the flow of traffic is negligible. I imagine surfaces such as this to be impassable in the height of the wet season. Small wooden bridges creak and wobble as we pass over them. Bamboo constructed dwellings have piles of bright yellow sweetcorn in their forecourts, while their separate husks provide a less productive stack. Pigs roll about in mud baths, flanked by more dominating beasts like oxen and cattle. The significant signs of a drop in wealth are all too apparent as I try and remain balanced through the deep ditches. In one unfortunate incident, my head nearly collided with a low-lying branch that forced me into drastic, evasive action after my frame is catapulted skywards during a particularly uncomfortable period. Long narrow canals that nurture the fields feed from the Bassac River that flows majestically to my right. Even in the dry season its imperious flow is a soothing spectacle.

It is early evening and dusk is upon us when we ride into Neak Luong after a testing two-hour journey. Phnom Penh is 65 km north-west from here. I'm in no hurry and decide to cross the river by ferry and spend the night. The shabby town does not match the smart ferry terminus on the other side and the hotels offer distinctly unappealing sleeping accommodation. My flea-ridden room is swarming with mosquitoes in the windowless hovel that is complimented by red see-through towels and thumping music from next door. The owner's offer of female company for the evening was teasingly deflected when I asked if that was included in the $12 rack rate. The less than inspiring, dimly lit restaurant attached to the premises did produce food of surprisingly very good quality. An intensely influenced lemongrass broth with moist chunks of fish is washed down with three Angkor beers and complimented by warm and cordial service. Back at my room, I switch on the old television that is perilously clinging to brackets on the peeling walls. With no little irony, channels one and two are dedicated to the flickering delights of hardcore pornography.

Undercover

Phnom Penh sprawls west from the confluence of the Mekong River and Tonle Sap, thus occupying a geographically significant point in my journey. The influence of the river and lake on the diet of the capital's inhabitants and many other Cambodians is reliant on these waters being healthy. It is not to be underestimated that without them their diet would not only be deficient in protein, it would be deficient, full stop. In early May, the Mekong's level is still low but by mid-June its rise accelerates to half a metre a week. What happens next is a natural phenomenon that has few equals. The Great Lake now being lower, the Tonle Sap goes into reverse. It is the most extraordinary of rivers that actually flows both ways. Now, instead of feeding the Mekong, it becomes one of its branches, drawing off its current and replenishing the Great Lake. By late August, both rivers and the lake will burst their banks and flood surrounding areas. The inundation of nutrient-rich water suspended with phosphates and nitrogen feed the land and creates the perfect conditions for growing the staple food of rice. As the rains cease, the Mekong falls. With this it retracts its floodwaters and the Tonle Sap starts to run back into the Mekong. Where once the Cambodian heartland was dry and lifeless, it re-emerges as a dazzling display of verdant paddy fields. It is due to this and the distinct possibility of a second harvest in the winter months, that allows Cambodia to reap all that it needs over an unusually long period.

The heat has been punishing since my arrival in Phnom Penh. Regular daily temperatures soar to over 40°C and leave me permanently seeking refuge in shady climes. The surprise arrival of a friend from back in the UK means that I achieve this quite comfortably in the laid back environs of the Foreign Correspondents Club. Jonathan, fed up with corporate life in

London, has done the wholly sensible thing and jacked in his job with a leading food retailer. He has just arrived from venturing around Vietnam and his presence has inspired me to discover something that eluded me in the delta. Jono, as he is affectionately known, is a bon vivant when it comes to anything gastronomic. If ever there were a man born into the wrong social group, it is he. A man as comfortable in tweed, as he is destroying a plateau fruit de mer in a high class London restaurant, he is, like me, in for a baptism of fire tonight.

Chhorda, who has kindly been seconded to me by Anthony the co-owner of the FCC arrives by our table at 7.30pm. Anthony, a tall, well-built man with a presence that fits his handsome features, has been extolling the virtues of Cambodian cuisine since my arrival. In theory, he has little time to chat with a food-hunting Englishman but his natural desire to promote its battered image flows readily from within. A fluent native speaker, he opened the FCC in 1992, turning the decrepit building into a comfortable bolthole for foreign journalists and embassy workers. Back then money was useless here and so the purchase was made in the more favoured currency of gold bars. Although European at his core (he was born in conservative Surrey in the UK), I feel sure there is Cambodian blood flowing through his veins, such is his empathy with its people. Chhorda, a smart, educated guy has been charged with introducing me to the flavours and elements that celebrate this forgotten cuisine.

Outside on the street, we ignore the ever-present pleas of moto and tuk tuk drivers and clamber on to the back of Chhorda's stylish 250cc motorbike. Jono, at first a little shocked at being asked to share the bike with two others, sits neatly sandwiched between Chhorda and myself. The international flags that line the Tonle Sap, wave in the cooler air of the late evening as we join the chaotic scenes on the wide boulevard roads. We head out of town and cross a bridge over the river where the streetlights cease and the glare of oncoming car and motorbike lights are accentuated. Weak, flickering lamps from passing restaurants offer little in the way of assistance. Chhorda had admitted to me earlier that he hadn't been to our chosen dining location before but was equally quick to reassure me that his sources were reliable and to be trusted. The mystery heightens as we pull over to a number of roadside restaurants where questions are asked and directions attained. Driving slowly, we all glance towards a dimly lit house that is secluded from the road. Surely this can't be it? A set of locked rusting gates blocks our entrance. Gentle chatter, the hum of the engine and powerful front beam are enough to bring an inquisitive lady from within the main building. It takes a few minutes of gentle probing and grilling before she releases the gates and allows us to park in the compound. Quietly she calls towards the house. A young girl precedes an older middle-aged man who appears bare footed, wearing black knee length shorts and devoid of any clothing on his upper body. He enters into light dialect with whom I presume is his wife and we are ushered inside.

Jono and I both look at each other with nervous bewilderment. What the hell is this place we both ask? The fusty room, with its old furniture is practically dark but for some feeble lights that allow us to make out a glass cabinet of Johnnie Walker whiskey bottles that is directly in front of us. When was the last time they had any customers I wonder loudly? It feels like we have just gate crashed the set of a horror film and about to be freaked out by some hammerhead nutter with seven eyes and hands bearing sharp metal gougers. Chhorda adds to our suspense by informing us that only people with a recommendation are allowed to dine here. Great, a bloody exclusive restaurant that looks like it hasn't seen a customer for at least ten years and is that secretive you need authority from the local Mafia to enjoy its sumptuous, relaxing surroundings.

Now he has got me worried. There are just two metal-framed tables and an ageing solid wooden one that occupies a spacious corner and this is where we choose to sit. We are offered several options from the verbally delivered menu. Here, it is not the food you deliberate over but the size and price that you plump for, that leave you with only one decision to make. The lady shouts towards a door to the side and her husband appears, this time wearing an open shirt. Accompanied by his daughter, he walks towards the exit and we slowly get up and follow. In the pitch of darkness, we pace gingerly to a grooved wooden plank that forms a bridge over the tiny water channel. He releases the lock from a wire-constructed cage and we follow them in. His daughter switches on a torch and with a long, hooked stick he draws up the hatch of an enclosure. He peers in and catches his target with nerveless efficiency. He quickly draws it clear and his daughter slams the door tightly shut. Jono and I reel away from the proximity of the writhing animal. It is calmly placed in a wide aluminium bowl where it proceeds to curl up.

Back in the restaurant, our sense of anticipation blends equally with trepidation. We watch as the beast is hooked on the wall and its head removed, along with the noxious venom that could pose a threat to our very existence. Deep, dark blood drains into a container and oval eggs inform us that this is a female. Returning to the table, the lady follows swiftly carrying clear glasses of the warm blood mixed to a cocktail with potent rice wine. The murky, almost chocolate red liquid looks distinctly unappealing. We raise our glasses and propose what must be the most peculiar toast of our lives. In comrade like unity we bring them to the cusp of our lips. I sneak a brief look at Jono and take my first sip. Our apprehension slowly drains away as the warm liquor connects with our edgy taste buds. Chhorda beams with pride and boasts that his powers of virility have officially hit the jackpot. In Cambodia, there already seems a cornucopia of food items that inflate one's sexual drive. The warm, sweet blood blends well and offers a surprising balance to the harsher liquor of the rice wine.

With no hint of any respite the real treasure from the creature is delivered. I look nervously up at the suddenly pale, stunned expression on Jono's previously tanned face. His eyes momentarily glaze over as I too contemplate the disturbing object that is on the plate. A sharp shiver is delivered to my spine, which freezes my body in temporary paralysis. 'Is it me mate,' I ask Jono, 'or did that thing just pulsate?' The nod of his head confirms my suspicion. 'This is the beating heart of the Cobra snake,' offers an excited Chhorda. I'll swing for him if he says it will increase the strength of my wedding tackle! I'm curious but definitely not thrilled at the prospect of that thing sliding down my gullet. I look up at a still stunned Jono. He wants nothing to do with it and is happy to pass the honour to me. He wouldn't be saying that if it were a perfectly cooked squirrel in a famous eating-house near Smithfield Market in London. Cheers mate. Still, these are exceptional circumstances. So, taking a deep breath I hover my twitching fingers over the thing. Positioning my glass of bloody rice wine like one would if dispensing aspirin, I pick up the throbbing heart. It hovers over my mouth as my breath shortens and I'm overcome with severe nausea. I try to imagine it is an oyster, for they too are alive. Defeat is not an option, so, in one quick burst I push the organ into my mouth. I struggle to force it down my throat and contemplate the inelegance of spitting it out. Will it start acting like a ping-pong in my mouth? The wine is my savour, I take a mighty swig and in seconds everything is racing down my throat. Paranoia rears it ugly head immediately.

The wait for the snake is preceded by something impressively normal and invitingly edible. A perfect circular, deep basket brings the colour back to Jonathan's cheeks. He glances admiringly at the golden shell made from rice. The thin rim is crispy and the base filled generously with chopped spring onions that were previously brushed with beaten egg. Brimming with exuberant delight, he expresses admiration for the creation and concludes that it is akin to eating cheese and onion crisps back in England.

Our long wait, nearing an hour, is finally over when the first, true snake dish is presented. The flesh is smothered in a deep brown coloured sauce of pounded onion, lemongrass and dried red chilli. The sauce conceals numerous off-white oval eggs and green bitter leaves. The rich, well-flavoured sauce offers fragrance and prominent heat from the chilli. The meat is stringy, tough and so dominated by small bones that our patient meticulous efforts extract very little worthwhile flesh. Its skin is totally inedible and my teeth would stand a higher success rate chewing on a bicycle inner tube. I clamp an egg between my chopsticks and have similar success. I watch Chhorda as he pierces the resistant skin and peels away its protective layer. Inside, reveals a dry, crumbly texture that Jono compares to that of feta cheese. The taste, while not sensational, is far from offensive and we happily eat all six. Sadly, the meat in the final dish, although a little more yielding, is just as painstaking to pursue. When I do manage to wrestle a bit away from the spiky, brittle bones, I discover a flavour not unlike chicken although delivering a more intense impact.

As we sit back in our chairs, now sipping on an excellent ginger flavoured, sweet palm wine, the bizarre events of the evening begin to line up. The bill is a whopping $75, well beyond the reach of the average Phnom Penh populace. Business cards are handed to each of us, offering instant membership rights to this inner culinary sanctum. The venue is hidden anonymously from public view and is shrouded in mystery. The Cambodians' revere snake and believe it has many magical powers when its various parts are consumed. The proprietors risk their lives to keep this tradition alive. Eating the deadly venomous Cobra snake is illegal in Cambodia. I've also been told of specialist crocodile restaurants in Phnom Penh. These too are illegal; the major disturbing difference is that during the Khmer Rouge years, these reptiles were used to consume humans as a sickening way of disposing those who opposed the regime. This shocking revelation turns the pit of my stomach and slams the door shut on exploring the town for any such establishments. To eat with a population's blessing, as with the snake, is fine but to blatantly ignore its wishes would be tantamount to abuse and I'm sure would bring a degree of negative karma.

As we take to the dark, eerily quiet night road I raise a gentle admiring smile. I won't be rushing to relive the experience but I wouldn't have swapped tonight for all the fish in the Tonle Sap.

Nighthawk Invitation

'How would you like to accompany me to my cousin's wedding?' asks Chhorda. Having only known him for just a few days, this generous offer surprises me with its complete open stance and the genuine warmth in which he conveys it. My other plans are swiftly dumped in favour of the excursion in a rural area near Kampot in the far south-west region of the country.

Since my arrival in Phnom Penh, any suggestion that the food isn't on a par with the offerings from its neighbour downriver has been swept away in an aquatic avalanche. Chhorda, who hails originally from the prolific rice-growing region of Battambang in the north-west of Cambodia, is proving to be an excellent companion. His honest insistence that he is not a professional guide holds no importance for me, for it is his powerful enthusiasm, impressive urgency and readiness to engage with my voracious appetite that makes him invaluable. This is a guy who makes things happen with a smart persistence that endears me to his educated spirit. I'm also pleased that Jono has decided to extend his few days in the capital (he actually ended up staying ten) and during this time we ventured to several rather upmarket establishments that are promoting and re-establishing the nation's culinary credentials. One such venue is called Malis, where a contemporary modern interpretation aligns with a cool sophistication that delivers refined Khmer food. The tranquil space is smart, the well-dressed clientele relax surrounded by fig trees, and a central pool illuminated by spotlights with calming white lilies floating within. The open kitchen gleams with brand new stainless steel appliances, while the immaculate cooks wear pristine crisp black uniforms. The evening began with Jono quizzing our waitress on the selection of sherries on offer. Her blank expression answered the question visually, which led Jono into an impassioned response detailing the merits of this fortified wine that takes its name from the town of Jerez in Spain. I'm not sure she was any wiser after the lengthy explanations but it was a priceless moment of cultural interaction that left me in fits of hysterical laughter. The only disappointment of the meal was a dessert of pumpkin crème brûlée whose grainy texture suggested it had been overcooked. Having yet to sample *amok*, one of Cambodia's national dishes, this first experience was a triumph. Small parcels of moist chunks of river fish cooked in a light creamy coconut sauce are steamed through wrapped in banana leaves and flavoured with lemongrass and basil. Jono, having previously voiced his disapproval, due to versions that were heavy and overpowering, announced it to be utterly sublime. A scooped out eggplant where the flesh is chopped up and mixed with diced mushrooms, crunchy green peppers, garlic, ginger, chilli, fish sauce and palm sugar is baked in the oven. Minced preserved fish and cooked pork are flavoured with pounded lime leaf, lemongrass, coconut, palm sugar, crunchy peanuts and pea aubergines. An exceptional dessert of pumpkin cake topped with a layer of condensed milk is served with light tapioca in refreshing coconut milk and polished off in seconds by an exuberant Jono.

Chhorda sounds his prominent highway horn as we zip past the immaculate modern airport on the outskirts of Phnom Penh. He sits tall and proud as he negotiates the throng of cars, lorries, motorbikes, bicycles and the odd stray cow that wanders into the road. Around town, he rarely employs a bash hat, today he wears a tough modern black helmet complete with a visor, a pair of thick yellow and black driving gloves and a lightly padded bright orange and black-sleeved jersey. His mobile phone is attached to the front left of the bike in a leather case. I sit firmly on the back carrying a small rucksack and shoulder bag secured over my head. I occasionally lift the visor from my helmet to relieve the stifling suffocating heat and feel the wind over my face. The road is in fairly decent order, helped by funding from the Japanese government who have invested a significant amount to help develop Cambodia's previously battered infrastructure. Children play dangerously close to the side of the roads as we motor through villages. The barren, flat landscape is dotted with tall, slender palm trees whose canopies hang like umbrellas and mitigate the monotonous wave of parched earth. In the distance I can just make out the outlines of hills that may inspire a more evocative backdrop during our journey. We pass several tired looking UN buildings that remind you of the impact and assistance offered in the reshaping of this beleaguered nation. Their role is vastly diminished now as foreign investment flows into a more settled environment.

After a brief stop for lunch in the town of Thmorsor, where I replenish my dehydrated body with vital fluids, we drive on for about thirty incident free minutes. An old lady, clutching bags of fresh herbs directs us to a wide track that stretches into the rural interior. Having relocated to here from Battambang, this area was once where Chhorda lived. Over lunch he had revealed the harrowing memories that it evokes. His story is not unfamiliar in a country with a fractured, torn society but every individual with equal tragedy feels the gravity of its consequences. The loss of his father at the hands of the Khmer Rouge was followed abruptly by the death of his mother to a serious illness and left a void unimaginable to me. His visits here are sporadic at best and while I wonder what emotions it may stir, I hold a respectful silence and leave him to his thoughts.

Traditional Khmer weddings typically last from three to seven days. We arrive on the second day and are greeted by both the bride and groom. The surrounding terrain is dominated by farmland, which is one of the factors that contribute to the timing of a wedding in these rural communities. Careful consideration is given to the date, which is believed to bring luck and harmony to the union and in the starting of a family. Rural families will usually not allow a marriage during the rainy season, as this is a very busy working period in the fields and also the conditions may seriously inconvenience their guests ability to enjoy themselves. We are ushered into a large tented area that precedes and joins with the main stilted wooden house. To my left, a full set of instruments is positioned on a specially erected stage, while on the floor, chairs backed with golden fabric surround red cloth-covered round tables, that at this time have a scattering of people who chat quietly and acknowledge us as we pass. The sedate atmosphere of the front is exchanged for bustling activity at the rear. A minor army of people, made up of local villagers, friends and family are busy preparing food for the feast that will feed up to three hundred guests at different stages of the day. Ladies squat on the rough ground while deftly shredding lemongrass, chopping green tomatoes, slicing carrots, splitting peppers and washing bunches of herbs, leaves and vegetables. Others feed lemongrass down the throats of sparkling wild snakefish, wash the innards of cows, pigs, ducks and chickens, while around the corner men butcher whole carcasses of animals that have been slaughtered earlier. A bare-chested blood splattered man smashes through the thick bone of a cow, as others sit on the rickety bamboo platform plucking chickens, splitting ducks and dissecting meat from a pig. A vegetarian's worst nightmare is a salivating prospect for lovers of carnivorous flesh. Everyone is in high spirits and the sense of communal purpose is fulfilling. This would be a major undertaking for one day but this wedding is running for three days. Further to the rear, to the right of the house, men stir enormous pots of bubbling food and fry mushrooms in industrial sized woks fired by charcoal that rages from beneath. The men seem to be taking a prominent role in executing the bulk of the cooking, which is one of the rare occasions this happens, as it is always considered the responsibility of the women. At major family events it is a point of honour for them to orchestrate the feast and the rare show of gastronomic testosterone is akin to the average Englishman proudly standing over his barbecue and turning sausages and steaks.

Arranged marriages have been the tradition in Cambodia for centuries and the courtship rituals and the wedding ceremony are very different from those experienced in the Western culture. Forced unions used to be commonplace, now though the modern way is to consult the individual and rejecting the parents' wishes is tolerated. The vast majority of Cambodians are Buddhist, so they are obliged to find spouses for their offspring and marry them into good families.

The ceremony, which I am invited to observe, is just beginning in the house, so I climb the steep sturdy wooden stairs and take my place inside. Gentle, soothing traditional Khmer music performed on original instruments gently fills the room. An array of spiritual offerings, with a decorated pigs head as the centrepiece, are laid out in front of a lavishly dressed Buddha statuette just to the left of the main door. The bride and groom, looking a little petrified and overawed, kneel in front of the priest surrounded by their parents, friends and family. Unlike Western ceremonies it is not considered rude to step out of the ceremony and return when you feel like it. Even those who have passed away are called upon to share in the celebrations, to offer their blessings and observe the wedding, if not in body, in spirit. In Khmer culture, family bonds are the ones that are the most important and a marriage is the inclusion of the couple into their new families. The couple is royally clothed, with the bride wearing a gold crown upon her forehead, long gold earrings and looks stunning in a white dress draped in gold cloth. The groom, in similar colours, wears a jacket with numerous gold bands around the arms and perfectly tailored trousers. The elders typically take this opportunity to explain the significance of the various customs to the bride and groom. The atmosphere is highly animated in a considered, balanced manner that is instructive in its meticulous planning.

Having stepped out of the ceremony, Chhorda has organised a trip to gather palm sugar liquid. First, a group of men invite me to join them in the first of many shots of Johnnie Walker that will inevitably be consumed throughout the evening, then, along with two of his cousins, we clamber back on the Nighthawk and drive off. A monk rests quietly under a tree as we turn off the main track and sweep through the monastery grounds. The wheels of the bike squeeze onto narrow, bumpy tracks that dissect and border the rice fields as we trundle through individual dwellings and scatter wandering chickens as we pass.

A short, wiry man, wearing an orange baseball cap and black cotton shorts, greets us near a condensed area of palm trees. A pair of torn pink gloves tucked into the front of his shorts doesn't detract my attention for long, as I stare at the aged machete blade that is clipped to a holder on his side. A frayed pair of cloth flip flops gives little protection to his leathery feet. A small group of kids play cheerfully nearby, gleefully launching stones and attempting to knock mangoes from the trees. Chhorda picks up a fallen coconut and throws it, connecting with a mango on his first attempt. His beaming smile is justification to himself that the country boy is still within. I'm handed a long wooden pole with a piece of wire on the end that acts like a hook, and prod a mango, twisting and coaxing the fruit from the tree. I too let out a smile. The Africans use a similar technique in the bush for removing oranges, so my previous experience fortuitously allows me to impress my audience. I rip the green skin, which reveals the deep orange flesh. The fibres are sweet, with notes of acidity and a heavenly fragrance that is the finest to touch my lips since my trip began. Excess liquid flows from my mouth, causing it to drip and stain my t-shirt. The kids eye me in silent fascination as I attempt to clean my sticky hands.

The man removes his flip-flops and lifts two worn bamboo containers from a long wooden carrier. The latter he utilises to transport, on his shoulder, a collection of the filled containers for processing back at his home. Carrying the containers by their tough, thin wire, he approaches the base of a slender palm tree. He begins to scale the trunk up a natural rope branched ladder that has tiny crafted pegs that jut out, which look barely able to remain in position, let alone carry the weight of a man. I nervously watch him from below, as he skilfully and nimbly scales the tree with such effortless precision that I'm sure being blindfolded would have not hindered him one iota. He positions himself in the canopy with the same ease and comfort of his ascent. Chhorda, keen to reinforce his country boy roots, now follows behind. Moving more slowly, I'm impressed with his degree of agility as he scales towards the canopy and even a momentary pause for thought to readjust his body, finds him unperturbed. He nestles in the dense branches and observes the man who has now begun to extract liquid from the palm nuts. Two is a crowd, three is company, or so the saying goes, which means maybe my feet should have remained firmly on the old terracotta. The urge to join them at the summit is much too strong, so I shout up to Chhorda and tell him I am on my way up. I decide to leave my trainers on, my first mistake, and the first few pegs prove little trouble. As I move tentatively from each peg, I try to concentrate on looking up and not down. At halfway, my second mistake is to look down, which causes an immediate jelly like wobble in my legs. I'm overcome with anxiety, which streams through my now hesitant body. This could get very messy indeed. Get the net ready boys, I could be down in a few seconds! I'm frozen, suspended and unable to move which really translates to a crisis of disconcerting proportions. Chhorda, realising my dilemma, shouts down and advises me to come no further. The mere idea of this fills me with dread, so I gather my thoughts and slowly begin to descend. Each nervous peg that I reach slowly restores a level of sanity that allows my confidence to flow a little more easily. I'm about one and half metres from the base when my size-eight left foot briefly connects with a minuscule peg that snaps clean off and I'm sent tumbling to the ground. The kids rush over and surround me. I drag myself from the dusty ground with nothing more than a severely bruised ego. I allow myself a smile that turns to laughter as the kids break their earlier silence and erupt into fits of giggles.

Chhorda and the man appear at the base in a matter of seconds, the former gently mocking my ambitious attempt and the fall from grace that accompanied it. The man passes me one of the cylindrical bamboo holders that are now full with a clear white liquid. I drink the luscious, sweet, scented palm juice directly from the container and nod in appreciation. The skies have darkened immeasurably in the last few minutes, so we hurriedly head back to his house and enclosure. We just make the safety of a thatched roof construction when the heavens open and torrential rain beats down on the sun-baked ground and creates tiny rivers in minutes. Cigarettes are lit and the man tells us about his work. These rains spell the end of the harvesting season, he will collect little more for now. During the dry season he will extract about 40 litres each day, which equates to around one tonne every year. Next, he processes the liquid by boiling it over his charcoal fire, which then produces the unique palm sugar that is synonymous with the region's cuisine. At market, his product will sell for a little over the equivalent of fifty American cents per kilo. With the rain persisting, the need to get back to the wedding party is accentuated by the fact that we have already sheltered inside for forty minutes. We dash for the bikes. I throw the plastic sheet, that our palm sugar man has lent us, over my head and we slide along the now more precarious narrow channels. I feel a bump as we drop down into a rice field where the Nighthawk accelerates through the mud until we are forced back to negotiate a bank where the bike, unable to grip in the conditions, battles to ascend. The back wheel is spinning furiously, covering us in a sea of spraying mud, while the front is not making any impact. The bike is now a cumbersome nightmare and begins to slide, dumping us both in the slick pools of the squelchy rice fields. I throw off the inadequate plastic sheet and observe the destruction of my only full set of clothes. I look like I have been mud wrestling with a hippopotamus or rolling around in the mud of a particularly bad year at a Glastonbury Festival. We push the bike up the bank and scramble back on. I sit sodden as the rain continues to lash our bodies. We are both a complete mess.

With nothing to change into, I have an embarrassing dilemma

to which I urgently require some answers. Chhorda comes to my aid and issues me with a set of dry clothes that I can wear this evening. My semi smart image is in tatters as I re-enter the arena looking like a victim of the late 1980s acid house era. Black baggy shell bottom trousers, a bright orange football jersey, wet socks and trainers that used to be blue is not an image I am particularly proud of but at least most of it is dry. It is a little after 4pm and the serving of food began hours ago. Tables littered with cans of German Park beer, bottles of Johnnie Walker whiskey and uneaten food have increased the atmospheric volume to a more animated tone. We are guided to a table under the main house. Our fellow guests, having already eaten, are getting stuck into the whiskey. Sitting directly opposite me, a loud and erratic young guy of about twenty-five years peers at me through his already bleary, glazed eyes and wildly swings a half filled bottle of whiskey. He pours hefty measures for everyone at the table and each person rises to clash their glasses in salute of the toast. It is their custom that when toasting an elder or an outsider, the rim of the glass should connect half way or below that of the other persons. This single gesture is a huge sign of respect and can be observed always at any social gathering. I'm not sure how many more toasts this young guy will be able to offer, in fact, I'll give him two more hours before he is flat on his back and curled up in a muddy field with chickens pecking at his hair.

The food is lavish, plentiful and arrives at the table in a flurry of activity. Bowls of steaming rice, succulent grilled fish with lemongrass, minced pork salad with peanuts and herbs. A rich intense broth with beef, carrots, onions and what appear to be shitake mushrooms is immensely satisfying and doubles to re-hydrate any lost fluids. Thick red chilli sauce clings to juicy grilled beefsteaks. We squeeze lime juice and fish sauce on the prime meat and eat with whole fresh herb leaves. Golden whole spit roast chickens, with a fine flavour, moist meaty flesh and crispy skin that I enjoy ripping from the bones. Duck, vegetable, noodle and more fish dishes continue the pleasurable assault on lucky stomachs. Food and drink continue to flow over the next few hours, while the band begins with a few early numbers.

Excusing myself from the table, Chhorda guides me over to mingle inside the tented area. 'Everyone wants to meet with you Mr Ian,' he exclaims, as he issues a huge pat on my back. I always find these situations rather embarrassing, as while I am thrilled to be here witnessing firsthand a wedding of a totally different nature to what I am accustomed to, I feel my presence is diverting some of the attention away from the bride and groom, which leaves me feeling modestly uncomfortable. I spend the next hour being shifted from each table. At one, I am briefly sat between a high ranking military officer and his son before they hit the stage and belt out a few classic Khmer songs to rapturous applause from the floor. People are now up and dancing, the rain has long since ceased and the sky has cleared to allow the stars to glitter over the countryside. The deluge has not helped with the condition of the route to the pit toilet, which looks hazardous. Situated next to the pigs pen, the ground is a bog, the emanating smell from the facility fights for supremacy with animal dung, cigarette butts, whisky and fish scraps. Add to that the fact that no lights persist either inside or outside and I only have a lighter for illumination, the circumstances are far from idyllic.

Interjecting with the music is a spectacle that is much more familiar to me. Placed on a round table draped in red silk cloth is a tall, elegant, elaborate three tiered cake that is brightly decorated with pinks, gold, a bell like pagoda crowning top and touches of blue icing that mask the sponge filled cake. Unlike Western ceremonies, both sets of parents are invited to participate in this ritual. An explosion of white snow greets the formal cutting of the cake, as excited guests wildly spray foam from spray cans that cover the jubilant partygoers. Only now, do the bride and groom appear to relax and allow themselves the indulgence of enjoying themselves. Chhorda, like me, suitably inebriated by now, leaps onto the stage and grabs the opportunity to duet with a very attractive young lady whose skirt is, well, just a little short. Enjoying the attention, he is quite the showman as he whips up the crowd to a minor frenzy with his infectious energy.

By midnight, I am starting to flag. My weary body and rapidly closing eyelids have begun the process of officially shutting down, so I stagger towards the refuge of the main house. A group of local young ragamuffin kids are scampering round collecting empty cans from the floor and tables. These they crush down and thread onto twigs and sell them for recycling to make a pittance of cash. Kids grow up quick here and in a country where education is still not a guaranteed right, I admire their entrepreneurial spirit. At the house I stagger up the stairs and turn my head briefly to focus hazily on a miraculous image. The young, erratic whiskey-swilling guy from earlier is staring up at me. Still hugging a bottle of whiskey, he holds it aloft in the air, as if in a sign of victory. I've no idea how he is still standing and I'm not about to find out as I virtually crawl into a space in the corner and lay down on the crude, hard lino floor with just a tiny pillow to rest my tired head on.

I'm woken by the sound of cockerels crowing, loud talking and the clatter of china plates. The time is 5.30am. I lift my head from the pillow and am greeted with sharp shooting pains. My sweaty body is bruised and twisted and I have a mouth that feels and tastes like a three-day-old ashtray would smell with dregs of whiskey and beer. The noise is relentless and irritates my sensitive mood. I attempt to close my eyes again without success. Deflated, I lift my sorry state of a body up from the floor and observe the scene outside. A full scale clean up operation is already in full swing.

Groups of ladies are huddled around massive aluminium bowls washing cutlery and plates. The tables have already been collapsed, leaving the ground strewn with food waste and littered with bottles and boxes. I have no idea where Chhorda is, and then I spot someone lying in a green cloth hammock under the house, his glazed eyes and drawn, pale features suggest the day ahead will be long and arduous. I splash my face with cool rainwater that revives me for a moment. For the next few hours we try to remain anonymous. For breakfast we eat a flavourless beef noodle soup that Chhorda describes as the 'lazy version' and some fried pork and snake beans. I have little appetite for food but I manage to force some down. The kind offer of a can of lager is declined with a tired look of resignation.

Having thanked everyone about fifty times at the scene of the wedding, thirty minutes later we are sitting drinking coffee in a restaurant in Kampot. Chhorda wanders about outside buying a pair of cheap sunglasses while I contemplate the day ahead. We are in search of the famous pepper and durian plantations of the region. The thought of smelling the insides of the latter creates an instant nauseous panic in my being.

Green peaked hills and islands dotted out at sea create an all-encompassing topography, as we turn off the main road and drive through a set of imposing iron gates. The 40 km trip from the town has delivered us to the heart of the pepper and durian plantations here in the province of Kampot. A group of military personnel, huddled in the shade, eye us warily while drinking tea and playing cards, as Chhorda smartly accelerates along the undulating dusty track and away from any problematic questioning. Shooting down a narrow trail, we eye a building up ahead and drive towards it. Men sit around rusting tables underneath an open shed as the farm manager steps from his office to greet us. He offers an elderly man to guide us to view the plantation. A traditional Khmer cloth krama drapes from his right shoulder concealing an area of the loose blue shirt that is open and flaps gently in the light warm breeze. Just up on the right is a deep pit that has a large blue tank at its head that furnishes the crops with necessary water and nutrients. Durian trees bearing this unique fruit have an almost ornamental quality with perfect neat circles of red soil that creates a deliberate border. The leafy cone-shaped short trees are said to produce fruits that are held in the highest regard by connoisseurs and Cambodians will pay a premium at market once they know the true provenance. As we draw nearer to the pepper trees, the sweet aroma of the spice invades my senses. The picking season finished last month, yet its beguiling fruity essence clings to the air and comforts my aching head. Orderly channels of tall erect trees, with their green bushy leaves that thin out at the top, producing a marlin like spear that points to the sky, are lined up in impeccable rows and stretch away in calming unison. This is the first time I've seen a pepper tree and ever since I landed in Saigon, the need to explore the impact of this special spice has grown stronger with each passing day.

Pepper originates from tropical forests and requires a hot and humid climate with a regulated exposure to the sun. The Chinese explorer Tcheou Ta Kouan described Cambodian pepper production as early as the thirteenth century, although people here suggest it could date closer to one thousand years. Intensive pepper production is thought to have began here as a result of the Aceh War in Indonesia (1873-1908) when the Sultan, who did not want to leave its wealth to its Dutch enemies, burned down the pepper plantations between 1873-1874 and then moved production to Cambodia in the Kampot region. Its geographical position between mountains and sea, combined with its special climate and soil type made this area the perfect location for pepper production. It was the French that really exploited and benefited from manufacturing it. At the beginning of the twentieth century, Cambodia was exporting about 8000 tonnes of Kampot pepper, with over ninety per cent delivered to France, where its quality and popularity made it the number one choice of cooks and chefs all over the country. They loved it for its strong aroma and pungent, fruity taste that distinguished it from pepper grown anywhere else. In 1960, as many as one million pepper poles remained in Kampot and the industry continued to flourish until the events that took place during Pol Pot's regime bought about its sudden demise. The effects were so devastating that by the end of the century the plantations were almost completely destroyed. The Khmer Rouge's destructive strategy of returning the nation to year zero was not just for the exclusivity of its people; the food and its cuisine suffered a similar fate. Farmers only began to plant again at the beginning of the twenty-first century and the trees I stand between at this moment are only seven years old. This peaceful area was also the scene of fierce fighting between Vietnamese forces and those of the Khmer Rouge. It is difficult to imagine, the now still land ringing to the sound of gunfire, grenades and rockets, which once again produces a hollow feeling within me. It takes three years for a tree to bear any fruit and after seven it will reach its maximum production potential. A pepper vine can live for more than thirty years, but its production decreases rapidly after fifteen and is almost nil by the time it reaches the age of twenty. At its peak, each tree can be expected to produce as much as 5 kilos per harvest. This plantation here has over 7000 trees and from February they employ about fifty local workers to pick what will become black pepper. When the fruit reaches maturity it turns a yellow colour and is then dried in the sun on bamboo mats for three days. Here they are further processed by the traditional method of crushing them by foot in wicker baskets, which removes the outer husk and reveals the inner corns. A further four days drying in the sun completes the process and their colour is now the familiar black that is in store cupboards all over the world. Green pepper, the young fruit of the vines, is collected from September to February and is sold fresh in the markets. I knew nothing of the fame of Kampot pepper until now and with a kilo secured for the journey back to Phnom Penh, I'm indelibly richer for the experience and the knowledge that is has brought. It also offers a clear demonstration that the pride in the production of this renowned spice is once again bearing fruit and helping to re-establish it in the hearts of its people that, like it, suffered a sustained period of brutal uncertainty.

The fishing village of Kep lies 25 km south-east of Kampot and makes a convenient place to stop for lunch, before driving back to Phnom Penh via Chhorda's uncle's in Kampot. Situated on the Gulf of Thailand, this former playground for the French colonialists is now a rather tired, decrepit resort whose imposing villas, although still standing, are a shadow of their former splendour. I'm not here to reminisce about its past, for me the real treasure lies in the waters and the delicious crabs that are plucked from them that make Kep an opportune diversion. Lined up along the shore, a series of basic, rickety, stilted bamboo constructed restaurants offer magnificent views to picturesque islands that dot the ocean landscape. Traditional fishing boats bob gently up and down in the calm waters near the shoreline that is flanked with overhanging palm trees. The proprietor steps down to the shore, wades into the shallows and hoists a cage from the water. A friend joins her to assist in carrying it to the littered, thin strip of sandy beach in front of us. Brilliant, shiny blue crabs energetically move about as she decides which to choose. She plucks several of the soft-shelled creatures from the cage and takes them inside. She fires up a wok and throws in the crabs and fries them for a few moments over a fierce heat. An abundance of green pepper, still intact on their stalks, is added along with pieces of spring onion, fish sauce and a pinch of sugar. From sea to plate in less than five minutes, the crustaceans are brought on an oval dish garnished with celery and coriander leaves. The influence of the pepper balances with the sweet, light saltiness of the crab, which I suck and chew every last scrap from the pliant shells. I slap my lips together in such appreciation; it leaves me in little doubt that what I have just consumed will register as one of the many highlights of my journey.

Caught in another downpour we arrive at Chhorda's uncle's house drenched and immediately strip down and dry off. The musty, unlit room we sit in is swarming with mosquitoes that feast on my exposed flesh with lightning ferocity and I spend the next forty minutes scratching and fighting them off. Outside a couple are preparing some intriguing, tempting snacks for customers who shelter under a canopy. A thin yellow batter sizzles as it hits a smoking wok and forms a pancake. Overlooking the Teuk Chhou River, which glides towards the open sea, the panoramic backdrop of the misty Bokor Mountains is set behind a classic low lying bridge. The light after the rain, produces shimmering water, forming a mystical idyll that is every landscape painter's dream. I'm shown to the back of the house where the foundation of the snacks being cooked begins. Raw rice is emptied into a bag, securely tied and placed in a water bath to allow it to swell. Removed, the grain is then ground through a hand-driven, heavy stone grinder that produces a fine powder. *Nom krouk* is prepared by mixing the powder with coconut milk, egg and onion leaf to form a batter. This is poured into a heavy black pan that has small round moulds within, like an old-fashioned egg poacher. Cooked over a moderate flame, each one is covered with its own lid, until lightly set and light brown in colour. *Bunch choov* uses the same base with the addition of freshly ground turmeric root that produces a yellow powder. Again coconut milk and egg are added and whisked to a light batter, which the lady fries into round, thin pancakes but only cooks them on one side. She fills it with a mix of cooked minced pork, dried shrimp, a pinch of sugar and salt. Next it is folded and placed in a bowl where it is garnished with fresh mint leaves, cucumber, bean sprouts, chopped peanuts, crispy fried chopped onion and a good splash of fish sauce. I don't care much for the *nom krouk*, with its curious savoury, soft custard but the *bunch choov* is a fascinating, unexpected combination, which delivers textures and flavours that deserve wider recognition.

After a few necessary repairs to the bike, we begin the drive back to Phnom Penh. We tail a brand new black station wagon for a majority of the way, which Chhorda pursues with the zeal of a grand prix driver determined to reach the capital in record speed. An impressive electrical storm illuminates the pitch-black conditions, while fires that send plumes of smoke from the roadside offer the only tangible light on our passage home. We reach the Cambodian capital a little after 10pm. Shattered, with my backside and spirit feeling the pinch, we enjoy a late dinner at a tiny roadside restaurant frequented regularly by Chhorda. A delicious seared steak, juicily pink in the centre, is a tender piece of beef that I dip in the fermented fish paste of prohok, which I find a little overwhelming. Soft, gelatinous eel in a well-flavoured, fragrant broth is boosted by the addition of chilli and washed down with a few well-deserved ice-cold Angkor beers. As we approach the FCC, my apparent tiredness is confined to only my exterior features, as inside I'm buzzing with enthusiasm for a trip that has shown and taught me so much. As I watch Chhorda roar into the city night, I feel I am now dancing to the rhythm of this captivating kingdom.

Perimeter Food

Chhorda urgently slams on the brakes of the Nighthawk, as a kid riding a bicycle crosses directly in front of us. Having paid no attention to his surroundings, the boy momentarily freezes, his eyes deep in his face as the shock registers. Chhorda reprimands him strongly for his stupidity. Clear of the wide boulevards, glittering Royal Palace and the smart international hotels at the centre of the city, we follow the road that would eventually lead to the area the world knows as 'the killing fields'. The suburban areas of Phnom Penh offer a more grubby, sparse outlook, although signs of economic investment are beginning to spread as new flats, houses and business premises are constructed, bringing the hopeful promise of a brighter future for its many impoverished inhabitants. Turning off the main road, before me is a flat and meagre wasteland, with huge piles of rotting garbage tumbling into ditches, giving off a foul stench that causes me to gag. Rice fields to my left, compete with new industrial factories as a brilliant orange sunset crafts a dramatic sky that ripples the clouds with hues of pink and creates a vaguely surreal moment of positive magic across an otherwise depressing scene.

The three-storey breezeblock house ringed with barbed wire, positioned next to a man-made lake has the feel of a house in isolation and coupled with the recent rains, it is the prefect environment for mosquitoes, which swarm in dense numbers. His brother, whom I had met at the wedding, opens the gates and greets us. The outside area is dominated by a raised bamboo constructed seating area, which doubles as a food preparation zone and is protected with a thatched roof. Three pieces of dried river fish hang from the left post, as numerous ladies and girls begin preparing the food for dinner. Equipment and ingredients are ferried from the house. Chopped duck, its beak protruding from the pan, is mixed with livers, heart, neck, and gizzards are sat on the ground near a charcoal burner that has yet to be lit. A young girl chops prohok, with raw pork meat, green tamarind leaves and spring onion until it resembles a fine, smooth pounded mixture. Earlier in the day,

Chhorda had driven me 25 km north-west of the city to discover the secret of prohok and impress upon me its own importance in Khmer cooking. Like the fish sauce of Phu Quoc, one can not be certain of when the tradition of this fermented fish paste dates from, however, many believe it to be in excess of 1000 years. The factory we visited is conveniently positioned on the banks of the prolific waters of the Tonle Sap, where small river (not sea) fish, form the basis of the fermentation process. Even in these premier fishing waters, stocks are under severe pressure, with years of over fishing and the irresponsible practices of electronic probing and dynamite, which contributed to levels of damaging depletion. To its credit, the government's stricter environmental initiatives are steadily eradicating such negative methods, so in the future stocks may reach much healthier levels. Traditionally cleaned by hand, this company employs a machine to remove the scales from the fish. One hundred kilos is then mixed with 20 kilos of salt that is tipped into deep square concrete pools and left to ferment for two to three months. The duration to maturity and ratios of salt to fish, may be less than the method employed for the Phu Quoc fish sauce but the nauseating impact is just as overwhelming. When the owner insisted I sample a fish straight from the vat, it took all of my resolve not to instantaneously vomit on the spot, whilst feigning a tight-lipped smile that was not in the least bit convincing.

I watch closely as a woman prepares the unique curry paste of Cambodia that is an integral part of many of its dishes. The paste known as *kreung* consists of many ingredients used by its bordering countries. What distinguishes it, is the surprising use of turmeric, that has muscled its way into an otherwise similar mixture to that of the various Thai pastes that I have come across. Turmeric is indigenous to South East Asia and India, the latter's influence on Khmer food and culture dates back centuries, when the first merchant ships arrived in the Gulf of Thailand to begin trading spices that became absorbed into native cooking pots. Blending lemongrass, lime leaves, spring onion, galangal, chilli and a good pinch of salt and sugar, the lady pounds it into a fine paste with fresh turmeric, producing a tantalising aromatic paste that will form the foundation of a duck curry. The duck, with a spoonful of prohok, is fried over a strong flame for a couple of minutes. Next, with a generous hand, she adds the kreung curry paste, stirs well and continues to fry for three more minutes, while her daughter brings a bowl of finely shredded leaves that have distinct sour qualities, which are added immediately to the pot and covered with a lid. After simmering for an hour, a good slug of coconut milk is added and left to cook uncovered for a further five minutes.

Tonight, the full moon shines down from the clear, starlit night, which illuminates the lake with a shimmering light and allows you to think the surrounding scrubland has been transformed to a paradisiacal showcase. Five years ago, this suburban area was a virtual no-go-zone, such was the endemic robbery, violence and underworld activity that was making it a dangerous place to live. Now, even with the barbed wire, a certain sense of community is being re-established and the security situation offers little risk, aside from minor incidents of petty crime.

The plates are spread out on a raised bamboo platform, the men sit cross-legged and sip on semi-cold Japanese beer. Having cooked all the meal, the females all disappear inside the house to eat together, while we eagerly tuck into the feast. It seems a trifle unfair and mystifies me that we don't all share collectively. Chhorda reassures me that this is perfectly normal, as due to this being my first visit here, tradition dictates that the men are left alone to dine. If I were to visit on further occasions, which I do, this situation would be reversed and in the coming days it is a theory borne out.

The food is quite simply sensational and the duck is the finest marriage to have passed my lips, not only in Cambodia, but also the excellent food of the Vietnamese Delta. The dense meat of the duck, fragrant balance of spice, the saltiness of the prohok, the clean sour taste of the leaves and creamy richness from the coconut milk is a palate busting work of genius, which makes me want to, inappropriately, hug all the women who prepared and cooked it. The minced pork and prohok mixture of earlier has since been wrapped tightly inside neat banana leaf parcels and grilled directly over the fire. The other ingredients mellow the strong intense fish and a fine sour note from the green tamarind leaves offers an intriguing balance. We dip crisp juicy vegetables including wing beans, green tomatoes, morning glory, white cabbage and pea aubergines in a sweet, salty, sour dip of prohok, sliced shallot, tamarind pulp and sugar. Salted, soft shell crabs, grilled fish with lemongrass and lengths of quickly fried lotus root combined with onion, salt and a pinch of sugar leave me beaming with enthusiasm for food executed by cooks with a natural brilliance, that puts a sledgehammer through any negative press of Cambodian cooking.

Skuon Snacks

Chhorda brings his bike to a halt and I step down to observe the undistinguished grey of the dusty junction. Pick-up trucks weighed down with patient passengers, whose eyes all seem to be inquisitively fixed on me, stand or sit as they wait to move on. Numerous packed buses, rammed mini-buses, private cars and pedestrians all congregate, besieged by a cluster of animated spider sellers, before continuing to Phnom Penh, Kompong Cham in the west or Kompong Thom directly to the north in central Cambodia. I'm 75 km north-east of its capital, standing at the crossroads of

National Highways 6 and 7 and I feel like I've stepped into a Wild West freak show. I had heard many stories in Phnom Penh about the fame attributed to Skuon and its bizarre rise to prominence as a popular gastronomic landmark that originally, through necessity, brought its desperate, starving people a source of food that virtually sustained their lives. Pol Pot's catastrophic bid to conform its people brutally back to an exclusively agrarian peasant society saw many of its inhabitants forced at gunpoint to survive in the fields and jungles. Food became scarce, pushing its people to gather what sources of nourishment that they could forage for themselves. With a seemingly never-ending supply, the harsh beginnings of a culinary delicacy took a unique grip on its ravaged people.

Skuon, an otherwise impoverished farming region, is recognised by all Cambodians as the finest place to consume grubs, insects and spiders. Phnom Penh residents will make special trips here, just to buy freshly dug or foraged specimens, rather than waiting for what might be inferior produce in the capital's markets. Eager passengers delight at stopping en-route to various destinations, just so they can engage in enjoying a deep fried tarantula or cricket. For many, it is simply impossible to deny themselves the opportunity of gorging on a selection of creepy crawlies. I'd been implored to come here, so had resisted the temptation of snacking on them in Phnom Penh, to allow my curiosity to be satisfied by eating potentially superior produce at this centre of excellence.

Three ladies, having responded to the sharp blast from the motorbike's horn, have scurried excitedly across the busy road, to surround us and begin their persuasive banter and parade today's special snacks. Lowering their heaped metal trays from above their heads, which were previously balanced on one hand, they allow us to inspect the produce. The choice is a tough call, as I am confronted with a selection of crispy fried creatures led by the venomous qualities of the black, hairy, eight-legged tarantula, the enticing prospect of crusty crickets and every chef's kitchen nightmare, the filth loving cockroach. If the choice were caviar, langoustine or foie gras, the difficult decision may be based on international acclaim or personal preference. I turn to Chhorda with a blank, befuddled expression and ask him for a recommendation. 'Try the tarantula first,' he says. 'Their taste is similar to the cricket, only far superior' he adds. Such a reply is really of little use, when I have no clue what that tastes like either and so he reassuringly removes the decision-making from my grasp and orders a bag of tarantulas to inaugurate me. The greasy, deep red-brown outer shell has been fried with lashings of garlic and salt and the true aficionado would insist on eating creatures plucked straight from the burrow and cooked without delay. I have no idea when these were prepared, although the constant trade and rampant appetite of the Cambodians would suggest the need for daily cooking is assured. The vicious, venom-soaked fangs of the 'the ping' as the locals commonly call these palm-sized tarantulas, are mercifully neutralised while cooking, leaving my mind reassured that this arachnid, common to the surrounding jungle, will not result in a hopeful dash to the local hospital. I pick one from the bag and examine it for a few seconds before biting down on a single leg. After the initial hit of garlic and salt, the sweet flavour of a light crab is boosted with a final delicate hint of chicken, which disappears to the pit of my stomach. The little white meat I extract is delicious, so I crunch through the body. The brown paste revealed within the abdomen is soft and gooey, and not dissimilar to the texture inside our own British native hard shell crab. The composition of organs and excrement, although, at first disconcerting is far from offensive and I eat several more in quick succession. The outer crispy shell left behind in my mouth is dry and unpleasant and I fail to swallow it. The curious locals and travellers who surround me watch as I hastily spit out the dry matter and swig on some water that Chhorda has fetched from his bag. My mind drifts back, trying to imagine the circumstances to which people, left with little choice, had to adapt their diet to provide any type of protein. It is impossible for me to comprehend the desperation that created this unique foodstuff, but easier to accept its enduring appeal to a nation that came to the very brink of destruction.

Back home in the UK the supermarket shelves are laden with food flown and shipped in from all over the world. The reliable flow of produce is never brought into question and, at this very moment, the way it is taken for granted leaves me reflecting and contemplating the balance of the human capacity for food. What would our actions be if we were faced with similar turmoil? Would we start digging for worms, foraging for insects and deep-frying ants? The strength of the Cambodian resolve is right here, dished up on metal trays heaped with an array of creatures that proved a saviour in times of scant choice and are now celebrated across the land as a magical delicacy that continues in more stable times.

One River

The Mekong River is by definition one of the major rivers of the world. In 1886, an ambitious exploration by a team of French explorers, originally commanded by Doudart de Lagree but subsequently led by the dynamism of the frenetic Francis Garnier, set out on a highly ambitious expedition to navigate and seek a trade route up the river into China. It was a journey of epic proportions that saw them map over 4000 miles of previously unchartered territory, over a two-year period. Although successful in many ways and indeed judged by experts to be on a par with the more publicised European expeditions into Africa, the commercial success was an embarrassing failure due to the river's resilience. Garnier's brave attempt to lead his team of six, enduring disease, lack of funding and overcoming great obstacles, including possible confrontation with tribal factions and the much better equipped British team further upriver, produced compelling evidence that the Mekong lacked any commercial credibility as a trade route. Over one hundred and fifty years later, the river holds the distinction of being the least utilised among the world's great waterways. In the 1860s, there were no bridges across the Mekong at all. In the mid-twentieth century, a rickety Meccano structure replaced a ferry service in the Chinese Yunnan; but below that, for over 3000 km the river remained a bridge-free zone until as recently as 1994. Although difficult to comprehend, a bridge only becomes necessary if the volume of traffic makes it economically viable to build. Engineering was never the problem, the non-existent traffic was the reason the river remained unspanned for such long periods. Kampong Cham boasts the first bridge to cross the Mekong in Cambodia, which is perhaps more a reward for its loyalty to the long serving Prime Minister Hun Sen, than for any vital strategic purpose. The first port above Phnom Penh is the hometown of the country's strongman, who, if local lore is believed, lost an eye in a fight with the Khmer Rouge. Across the river, on its east bank, stands a solitary brick tower, said to be the scene of the incident. Built by the French as a bell tower in the 1940s, it has long since been of any importance. What ever happened here, the three tiered tower, that leans ever so slightly, was clearly the scene of fierce, violent exchanges. Permanent scars of machine gunfire across all four sides of the tower's exterior, pepper its brickwork. I had read of scenes of a river busy with traffic during the rainy season. At this time, its waters are lifeless by the absence of boat activity. Sandbanks protrude along the Mekong's withered shores supporting a collection of floating houses that, for now, sit firmly on the dry islands. Any remote hope of journeying onwards to Kratie by boat seems dashed as I stand on the bridge and look towards the sweeping bend upriver. The bridge may well have engineered the death knell to any further passenger services but the population of Kampong Cham may well benefit from its connection with the country's power base.

Earlier, I had checked into The Mekong Hotel, which overlooks the river. A modern, functional building that has corridors that would accommodate a full size soccer pitch and an eerie chill in its echoic chambers. The end of my two-week association with Chhorda is nearing its conclusion. Tomorrow he must return to Phnom Penh, while I continue further north to Kratie. The close bond we have formed during the short, yet productive and illuminating period will leave an empty void; my gratitude towards him is immense. His willing, warm straightforward approach underpins a smart brain that I hope will serve him well in the future. His generation of twenty-something Cambodians, while grateful for the increasing stability created over recent years, is fiercely ambitious. He has a cautious optimism for his own future prospects. Poverty levels in Cambodia, especially in rural areas are endemic, allowing little time for day dreaming and Chhorda knows the battle to prosperity will be a long hard slog.

The chef stands before a row of three woks powered by gas flames and ladles steaming, evocative stock from one of the deep pots to his left. A tray of seasonings, herbs and vegetables are conveniently positioned behind him, allowing him to spin on a six pence and reach all he needs. Into a dry wok he throws lime leaves, a few slices of unpeeled galangal, pieces of turmeric root and begins to toast them. In the fashion of a Mexican cook toasting chillies, he allows them to char until lightly blackened before adding chopped chicken, white pork stock, a pinch of sugar and salt. He smells and observes the aromas while it rapidly comes to the boil. In two bowls, he adds what appear to be an excessive quantity of whole, tiny, fingernail sized green chillies, two whole red chillies and a few slices of green pepper. Turning back to the boiling broth, he dips in a ladle and slurps liquid into his mouth and intuitively adjusts the seasoning with a liberal dash of fish sauce. I stand and watch the combination of intriguing technique and imagine the copious amounts of chilli that are about to incinerate my palate. Having followed the river's path from the depths of the Vietnamese Delta, I have yet to witness such a style of cooking. The Khmer Food restaurant in Kratie is thus scribbled in my pocket sized diary and etched with a star of compelling recommendation. As the chillies are whole, the majority of heat within the inner membrane and seeds is imprisoned, so that when I sip the liquid, I'm hit with a clean snap of fresh sourness and a mellow smokiness from the charred aromatics. I jump from my stool, head back to the street side cooking area and beam congratulations at the cook while two whole fish hit a smoking wok. Over the coming days I eat here on numerous occasions, extolling its virtues to many of the aid-agency expatriate community that work in the area. The very next lunchtime I enjoy a broth with chopped chicken, livers and heart that has chewy, crispy pieces of nutty garlic floating on the light oily surface and thickly sliced pickled lemon rind, that sends my mind drifting to the incense filled souks of North Africa.

The depth of the Mekong at Kampong Cham is about two metres during the dry season, but further upriver as far as Kratie, this level is only attained during the rainy season. As I sit on the veranda of my sturdy, traditional Khmer bungalow, the receded river's main channel seems barely navigable. Huge flat sandbars stretch out in front of me, where, during the early evening, dogs come to play in the shallows and gleeful children splash about with carefree pleasure. I watch as monks gently stroll to the edge of the main passage of water pausing for spiritual reflection, lingering until the onset of dusk. Great flocks of cormorants, flying low over the water, commute back to their evening resting spots as the sun dips and the light fades. Dramatic deep red-orange colours deliver a blaze of brilliant radiance that shoots across the water from the steep bank on the opposite side. The tricky, precarious levels of the river subdue the activity on the water and only the most skilled or foolhardy captains can be seen attempting passage at this time of the year. Vietnamese fishing boats occupy the shallows and wait patiently for the river to swell, bringing the promise of a surge in fish stocks. Over the coming days, I watch the phenomenal, natural spectacle of the river's dramatic rise as it visibly swells. In just four days, the great stretches of sand bars, so prominent now, are submerged as heavy rains bolster the Mekong and the melting glaciers of the distant Qinghai Tibetan plateau feed this mighty river.

'I am the only female guide in Kratie' announces a proud Dary as she arrives at my bungalow. Tight stonewashed jeans, a black t-shirt and white baseball cap, dress a petite figure whose facial features manifest a look of deep anguish. After attending to my dwindling cash pile in the town, we drive back to a local market situated near my peaceful accommodation. The market is an unkempt line of stalls numbering no more than ten, where the lightly sodden ground is littered with food waste and garbage that encourages a rampant insect community. During my stay at the FCC in Phnom Penh, where I would have breakfast most mornings, I was introduced to the popular dish of *bor bor*. I remember juicy chunks of river fish in a light rice thickened broth and the warming heat of shredded fresh ginger, sprinkled with spring onions. The version I'm served in these more modest surroundings is a thick glutinous mass of rice with a feint hit of ginger and meagre scraps of bony fish. The refined bowl that had become my chosen staple in Phnom Penh now sits undesirably in front of me, half finished.

We arrive to the village of Tagoun a little after 10am to be greeted by a group of boys playing an animated game involving sandals and rubber bands. In Phnom Penh, kids would play on the street and even gamble for a little money, causing you to walk around their small huddles. Here, it is for pure social entertainment and involves kids throwing their sandal towards a bunch of elastic bands. The object is to reach the target without any hindrance by rival footwear, which, if a sandal were directly hit, would disqualify them from further action. The village occupies a shaded position by the banks of the Prekte River that is reached by a narrow dirt track, fit only for two-wheeled transportation. Entering an encampment of five wooden, stilted homes we are greeted by the men, who have paused from working on a dugout canoe. A bare-chested man, wearing a black peaked police inspector's hat (I can't help but think of The Village People, the camp band of the 1970s, when he acknowledges my presence), places down the tool he uses to plane with. Another sits on a thick, solid log using an axe to construct a long cooking implement that is used for pounding rice from its husk and stirring the bubbling cauldrons of green leaves that feed the animals. A red-checked traditional krama cloth is all that covers his modesty as he skilfully shapes the tool. His lean body ripples with taut muscles, while his bulging calves suggest a man in prime physical condition. Ladies peer curiously from the havens of the shuttered window and remain there for the next hour as I chat, through translation, to people who have lived in this way for centuries. In scenes repeated all over rural Cambodia, this subsistence way of life is poles apart from the increasing economic prosperity beginning in Phnom Penh. There is little help from the government and what help there is, is totally inadequate. The shabby local school employs two teachers who have no funds for any educational material, are poorly paid and rely on donations for any educational resource, from anyone generous enough to offer. At the height of the rainy season, the possibility of any teaching is at the mercy of the weather and the flooding river that can close the school for months. My donation of textbooks, pens and pencils from the modern market in Kratie, are greeted with squeals of delight from the appreciative kids who sing a song as a thank you.

Food, for this particular rural community, is fortunately now not a problem. Their yearly supply is rarely supplemented with produce bought in from markets and a healthy balanced diet is quite normal. Fresh, dried and smoked fish, pig and chicken meat from home reared animals, wild birds shot from the trees with catapults and frogs in the wet season, yield a plentiful supply of protein. Trees laden with mangoes, bananas and coconuts, large juicy pineapples and fresh vegetables like corn, onions, garlic, pumpkins and mushrooms provide important vitamins, while rice from the fields contributes carbohydrates. I'm invited to share lunch with them, which is always served at 11am and constitutes the main meal of the day. Days here are dictated by the weather and utilise the most favoured conditions for working the fields, which means everyone is active by 5am. The easier, bearable morning climate allows for increased productivity before the sun begins to rage down from above. Just now, the main activity is building and repairing the dugout canoes or ploughing the fields in preparation for the rice-planting season. The ancient method of the water buffalo-drawn, wooden plough remains the most reliable and economically sustainable to perform this arduous task. Among the rural population, the respect for this powerful, steadfast beast is unequivocal and I recall Chhorda naming them 'everyone's best friend.' Water buffalo is rarely given to the pot and almost never in rural areas where, by virtue of its importance, such an act would be like British people striking out and having roast horsemeat for Sunday lunch.

Living with Dolphins

The knock on the door and gentle calls rouse me from my deep sleep. My alarm is yet to be activated on my mobile phone, as I wipe my bleary eyes and focus on the digits 05.55. I release the mosquito net from underneath the pink mattress that I have slept on for the past four nights and grab a t-shirt from the magnificently created bamboo chair that is set before a low slung table in front of my bed. The moist air from heavy rain fall in the night greets me as I unfasten the solid wood doors that reveal a coy Dary diverting her eyes from my hairy, bandy legs. A gentle light mist shrouds the Mekong's waters as it glides by with an increased vigour that leaves me transfixed and my mind speculating about the sight of the mighty Khon Falls that wait over the border in Laos. Today though, I am grabbing the opportunity to join the project coordinator from the Cambodian Rural Development team, who, after gentle persuasion has agreed to let me accompany his team on a three day trip beginning from Stung Treng. I met Sun Mao a few days ago, when Dary had invited him to have lunch with us. I was immediately impressed with his knowledge of the surrounding area, its people and his impassioned disgust at the overt use of Monosodium Glutamate or MSG by many of the cooks, who, he says, with such fresh ingredients to flavour the dishes, should have no necessity for the shards of white crystals.

Heated debate of the use of MSG in the western world has led this flavour enhancer to be banned in many foods on our shelves.

Here and all over Asia, this fact is lost and of little interest to people who have no fear of MSG. To fully understand MSG, it is necessary to trace it back to its original conception. The first steps of discovery began in Japan just over a century ago at the Tokyo Imperial University, and were inspired by the bespectacled, mild, biochemistry specialist, Professor Kidunae Ikeda. One day, as he sat down to eat a broth of vegetables and tofu, he turned to his wife and enquired about the secret of her wonderful soup. Mrs Ikeda directs his eyes to the store cupboard and points to the strips of dried seaweed that she kept. This is kombu, a heavy kelp that when soaked in hot water delivers the essence of dashi, the stock base of the tangy broths the Japanese love. Professor Ikeda, having already been one of the many scientists to identify the crude whereabouts of the tongue's four accepted primary tastes, thought this matrix missed something. He noted, 'There is a taste which is common to asparagus, tomatoes, cheese and meat, but which is not one of the four well-known tastes of sweet, sour, bitter and salty.' He immediately began work on kombu seaweed and succeeded in extracting crystals of Glutamic Acid that produced the Glutamate he required to progress his research. He decided to name this fifth taste 'unami' – a common Japanese word that is usually translated as 'savoury' – or with more magic as 'deliciousness'. Having successfully isolated unami, the professor hoped it might be able to improve the standard of food of Japan's rural poor. Further research was completed on stabilising the chemical, which was easy. Mixing it with ordinary salt and water made the monosodium glutamate – a white crystal soluble in water, which had excellent storage properties. His new seasoning was an instant success and with the commercial insight to patent his discovery, Professor Ikeda's 'eureka!' moment led him to his fortune and changed the nature of twentieth century food. He remains to this day, one of the top ten greatest inventors in Japan's history and left a legacy that was to become one of the longest lasting food scares in the western world.

In Edward A. Gargan's excellent book, *The River's Tale,* his description of Stung Treng makes for gloomy reading. When the French were there, the town had a central green and a degree of order. What he found was a bleak, dusty place, connected by dirt tracks and pummelled by a searing, unbearable heat. When I arrive it is easy to imagine what he meant, with the swirling dusty air around the market a clear indicator of the past.

Six years on and Stung Treng still has the aura of a shabby town, although now with a few modern hotels, better selection and quality of food than what Gargan went on to describe in his quest for any sustenance. The Khmer Rouge, who used the thick surrounding jungle and forests to hide in, was still creating anarchy, thus, only a fragile stability was in place. Gargan also describes the unnerving feeling of travelling on to Kratie, with stories of robbery and banditry rife on the ragged roads and his discomfort at not seeing any boats tied up in Stung Treng. The road from Kratie is now a brand new stretch of slick tarmac funded by the Japanese and the only robbery I witnessed was a passenger intent on sharing the driver's seat by squeezing his frame between him and the door. As we get down from our comfortable Toyota taxi, the numerous boats tied up offers me a far more comforting outlook than which Gargan encountered.

By a tree, a group of chickens sit tethered and peck at the scant rewards on the dirt surface, as a man inspects them and chats with a lady who is busy stripping bark from sugar cane in preparation for juicing. I help Sun stack the goods he has brought on the pavement, before heading across the narrow road to purchase lunch and fluids for the short journey downriver. Upriver, people shuttle across in ferries amidst the mass of steel that now spans the river, forging a new road link with neighbouring Laos. For very different reasons than Gargan witnessed, these waters in the future might become just as redundant as the inevitable road traffic increases. Sun points to our vessel as we gingerly negotiate the steep, muddy bank that brings us to the shoreline, to be greeted by the skipper of his functional, if a little dilapidated, long barge. Sun helps the skipper secure a blue, thick plastic canopy across the hull in order to protect the fifty kilo bags of cement that must be delivered en-route. I position myself on the raised platform that precedes the skippers wheel, the incomplete roof has glaring gaps that offer no shelter should it rain, the wood is warped and worn from years of plying these waters and its elements. The skipper, having checked and adjusted the engine, launches the Chinese 7hp diesel motor into spluttering action. The loud clanging noise from the engine rings in my ears, reverberating as we sluggishly draw away. The deck hand, slouched in a hammock under the roof seems oblivious, except for bringing his pocket radio up to his right ear. The skipper stands and peers out over the roof while steering casually with his right foot, directing us to mid-channel and through the confluence with the Mekong's tributary, that of the Sekong. The wide channel is congested with local fishing boats, as people deftly balance in their low-level crafts and launch nets high into the air, which spread across the water. Dugout canoes look on in awe of the more sophisticated engine-fired longtail boats that have arched plastic canopies to the centre to offer respite from the crucifying sun. I admire the beautifully kept banks to my left, terraced to enable the growing of vegetables and herbs that benefit from the nutrient rich waters of this river. I look back towards the slowly disappearing town and for the first time realise that I am heading with the river's flow and not against it.

After a brief heavy downpour, the sun appears from the clouds and bakes the battered wood of the boat's decks dry in less than ten minutes. The captain is now sitting upright across a string hammock with his left leg tucked behind him and stares straight ahead while drawing from a cigarette. Up ahead, lay the indomitable fast flowing Preatapang rapids, interspersed with tiny islets of hazardous flora that break the white water's flow. These torrents are perilous and require exceptional navigation skills to defeat their ferocity. He plots his course, carefully and with exact precision, so as to avoid all the obstacles, and we pass with little drama.

During our journey we deliver the sacks of cement to various points along the river. The steep banks prove problematic on each occasion and in particular the second dropping point. The looming dark skies cast a deep, unsettling black shadow, as further rain brews. As we peer up the bank above us, a man rests under a tree and explains that no one is on hand to shift the heavy bags, so we climb the bank and go in search of assistance. The elevation is almost vertical here, as we contend with the slippery mud and I struggle to believe anyone could be successful shifting anything up its sheer incline. As we walk through the rice fields I spot a few broken shells nestling in the bare soil, which appear to belong to giant clams or mussels and I question Sun with the enthusiasm of a kid discovering candy for the first time. He confirms my curiosity and my mind rushes at the prospect of what I imagine to be a large, juicy, meaty mollusc contained within, as I quiz Sun on the likelihood of obtaining some for a freshwater shellfish feast. We enter a school encampment just as the heavens open. A child with one leg (not as I suspect due to the horrors of leftover landmines) hops about on his crutches and brilliantly executes accurate kicks of a sandal, as two dogs fight ferociously for supremacy, with the smaller one eventually hobbling away licking his blood dripping wound. After thirty minutes of torrential rain, three men appear and talk with Sun, and then begin walking towards the river. They stand and examine the bank closely and conclude that in its present condition it would be impossible to haul the bags up it. Not to be defeated, a few pick shovels are sent for and the men commence fashioning neat flat grooves that create steps to stabilise their footing. A human chain of three is formed to allow for less movement of each individual and the task is completed with no more unnecessary fuss. As we depart, I watch as kids slide down the banks, filthy with mud, shouting and squealing, exalting the pure pleasure of splashing in the water and popping up seconds later, ready to scramble once more to the top.

The flat, grassy pointed beginning of Buddha Island introduces my home for the next few days and as we once again navigate through water borne flora, I ask Sun how it got its name. The island, once densely populated with trees, received its name from Buddhas that locals saw floating past one day and which they gathered to distribute around the length of its 12 km landmass. Sadly, none remain now, all of them being destroyed during the Khmer Rouge period and thus robbing the island of its very identity. They also tried to wipe out something else here and very nearly succeeded in annihilating one of the Mekong's greatest living creatures – the Irawaddy Dolphin.

The Irawaddy Dolphin is central to the projects that Sun and his team deliver to these remote areas of Cambodia, helping to bring an educated, sustainable alternative to practices that cause harm to the dolphins and create practical managed solutions to avoid conflict between man and this rare species. The quarrel is not one of respect, for these dolphins are revered by the locals and held in traditional folklore as lucky charms, so they are never hunted, killed or eaten on purpose. The issue, after the destructive regime of Pol Pot's Khmer Rouge left the population close to starvation, is one of pure survival. The people who reside on the island and surrounding banks of the Mekong all traditionally relied upon fishing to support and feed their families but in recent years measures have been introduced by the government, under pressure from conservation groups, to ban fishing in the areas that the dolphins populate. With fishing as their only meaningful way to earn a living, the locals turned against the very creatures that have been held so sacred and erupted in fury towards local officialdom. Once upon a time, the Mekong's vast waters and tributaries were home to a significant population of these dolphins but recent history has not been kind to them. During the periods of the 1970s to 1990s, large numbers of dolphins were known to have died through human-induced mortality on the Mekong River. These threats included direct killing during the Khmer Rouge era in the Tonle Sap Great Lake area for their oil, being shot at for target practice by both Vietnamese and Khmer in the 1980s and killed accidentally through the destructive practice of dynamite fishing. Today, there are said to be no dolphins in the Great Lake and as little as one hundred surviving from south of the Khon Falls in Southern Laos and perhaps as far as Phnom Penh, although this is most unlikely according to experts. Indeed recent analysis indicates that even during the wet season, when the river level rises significantly, the dolphins no longer venture downstream of Kratie, preferring the familiar pools of Kampi, which they inhabit during the dry season. The characteristics of these dolphins are far removed from the images of their ocean loving cousins. The Irawaddy dolphin is a shy, retiring mammal that moves slowly in the water and never leaps from it; this may only be occasionally witnessed when a very young dolphin may perform this act. This dark grey creature has a blunt, bulbous forehead, an indistinct beak and a dorsal fin situated three quarters back on the body, is small and rounded in shape and bares an uncanny resemblance to the Beluga Whale in its appearance. Its existence depends upon the survival of the human population around it and their growing need to explore other means of sustenance and of better, less harmful fishing practices than the reliable but harmful method of gill-netting. As I stand on the bank, the evening sun shrouded with clouds reflects from the water, its surface smooth like a mirror, as it effortlessly drifts forwards to Kratie.

Nine years ago, this island supported only very modest vegetation, the thick forest sustained monkeys, bush deer and even elephants throughout its towering, strong trees, which in turn were utilised for building and crafting dugout canoes for transportation and fishing. Now, in 2007, the natural forest has been partially sacrificed and chopped down to allow new plants and crops to flourish as part of the wider food initiative. The island drips with mango, papaya and banana trees, morning glory, galangal, lemongrass and wild and cultivated herbs, which lend it a tropical air of culinary heaven. And the encouragement to rear livestock has introduced pigs, chickens and more recently ducks that command a massive premium at the markets in Stung Treng than that of intensively reared equivalents. This sustainable method of conservation is slowly reaping rewards for the islands impoverished inhabitants, who no longer solely rely on fishing to generate any income.

As night falls, the battery-powered generator supplies a limited flow of electricity to power a few lights and the laptops that Sun and his team bring to log any necessary data. The mosquitoes are rampant tonight, thriving in the damp humidity that offers ideal conditions for these blood-sucking pests; they attack my ankles with annoying relish and battle for supremacy with a blanket of bugs that have massed on the round table in the centre of our stilted-raised room. In an adjoining room, a petite, elderly lady sits cross-legged on the bare wooden planked floor, her teeth stained a deep red colour from the beetle nut she chews. Her calm silence soothes and relaxes me as her meditative aura fills the room. Peeled garlic, bought from Stung Treng, boils in water over a charcoal flame with sugar and salt, which both enhances and preserves it for future use. Another lady crouches down beneath a row of blackened pans; she washes the rice for their evening meal with the meticulousness that an engineer would show while fine-tuning a Formula One racing car. For our dinner, we must take the short walk to another hut following the muddy track that intersects the villagers' dwellings.

A drunk, yet warm, laid back man greets us with genuine enthusiasm as we climb the solid plank stairs to the house. The quiet, whirring sound of a generator that is housed to the rear of the property is a rare sound on this island. I watch as the man's wife splits coconuts and presses the milk from the succulent flesh into a wooden bowl, while beside her, her daughter pounds galangal, fresh peanuts, lemongrass, red chilli and garlic. She mixes it together in a saucepan with tamarind paste and adds the heads and bones from fish fillets that lay on a plate beside her, while spooning in a spoonful of prohok and a pinch of sugar and salt. This family has the luxury of gas burners, which surprises and delights me in the same breath, she brings the contents to the boil and simmers for about thirty minutes.

We gather for dinner in the large main room. A slight breeze wafts through the humid air as we sit on a single bamboo mat that is laid out with forks, spoons and plates. We joyfully tuck into the richly flavoured fish, peanut and coconut broth, adding marinated strips of fish that has been mixed with egg, sugar and salt and an abundance of fresh and wild herbs, the latter containing a distinctive sour note and morning glory. The strength of the chilli heat is more prominent than I have been used to in Cambodia, (where it is usually dictated by your own preference for condiments added at the table) and it causes me to sweat, something that only the humidity has induced thus far. The idea of adding marinated fish to the broth as you eat is well merited, the flavour already entrenched in the liquid is then supplemented with the fresh flavour of delicately poached fish that allows my palate to wallow in both depth and lightness. Earlier the man's elderly mother was cutting watermelon into chunky wedges and painstakingly grating coconut to a fine pulp, which she then squeezed in her hands to release cool liquid and mix with the ripe fruit. After the unexpected blast of chilli heat, the refreshing juicy watermelon makes for a dessert that readily nullifies the burning sensation in my mouth. After dinner, I'm invited to sit and relax in a chair by the open window to enjoy what cooling breeze there is, as smoke wafts from incense sticks beside lucky charms said to ward off any evil spirits.

Tonight is a special night for many who live on Buddha Island and for me to be present to witness such an event, an unexpected highlight that registers how wide the gap in materialism is with the world I am used to. Heavy rains begin to once again pummel the tin roofs, as sodden locals dash through the slippery mud holding small petrol lanterns and climb the stairs to the house. Swarms of mosquitoes begin feasting on my ankles as I furiously swat them and try in vain to halt the onslaught. Sun busies himself with his laptop, while his colleagues help to set up a video projector and attempt to hang a plain white sheet from the ceiling and weigh it down with a long bamboo pole. News of this event has spread as rapidly as the mosquitoes that continue to flock to any part of my naked flesh and at 8.30pm, what would normally be a village thinking about retiring to sleep, is full of excitement as the people are absorbed in the proceedings. Kids, as young as four, huddle together on the floor and stare at the blank white sheet, while their mothers and fathers talk to the elders and sip clear hot tea from chipped glasses.

After a few technical difficulties are ironed out, the first images appear on the temporary, functional sheet and the wonders of modern technology leave its audience just as transfixed as I would undoubtedly react if an alien unexpectedly knocked on my front door in South London. The inhabitants of Buddha Island have never before watched anything on screen, let alone have access to regular television programmes. MTV, BBC, ITV and Sky are as unfamiliar as toiletry facilities, air-conditioning or a Saturday night spent having dinner in Pizza Express. Before my eyes, faces, young and old, illuminate with a mixture of hesitant glee and outright jubilation that produces in me, a smile as wide as the Mekong's substantial girth, as we watch clips of promotional and celebratory activities filmed on this very island. Members of the audience squeal loudly with excitement when they recognise familiar faces, who, at first seem a little embarrassed or shy of their newfound fame, but visibly relax and eventually rather enjoy the acclaim. The main showcase of the evening, which lasts well past midnight, is a tragic love story involving a randy penniless monk who falls in love with the daughter of a wealthy business woman, who has a much grander suitor from a prominent, prosperous family. The movie blends unashamed slapstick humour (imagine Benny Hill or Dick Emery in their prime) and heartfelt, emotional tragedy that follows the playboy monk and his friend as they hound much younger, beautiful women, who ridicule their advances through blatant social embarrassment, as the cunning social duo pursue their fanciful flights of passion. After the film, everyone drifts silently off, some cradling kids in their arms and disappear to their respective huts. That night I lay under a rather nifty fetching pink pop up mosquito net listening to the addictive, recurrent audio melodrama that is forest nightlife. With my head propped up on my towel, I lay on a padded bamboo mattress and drift slowly to sleep.

Predictably, the late night of before does not permit anyone a chance to sleep in, as the first murmurings of the day announce themselves at 5.30am with the shrill blast of a cockerel's alarm clock that jerks me from my slumber. Reluctant to move, I doze for another hour before escaping the confines of my glamorous repellent mosquito net, rolling up my mat and tearing open an instant three-in-one coffee to make a morning drink. The taste is as good as it ever will be, suffice to say, very hot, sweet and familiar. The rain from last night continues to persist in the form of a light blanket drizzle that casts a heavy gloom over the forest. We trundle slowly back to the house of the previous night to eat breakfast, which consists of last night's leftover soup, freshly fried fish and my first encounter with (what in the coming weeks will be a staple) sticky rice. As we leave after breakfast the rain has gradually halted and the first glimmer of the sun's rays are breaking through the forest's drenched canopy. We pause by a family, where a lady is nursing a sick piglet that she keeps warm in a torn blanket. The young pig is suffering from a potentially life-threatening virus and needs urgent treatment with antibiotics to have a decent chance of survival. I look up at Sun, who shrugs his shoulders with the stance of a man who wants to help but does not have any effective drugs with him. I explain that I have antibiotics for human viruses in my luggage but feel reluctant to administer them, as I have no knowledge to the effect they would have. I discuss it briefly with Sun, who in turn explains this to the woman and between us we decide that the pig probably has a ninety per cent chance of survival without them, so I saunter off to fetch them.

The main role of the Cambodian Rural Development team is to educate, promote and offer tangible, practical advice and assistance to benefit the communities they come into contact with. This morning I'm invited to join them on the short trip across river to the village of Ben Tang. A motorised longtail boat is waiting for us at the shoreline as we appear down a gentle gradient to the water's edge. I stand for a few moments and scan the serenity of the river here and admire the flat surface that is deceptively swift to the naked eye. At this moment, its tinted waters are unperturbed by boats and as it flows by, I'm wholly convinced that this is much the most splendid view I have yet had of this mighty river and begin to wonder what its trajectory will become in Tibetan waters, as I edge closer to the source. As we gently motor across, I peer over the water, scouting for a view of the rare dolphins that alas do not materialise. At the other side, we alight and walk up the slope to a prominent communal shelter, that doubles as the village hall. About fifty locals are seated, cross-legged, on the bare wood floor in mini groups that do allow for both genders to sit in the same cluster. The men sit quietly whilst rolling trumpet like cones of banana leaf filled with tobacco and chuff away casually, interjecting with occasional curious glances towards me. The village chief appears from up the stairs, so I stand to greet him with my hands clasped together, like two open books and motion a respectful, greeting. He slouches to the floor and rests against a supporting pillar, his presence seems subdued and he wears the look of a forlorn character seeking respect and recognition for his status. The meeting begins and it is soon evident that immense patience is an essential part of the team's job, as women fuss over babies, men chat and smoke and a man walks in clinging to a bottle of rice wine. The discussions are generally light hearted, anything more would lose their interest, and so the overloading of factual, precise in-depth information is kept to a minimum. The wife of the chief seems to exercise the most control in creating a positive response from fellow villagers. She looks resplendent in a traditional blue and gold wrapped skirt, smart black top and her beetle stained teeth compliment the look as she helps dictate proceedings, which at times are slow and cumbersome.

The main issue they tackle is the lack of any form of basic education here, which has resulted in years of neglect towards any progression. The discussions are set to be very long and Sun is keen to show me around and impress upon me the extent of the problems that face this community. We meet villagers who are digging and widening the paths into more accessible corridors and men who make new ploughs for the fields and those who just lounge in the shade, who Sun tries to cajole into making meaningful use of the morning. He shows me half-finished projects that villagers have abandoned such as a frog pool that lies idle, which Sun says could begin to provide them with an income if completed. 'Giving them back their pride, remains our biggest challenge' he tells me. Some have responded to the assistance they have received, one man I meet proudly shows off the progress he has made. His proud new house will be finished in the next few months and is surrounded by pigpens, chicken sheds, a rain well and an abundance of banana trees. His future plans include a vegetable patch, a toilet to improve sanitation, superior rearing methods for his livestock, more fruit trees and to increase his rice production. The man's grit and determination is a testament to his motivation and the help offered by Sun's organisation, which it is hoped will lead many of them, if not directly, out of poverty towards a brighter, more prosperous future.

Sun returns to conclude his business with the villagers at the central meeting hall, as I take refuge under a mango tree from the midday heat. As I gaze out across the water, I'm lucky enough to spot my first dolphins and although only a distant glimpse it feels as though I could touch them. The three mammals include a young juvenile, which breaches the water gracefully while his parents glide through and disappear as they head to the safety of the deep pools after a feeding mission. Sun had earlier told me that the government is employing over seventy-five guards to patrol the areas that the dolphins inhabit, which he says would be an excellent measure if the plight of the villagers who live alongside them had also been considered, which may have prevented the unnecessary collision course with the traditionally revered dolphins.

Back on Buddha Island we have a scrumptious lunch of fried chicken. The bite-sized pieces on the bone are fried with a pounded paste of peanuts, red chilli, lemongrass, galangal and turmeric, to which a fragrant wild leaf, with a hint of bitterness and the texture of spinach, contributed to a dish that again was fired by the heat of the chilli. To counter-balance that, a soothing, light, fresh soup with thick juicy pieces of Basa fish, lemongrass, lime leaf, shredded ginger, chives, spring onions and a generous hand with lime juice offers me once again evidence of Cambodia's excellent cuisine. The fact that all of the food cooked for lunch was grown on the island or caught in the waters surrounding it, fills me with an enormous degree of satisfaction. What also gives me and my stomach great pleasure is that after eight weeks of travelling in and around the river, I have still yet to fall foul of any food borne illness. Is that such a surprise? If you think about it logically, it doesn't strike me as so, for all the food I have eaten has involved ingredients at the peak of freshness, which easily compensates for the lack of refrigeration and in the case of this island, picked and cooked at source. It doesn't get much better than that in my book.

Since I first saw that giant mussel shell on our trip downriver, I have continually bugged Sun to ask if we could take to the river and forage for these molluscs and the snails that are popular in these areas. After lunch, news of a rummaging mission has spread and plans are in place to leave about 3pm. We meet back at the boat and our numbers have swelled from four to nine since our trip this morning. I've changed into my swimming shorts and for now, cover my legs with my Burmese green Longyi and secure everything else in my red waterproof scuba diving bag. The four young ladies that accompany us have already donned their life jackets as we move away and motor noisily downstream. My extended time spent on the water has been precious to me, while the opportunity to step into it an added bonus that I had not expected when I left the chilly climes of England.

We drive slowly and scour the river positions that are adjudged, historically as good hunting territory and stop first at a location only ten metres from the bank of Buddha Island. The skipper grabs the long rope attached to our boat and jumps into the water towards the trees that fight the force of the river and to which he will secure us to, prevent a rapid passage downriver. He stands with the water rising to his chest and battles to the trees where he leashes the rope to a tree, which, due to the strength of the current, tugs at the flora. In quick succession we all jump into the chilly waters to begin foraging. Due to my size the water level brushes my chin as I struggle to even walk against the flow. The impact of this river's strength is fully understood when I attempt to dive beneath the water and briefly scrape a rock with my hand, before hopelessly aborting and clinging with my right hand to anything that is stable below and popping to the surface. I struggle to maintain any grip, as my hand is wrenched from the stone I hold and I'm sent hurtling downriver past the rear of the boat, before I frantically swim back upriver and grab onto the safety of the boat. The energy I have just asserted leaves me panting and my arms and legs burning, as I watch the skipper rise from below with a solitary mussel that is scant reward for his perseverance. We clamber back into the boat, unleash the rope and move back to the centre, where we move upriver to another site. The same routine is repeated, the depth of the water identical to the previous position closer to the shore and the results equally predictable. The skipper enters into a discussion with two of the ladies aboard and motions a finger to indicate that we should head downriver once more and try the other side of the island to see if that improves our chances. Our total haul of three mussels and about twenty-five minuscule snails doesn't inspire any confidence, particularly as we have three big buckets to fill. The hot sun bakes my wet skin in seconds as we head to the corner of the island, Sun points to an area in the river where dolphins might be, relaxing in the deep pools that enable them to reside here all year round. Ominous dark clouds have closed around us as we head round the bend of the island and back up river. Approximately 4 km and almost dead centre of the river, we lash the boat to a small forested area, that upon testing the depth with a paddle, indicates a very shallow site. Everyone is in quickly and a boost to our meagre pickings comes in the form of a grandiose show of exhibitionism from the skipper who hauls up a gigantic rock covered in snails and mussels and holds it aloft in triumphant glory. The water only reaches just above my waist here, so the need for diving is thankfully not required and a convenient sheltered area of trees circumnavigate our bodies enabling us to pick without too much fear of shooting downriver. When I finally pick my first mussel I let out a whoop of ecstatic joy and receive congratulations from everyone as I toss it into a bucket that Sun holds in his hand. The two youngest foragers, aged only nine and ten respectively, are easily the most prolific pickers from the sandy, rock strewn bed of the river but I couldn't care less, just being in the water is reward enough at this moment. For the next two hours we continue to hoover up good quantities and although I insist that any undersized mussels go back, our haul is now an impressive two and half buckets. A light rain is now beginning when the decision is taken to head back. Foraging for you own food is immensely gratifying, picking from the bed of one of the worlds great river's a tough, pleasurable challenge that will only be complete when we have cooked our catch.

We arrive back just after 6pm. As I step from the boat, the full impact on my calves and thighs becomes all too apparent as a burning sensation rips through my aching muscles. The constant pressure of water battering against them has taken its toll and I scarcely manage to hobble back up the slope to the house. We place the buckets near the water butt, where the cleaning of our mussels and snails will commence before cooking. After a well-earned cold bucket shower, I dress and join the others for dinner with the appetite of a crocodile that has just finished fasting. Tonight, the man of the house is curled up in the corner, his shivering suggests a fever and he also complains of feeling weak and sick, the instant diagnosis is he may have malaria, which regrettably is still a major threat here and will continue to be for many years to come, I fear. Our dinner consists of sweet fried fish which we wrap in sour wild leaves with mint and basil, then dip in a heavily lime influenced dip flavoured with red chilli, crushed peanuts and fish sauce. Next comes a soup that has a heavy reliance on turmeric, which I find a touch overwhelming, is packed with the green leaves of the tamarind plant, which introduces a hit of sourness, and moist chunks of fish. We don't linger tonight and head straight back, where the colleagues hold a meeting until 9.30pm and I catch up on some writing. The mussels seem destined to be cooked tomorrow until the idea of a late night snack is introduced.

We enter into the back of the dimly candle lit room, the glowing embers of the charcoal stoves in the corner flicker faintly, as Sun stokes them ready for an unexpected night time feast. Thus far, throughout my journey, I have yet to prepare or cook a single item of food, so, the opportunity to hone my skills on unfamiliar shores is seized upon without hesitation. I volunteer to cook the oval mussels and begin by scanning the preparation area for ingredients as inspiration. The mussels and snails have been thoroughly purged in three separate stages to remove any grit or minute gravel. It is no exaggeration to mention, these mussels are specimens that would compete with the size and weight of a pacific oyster and surpass any 'green lip' variety that I encountered in New Zealand. I grab some long stalks of lemongrass, several limes, freshly harvested galangal root, garlic and a few red chillies and squat over a round log chopping board with a heavy cleaver. At this point, I figure if I have learnt anything in Cambodia, it is that their love of pounding ingredients to a paste is often an essential foundation to much of its delicious food. So I pick up the solid round mortar to my left and my selection of ingredients and begin bashing them. Everyone watches me intently, curiously scrutinising my every move and probably wondering if I have any clue to what I am doing. With my paste ready to use, Sun suggests I may like to add some kaffir lime leaves to boost further the aromatic essence of my dish. I quickly shred them with the cleaver and sprinkle them onto the paste and blend together with my fingers. As the two fires are now ready, Sun offers me a pan, which I dismiss quickly as too small for the task and instead point to a deep wok, which he places directly on the heat. I add a splash of palm oil to the smoking wok and the paste which I fry for about a minute, followed by good handfuls of the black shelled mussels, before slamming down a makeshift lid that is far too big for the pan. On the adjacent stove, Sun's colleague is gently steaming the snails with lemongrass and galangal. After a few minutes I check on the progress of the mussels, which I mix and turn over with a metal spoon before replacing the lid. It takes about five to six minutes until they are all fully open and I lift them from the roaring orange glow of the fire. In a bowl, I prepare a dip by squeezing plenty of juice from the limes and mix with cracked black pepper and salt. All four of us sit cross-legged in the centre of the room, burning incense wafts gently through the air, as we dig into the steamy pots before us. I choose the biggest mussel first, release the meat from its connective muscle and drop it in my mouth and begin chewing the flesh. Its texture is closer to that of a large clam, and after the initial flavour dissolves, it's bland and uninteresting. It sounds ludicrous, especially as I know they live in freshwater, but my baffled brain has sent a message to my palate to expect a salty, sweet hit of shellfish glory, much the same as when I eat crayfish from the River Thames and unfairly compare them with the sweeter impact of an ocean langoustine. Sun and his colleagues graciously congratulate me on my cooking, which I'm happy to accept, as I dip another mussel in the citrus, peppery dip that cheers up an otherwise unexciting foodstuff. The insipid liquid is not slurped or drunk but left hopelessly abandoned; to be discarded outside before we retire to bed. Tomorrow, we must travel upriver back to Stung Treng, where I will say farewell to Sun, his colleagues and the intriguing Cambodian cuisine, as I continue my pursuit of culinary adventures up the Mekong and enter the land-locked country of Laos. I've witnessed the rebirth of Cambodian cuisine that for so long has lived in the shadow of the widely recognised Vietnamese fayre but is now ready to ignite the passions of its people and all who travel this Golden Kingdom.

Laos

The Bolaven Secret

My entrance into Laos became a slow, tedious journey of mishap and opportune travel fortune that took far longer than I had originally anticipated. The morning began with a simple crossing from the river's east to west bank on one of the passenger ferries heading for the Laos border or surrounding villages. Yet to arrange a ride, I became engaged in a conversation conducted in broken English dialect with a tall, lean Cambodian man who, for a respectable fee would offer me a space in his pick-up truck. His white Toyota certainly seemed in decent condition, with a few minor scrapes and dents, but overall the white four-wheel van appeared to be roadworthy. That is, until he lifted the bonnet and discovered that a fundamental piece of kit was missing from its dangling leads. He offered me a look of embarrassed resignation as he informed me that he forgot to bring the battery with him. I thought his mind may have been triggered, as when we embarked on the journey across, he nearly fell arse over head on a dozen or so. While I wait for another vehicle, I mosey over to a bamboo shelter and order a bowl of decent noodle soup and smoke a few cigarettes. Smoking is a habit, that I invariably ease into when I'm on the road; I'm not sure why, as back in the UK I'm a very casual smoker at best. I have though, always found it a simple social icebreaker, particularly among men, who after an effortless spray of tobacco often register you as a convivial intruder into their world. An hour passes before a suitable vehicle arrives that is going the full 40 km to the border post and whom I negotiate a lift with. Heavily laden with sacks of merchandise, the battered truck doesn't inspire confidence but after a much-needed inflation of the back tyres, we begin trundling along the bumpy dirt road.

I sit crammed in the back between two middle aged Cambodian men, who, like me, have to endure the screeching voice of a woman in the front passenger seat, as she maintains an Olympian pace of verbal diarrhoea that leaves my previously relaxed persona in a state of fractious meltdown. I clear customs quickly and without incident. Nearing the Laos customs post, I'm greeted by herd of goats, which immediately scurry into the forest, pay the customs official $1 to stamp my passport and join a group of men sheltering a few feet away on a bamboo platform. I'm officially in Laos, happy and contented, but for now with no means of forward transport and a serious shortage of passing traffic. Next to me is a dead creature slumped over a catapult; the freshly shot reddy brown animal is a type of squirrel that is clearly destined for the pot later. After a considerable session on the 555s, gentle banter with the customs officials and a couple of hours later, two brand spanking new land cruisers appear from Cambodian territory and I ease to my feet ready to negotiate a ride. Two key factors are certainly in my favour here; firstly I'm a lone traveller and secondly I always present myself at official custom posts wearing the smartest clothes I possess. This latter point is a key lesson from my African travels of eleven years ago, that at least afforded me a scrap of dignity in otherwise often humiliating circumstances. These are clearly wealthy individuals, who initially seem reticent to even communicate with me, then inform me that they have no room, but with gentle persuasion relax enough to ask me where I am heading. Just above the Cambodian border, lay the enticing prospect of the Khon Falls and the labyrinth known locally as 'Si Phan Don' or Four Thousand Islands. I had planned this to be my first destination in Laos and all seemed to shape well, when one of the men finally agreed to allow me to travel with them to a point near the falls. A green military jacket hangs from the back of his supple leather driving seat indicating this man holds notable rank in the army. His attractive wife, a faultlessly fluent English speaker sits with cool posture, while their three children watch DVDs on flat screens and I congratulate myself on my good fortune that this luxury air-conditioned carriage affords me.

After bumping along a ditch-riddled, muddy dirt track we are soon cruising on perfectly smooth tarmac heading to our mutual destination. However, the events of the next half hour conspire against me and numerous junctions later, it becomes evident that the Khon Falls have tumbled from the agenda and Highway 13 is now guiding us further up to Pakxe, 120 km north of the border post. The disappointment I feel at this point is comfortably cushioned by the recollection that this is an area I have once visited before, so the temptation to remonstrate and kindly ask to be dropped close by passes without a word being spoken. It was back in October 2002 when I spent a peaceful week beguiled by the magical landscape of an archipelago that carves the Mekong into a 14 km wide web of rivulets dotted with islets, rocks and sandbars. Days spent lounging in a hammock attached to my $1 per night stilted bamboo hut, idly observing life drift by on the island of Don Det, while eating the best coconut curry that has ever passed my lips. I can still taste the succulent chunks of fatty pork in the blissfully creamy aromatic broth, with ingredients dug or picked from their garden and the coconut pressed by hand only when the dish was requested. It was the finest ensemble I have ever had the pleasure to wait over two hours to eat and I've still to taste anything similar that even comes close to matching it. I remember motoring gently through the channels, to view sunsets at the north of the island that lit up the sky, tinting it deep red and orange that gleamed down with mesmerising brilliance on the shining water. The swaying palm trees of coconut, cede to jade and emerald coloured rice paddies in their interiors, while the placid waters flow into the ferocious low level Khon Falls that would scupper any ambitions the French had of transforming this through fare into a commercially successful waterway. To compensate, the French constructed a railroad to haul cargo from beneath the falls, up Don Khon and across to the wharf on Don Det Island. It was and still remains a colossal work of engineering that for a time extended France's influence in Indochina, before its dream faded and died. Back then, it benefited only the French, while the Laotians, who laboured in the gruelling heat to complete the work, received little advantage. Today the narrow-gauged railroad is a colonial relic, its steel rails long gone with only occasional glimpses of wooden ties surfacing from the railbed, while a structure used for hoisting cargo from the train and a rusty, black locomotive are all that remain of a project that offers its gentile residents only reminder of the toil under colonial rule. The falls themselves are not that spectacular but while this maybe true, the Khon Falls offer a powerful reminder of natures ability to wrestle the initiative from this human encroachment and preserve part of the river's spirit and integrity.

Arriving in Pakxe, around 2pm, the dusty city (as in the whole of Laos, the term city is used loosely, as with even the capital Vientiane, none of them truly merit the term, being as they are, large towns) is much as I remembered five years previously. The main drag is an undistinguished, drab collection of buildings except for the elaborate, fairytale carbuncle the Champasak Palace Hotel, which looks like a giant wedding cake and was the brainchild of an eccentric Prince who commissioned it so he could entertain in lavish surroundings. However, Pakxe is not without significance and the city that sits on the confluences of the Xe Don and Mekong rivers is an important commercial and transportation hub and profits from its proximity to the Thai border and the fertile plains of the Bolevan Plateau. It is the latter that is the big draw for me and I have been keenly anticipating discovering its delicious, mouth-watering secret since this trip's inception. Having thanked the owner for the lift, I hail a tuk-tuk and with curiosity reigning supreme, noisily rattle off back towards the Champasak Palace Hotel. The hotel certainly bestows the sense of grandeur as we splutter up the sweeping drive to the entrance but as I step inside the foyer, a sense of anticlimax hits me as the stale atmosphere presents itself in the unenthusiastic staff that echo the hotel's decline. That said, the large, airy bedrooms are still well kept though and the crafted wood panel interiors and substantial shutter windows open out onto decent views of the Mekong allowing me to imagine briefly the lavish parties this building was destined to hold.

Ariya arrives at 10am sharp in his father's Toyota station wagon and steps from the cabin in a crisp white shirt, blue slacks and polished shoes. Having advised me to check out and move to a brand new Thai built hotel, he lifts my tired, tattered blue Berghaus FGA rucksack and rests it on the back seat. Before I left England I made several key contacts that I felt might be useful in order to make my trip as fruitful as possible, the rest has occurred with the organic spontaneity that I relish and could never shun. Ariya is one such person, introduced to me by the Thanksgiving Coffee Company, which works in union with the Jhai Coffee Co-Operative, who in turn represent hundreds of individual farmers who grow and harvest coffee in the higher grounds of the Bolevan Plateau. Since my first visit to Laos and a subsequent one to Luang

Prabang in 2006, I've longed to discover the secret of the fabulous coffee that is produced here and with Ariya to guide me I might be about to find out.

Turning off the highway, we join the road to Pakxong and begin climbing gradually on the winding roads, passing roadside stalls stacked with magnificent looking pineapples in rows of neat symmetry. The stifling heat of the Mekong basin gradually subsides, as Ariya switches off the air-conditioning and we both wind down our windows to allow the warm breeze to waft through the cabin. The same feeling must have been felt by the first Frenchmen that ventured to the cooler climes to escape the searing heat and to whom this area became a pleasant haven during the punishing months that made it excruciating to remain in Pakxe. Ariya points out factories and processing plants, not necessarily of any great size but significant in the development of infrastructure and evidence of increased investment in this region. Trucks laden with cabbages rest by the roadside and at varying points, sacks of the round pale green vegetables are dropped ready to be picked up by passing trucks on their way to the main market in Pakxe or further afield across the border to Thailand. Masses of trees line the roads with an array of ornamental flowers that hang upside down and appear like giant courgette or pumpkin flowers, for which the local name of 'speaker flower' is brilliantly apt. Cows, the exact colour as our native Jersey cow, huddle by the roadside and take advantage of the excellent grazing pasture at this higher level. I ask Ariya if they milk the cows here? 'No, not really, they are predominantly reared for their meat.' Which he tells me has a fine, rich flavour. We journey through the main settlement of Pakxong, an unassuming town that is only of any significance due to its large market, where buyers bid for coffee.

As we reach the tiny hamlet of Thonset, Ariya pulls off the

main road and turns right down a muddy track, where we come to a stop at a peculiar house that appears to be only half built. The cool, clean air is blissfully invigorating, as we are now at 1300m, almost the highest point on the plateau. We step through the sparsely furnished interior, where a bare-chested elderly man sitting on a wooden stool, grinding freshly roasted coffee beans to a fine powder using a pestle and mortar, greets us with warm affection. The old man is part of the 520 strong Jhai Coffee Farmer Co-Operative (JCFC), to which Ariya is the general manager. The cooperative began back in 2001 with the aim of securing exploited farmers a fair deal for their coffee and to foster new methods of production, technical expertise and quality control that would lend more credibility to the undoubted excellence of the coffee produced here. French Colonialists were the first to identify this region as having the potential to grow coffee. The plateau, with ample rainfall, cool temperatures and rich volcanic soil, reaches an elevation of over 1300m at 15 degrees latitude – perfect conditions for growing world-class coffee. The first trees were planted in 1915, but this initial experiment failed and another attempt was made in 1917, when both Arabica and Robusta plants were selected from Saigon's botanical gardens and planted in Thateng, a village in the north of the plateau. This was once again a failure, although many believe due to lack of care more than anything else. The real breakthrough came in the late 1930s with the trees planted in 1936, although it would be three years before the trees bore fruit and a further three until beans were produced of drinkable quality. Colonial rule can certainly be blamed for many poor selfish acts but the decision to plant coffee has left a lasting legacy that could benefit the inhabitants of the Bolevan Plateau for centuries to come. In its first year the JCFC collectively produced 1.7 tonnes of coffee, rising to 9 tonnes in 2002 and increasing year on year, recently to an annual level of 46 tonnes and this should remain on an upward trend for the foreseeable future. In total, the yield of coffee produced throughout this fertile region was approximately 20,000 tonnes in 2007 and it has already bought wealth to a number of budding individuals. Eighty per cent of the coffee is produced from the taller trees of the Robusta, which many growers prefer, not for its superior quality but for its high resistance to disease. However, Arabica is the most prized and at double the market price, farmers are slowly beginning to reverse this trend. Real coffee connoisseurs, fortunate enough to have tried it, revere the Arabica Typica grown here which balances acidity and body with a unique palate of light lemony citrus, floral and chocolate notes.

The harvest here commences in November with the heavy yielding fruit of the Arabica and runs through to January. In February the Robusta is picked and this continues into March. The farmers now have a choice, either sell the fruit in their natural state or process it to maximise their income. To achieve the maximum price, great care needs to be administered while preparing the fruit and this crucial stage has been the focus of the experts' time spent educating the growers. The Robusta employs a natural process, where the cherries are laid out directly on the drying surface in the sun for about twenty days and the entire fruit, with the beans inside, are hulled, graded and sorted for selling. To produce the best Arabica, the beans must first be squeezed out of their husk by a pulping machine, then left to ferment for a day, before being washed and laid out on raised netting to dry. When the beans reach eleven per cent moisture, they are hulled to remove the parchment, graded by size and sorted to remove damaged beans. This process produces a clean, smooth cup of coffee that balances acidity and body, allowing the true aromas and flavours of the coffee to blossom. Ariya confessed that it was hard work, requiring unending patience to convince farmers to embrace these more painstaking methods and he is justly proud of their significant achievements as a cooperative.

We drive the short distance back to Pakxong to have lunch at a roadside restaurant. It is one of only a few eateries in town and specialises in deer meat and other wild game from the surrounding forests, which strictly speaking should not be hunted anymore and is officially illegal. The local inhabitants uphold a long tradition of hunting, so in practice the laws are overlooked and it flourishes in much the same manner today. The hunters bring their kill directly to the door and as we walk into the small dark, dingy room, one is just leaving with a gun levelled on his right shoulder much to the appreciation of a group of Thai businessmen who are enjoying their lunch in the annexe. The fierce brew of fermented rice whiskey, known as *lao-lao,* is lined up in large glass jars on the shelves nearby. Ariya greets the owner and a jar is lifted from the shelf and placed before us with two tumblers. The Laoation people adore rice whiskey with the same passion as a Scotsman loves malt whiskey and while it lacks the international reputation of its cousin, it is woven into the patchwork of their society. The one I am about to sample is fermented with the genitals of a goat (as I travel through Laos, their fondness for fermenting with unappealing parts of an animals anatomy becomes an everyday occurrence). Ariya pours a healthy measure, while a lady brings honey from a bucket on the floor and adds a generous spoonful to the alcohol. Before I taste the sweetened liquor, I walk over to four white buckets on the floor, one of which contains the honey and after receiving permission, dip my finger into the golden nectar and savour the sticky taste of wild flowers that give this honey its identity. Mixed with the whiskey, it adds a delicious counterbalance with the harsher alcohol and instead of ripping out my throat, just mellows soothingly in the mouth. Thick medallions of deer meat arrive coated in honey; the juicy, forgivingly pink flesh is superb, offering flavour of intense gaminess with livery back notes. Last night, Ariya had introduced me to the popular Laotian creation of *lap,* which is created using either raw or cooked minced fish or meat. Here we receive tiny flash-fried cubes of deer meat tossed with fiery red chillies, torn mint leaves, chopped spring onion and plenty of lime juice, that is not served hot but at room temperature as a salad. The heat from the chilli makes my eyes water, the freshness of mint and sapping citrus sour lime notes deliver a counterpunch to my invigorated palate. Finally, shifting away from deer, to a wild bird that lives in the tops of trees high in the forest canopy, similar to that of a small eagle and sporting a wingspan of colossal proportions we delve into a murky, unappetising grey broth. Flavoured heavily with lemongrass, galangal, lime leaves and supplemented with spring onion, shallot and a sprinkling of sticky rice, the liquor is intensely rich, its deep flavour indicative of a stock made from pheasant, partridge and grouse carcasses but alas, it is let down by meat that is as tough as the rubber produced in the plantations that occupy the lower plateau reaches. It had been cooked over a fierce flame that has not allowed the protein to soften, as it would over a slow, sympathetic flame.

It is not just coffee that the Bolevan Plateau is famous for. This area also supports many excellent tea plantations that thrive in similar climatic conditions and enjoy the organic matter in the volcanic soil. The picking season is a different cycle to coffee and is now in full swing, the rains helping the leaves to flourish and harvesting continues through to July. We drop in briefly to the factory operated by Batieng Products and witness around eighty employees laying out green and red tea leaves on large wooden, slatted tables covered with blue plastic canopies, where the leaves dry for three days before sorting and packing. The coffee I had previously heard of, but I had no clue that high quality tea was also produced on the plateau. In the pack house, I watch as workers weigh two gram portions into individual bags on electronic scales, then pack twenty into neat, handmade bamboo boxes that receive a manually administered label. Only a fraction of this tea will be distributed in the domestic market while the bulk is exported, mainly to France who will receive sixteen tonnes this year. Their long-term goal is to market their tea, like coffee producers, as a high grade, premium product that can stand with the best in the world.

As we drive away from the tea factory, Ariya and I enter into a very different discussion about this area and talk about the horror of the Vietnamese war that spilled over into Laos. From 1964 until the ceasefire of February 1973, the United States air force flew 580,944 sorties (or 177 a day) over Laos and dropped 2,093,100 tonnes of bombs – equivalent to one plane load of bombs every eight minutes around the clock for nine years. This region bore the tremendous brunt of those despicable attacks. More bombs were dropped in Laos than on Germany throughout the whole of World War Two, making Laos officially the most bombed country per capita in the history of warfare. The war in Vietnam was a very public, media frenzied affair, images of which are etched in the archives of American and Vietnamese history. The bombing that took place in Laos was never made public, carried out in total secrecy in a country that had officially become classified and in what became known as the Secret War was the official dumping ground for any bombs that the Americans failed to drop on targets in Vietnam. The Lao people paid a heavy price, a neutral pawn in an evil game. The eastern areas of Laos, connected as they were to the Ho Chi Minh trail, became a mass of misery and death that continues to this day through the horrors of landmines. As we continue our drive, I scan the fertile landscape with agonising thoughts of the unnecessary hurt that afflicted an innocent population. It is wholly depressing.

We drive on and stop briefly at the cooperative's house in Phouoy village, where Ariya checks a few things. Old Arabica trees surround the solid wooden, stilted construction, some dating back fifty years, while under the house a brand new grading machine and bamboo matted tables for drying the beans lay dormant for now. I had expected neat rows of trees in immaculately maintained plantations carefully groomed by the farmers, but instead there is a rugged wildness to their formations. Several farmers have now opened nurseries to sell young coffee plants for extra income and the preferred method is to raise them in the wilds of the forest canopy, offering the protection in a free, natural environment. The whole process feels and looks so organic, that as we drive on it shocks me when Ariya directs my gaze to a clearing that is anything but. Industrial tractors are hard at work preparing the ground for the invasion of Vietnamese growers that are snapping up land here, enticed by the prospect of a quick buck. In the last few years they have bought a total of 700 hectares in order to grow coffee here but their interest is not in tune with the local habitat and much angst is felt by farmers, who worry about the impact of aggressive, chemically induced farming. The Vietnamese want rapid returns and are not too fussy about the quality and Ariya fears their presence could harm the future image that has slowly been developed to promote coffee of world class standard. He does admit, reluctantly, that some of their methods, particularly relating to efficiency, could benefit the wider community but hopes the wild integrity of the regions plantations will be preserved in harmony with the forest. We drive further into the interior, along red brick dirt roads that occasionally hamper our progress with waterlogged ditches that send flurries of mud skyward as our vehicles wheels spin hopelessly and I jump out of the cabin to assist us through. Our final stop delivers us 10 km from the main road, to the village of Nont Luant and as we park up, two hefty dirt bikes career around the bend ahead of us and grind to a halt. Covered from head to toe in combative padded leather riding gear, Jeff, a giant of man, standing at least 6 ft 10 inches, climbs from his machine and lifts his mud-splattered visor. Jeff is a Londoner living in Phnom Penh, where he works as an architect and is on a week's adventure with a mate, Clive, a Kiwi, who resides in New Plymouth. Clive has already broken down twice in three days and Jeff now has a faulty clutch, which is causing him grief. It is a little after 5pm and they are seeking accommodation, which, with Ariya here represents little problem. We walk to a small shack on the corner, where a man, a member of the cooperative, greets Ariya and begins brewing coffee for us all. Excited children appear from houses, scurrying along the track with frantic energy and frighteningly cower away when the lanky Londoner stands and towers above them. In the cool of the evening air, I sit and chat, sipping on Beer Lao and nipping down the odd glass of lao-lao. At about 7pm Ariya and I rise to depart back to Pakxe. The drive back is conducted under cloudless sky, the darkness lit up by a blanket of stars as we gradually descend back to the river basin. As we enter the outskirts of Pakxe, a horrific road accident has occurred, the inadequate police presence guiding cars around the scene. Pools of red claret offer no comfort, as a lady kneels over a body and covers it with a yellow blanket. This type of fatal occurrence is shockingly frequent says Ariya and this strips the gloss from an insightful day in the Bolevan Plateau. After seeing this the thought of food leaves me a little cold but Ariya insists we stop at a favourite haunt of his and I'm glad he twisted my arm.

The Asia Restaurant is situated about 1 km from the centre of town and is an extremely popular destination that is very busy when we enter. The dining area, with areas both covered and uncovered specialises in food that was to become a firm favourite in Laos. Our table has a deliberate hole in the middle, to which a waitress brings a gas burner that nestles in the centre. A pan of grainy, clear stock is brought and placed on top, the flame ignited and the liquid coerced to the boil and then left to gently simmer and wait further instructions. Neatly sliced, thin pieces of fish are presented, fanned on a plate with a whole uncracked hens egg wobbling in the centre and a basket full of oyster mushrooms, morning glory, sweet green cabbage, water celery and uncooked strands of rice vermicelli, that stand ready for cooking. First the egg is cracked over the fish and Ariya mixes it thoroughly with his chopsticks. We mix our own dips at the table, firstly blending chopped red chilli, fermented fish paste, smooth pigs liver and sugar, and secondly one with just crushed peanuts and coconut water. With the stock simmering, Ariya adds the mushrooms, vegetables and rice vermicelli to the pot and allows them to wilt and cook for a few minutes, before we lift some egg coated fish slices and watch as the protein coagulates as the fish hits the steaming broth. The simplicity and immediate freshness is stylish, effortless communal food executed by anyone at the table. The pork-flavoured broth is light and subtle, tinged with sweet essence of coconut water and the cabbage the finest I have eaten thus far. Like the dish that was prepared on Buddha Island, the power to add your own fish at one's convenience is ramped up further upon dipping in the curious combination of fish paste and pigs liver. With a glass or two of the ubiquitous ice cold Beer Lao to wash it all down I leave the restaurant a contented man.

Dung Beetles

I'm standing in Pakxe central market staring down at a basket, next to a lady selling squawking live chickens, that contains tiny, oval black bugs that thrive in water buffalo dung and Ariya is trying his best to convince me that these bugs taste good. Is this guy serious, how an earth can something that resides in shit, any shit, let alone water buffalo shit, expect to taste of anything else than, well, shit! It doesn't help that after a mighty drinking session with Ariya last night, I am nursing a slamming hangover and can still taste last nights rocket fuelled lao-lao. The lady looks up at my startled, ashen expression, the smirk on her face beginning to crack as it breaks into laughter that encourages other traders to join in. Ariya goads me, mocking my hesitation as I stand and contemplate my decision. I think back to the grubby junction in Cambodia at Skuon, with its selection of creepy crawly delights that were easily palatable and, with a nod of my head, the astonished female trader begins ferrying the little mites into a plastic bag. I walk slowly away, not in the least convinced that these creatures might surprise me.

Markets in these regions of the world are generally not for the faint hearted and best avoided totally, if like me, your stomach cannot stand the punishment of looking at slabs of congealed blood and trailing innards of a pigs guts, while overcoming the alcohol excess of the night before. This is what I signed up for when I left the familiar, conservative shores of little England, so with a typical stiff upper lip I trudge over to the fish. I came here yesterday on a recce and was instantly stunned by the sudden increase in the size of the fish. There are species here that weigh in excess of 25 kilos, much larger than those I came across in Vietnam or Cambodia. Maybe the simpler less aggressive fishing methods allowed for species to flourish and mature or is it that the population of Laos, at only 5.25 million, is small enough, that the fish stocks may never come under pressure as they already have in the Vietnamese Delta? The Mekong is the lifeline of Laos and runs the length of this country, feeding from its tributaries and branches, which yield a ready supply of protein rich fish to the diets of the Lao people. We buy a 4 kilo fish called *pa nant* or 'skin fish' for 90,000 Kip (about $8). Its smooth, silvery skin gleams as the lady puts it head first into a plastic bag. The majority of fish here are not alive but turnover is rapid, boosted by eager Thai buyers with money to burn. Strings of red sausages, offal and dried meat hang from stalls as we purchase half a kilo of beef from the orderly line of traders. The market is busy, but as is the Laotian style, the pace is deliberately not frenetic, shouting is limited and negotiations are conducted calmly and quietly in order to maintain the equilibrium. Sacks of fresh green and red dried chillies sit alongside buckets of various forms of fermenting and dried fish, neatly arranged on rectangular wooden frames and herbs like holy basil, mint, coriander and for me, most surprisingly, dill. The dill is promptly bought, for no other reason than plain curiosity and joins our bulging bags of green vegetables, fruit and snails that Ariya purchased on the fringes of this exciting market.

Ariya's family home is set back from the main drag, the end where the bridge crosses the Xedon River and the road continues to Savannakhet and the capital Vientiane. The clapboard house has bottle grey wooden shutters with purple frames, while the exterior walls are awash with yellow paint that blends into the courtyard feel of this neat dwelling. Inside, a stuffed deer's head stares down at me fixed on the fading orange walls and complimenting the cow's head hanging opposite. The tops of the walls reserved for family portraits accentuated by a gold-framed picture of his parents, who seem to be inspecting my appearance when I enter the house. Ariya's sister comes to greet us; her pale complexion, due to morning sickness does nothing to hide her brimming smile. We walk across the wood-effect lino floor to the kitchen and preparation area, with an upright fridge-freezer and a deep sink for washing vegetables is positioned against the back wall. Ariya begins preparing the skin fish, by attempting to pierce its skin with a knife that makes no impression. I can't bear to watch as he forces the blunt knife into the silver skin of this fine specimen and begins tearing at the fish, ripping the flesh, a sight that almost makes me weep and to coin a phrase of many a chef at witnessing such an act 'he's bloody well murdered that'. His sister is far more accomplished and attempts to resurrect her brother's ham-fisted handling of the fish, as she trims and glides her sharp knife through the flesh, cutting thin slices across the grain and piling them carefully on a plate. Ariya's youngest sister washes all the herbs and vegetables in the sink, while Ariya slopes off to watch TV on the sofa.

As the cooking commences, I stand over his sister and observe, step-by-step, dish-by-dish, every detail of the cooking process. A pan of water simmers on the double gas burner to which she adds a pounded mix of lemongrass, onion, red chilli, galangal and garlic, a few lime leaves and handful of raw sticky rice that she previously soaked for ten minutes, drained and pounded to a rough powder. She drains some fermented fish through a bamboo sieve to remove any bones, into the pan, with a little salt, two handfuls of nutty coloured mushrooms and chunks of the white fleshed skin fish. This is left to simmer for thirty minutes, before a final addition of small, sweet leaves called *phai van* which she will stir in towards the end of cooking.

The acceleration and greater emphasis of fiery chilli heat in my early experiences of Laotian cuisine is rubber-stamped by the preparation of *tam mak tant,* an alternative to the more widely held version that uses green papaya. First, she peels two short, stubby, thick-skinned green cucumbers – different from the slender, fine seeded variety I am used to – and shreds them into a heavy mortar. What seems like an avalanche of cascading lime juice comes next, followed by sliced red tomato, tiny red chillies, fermented fish paste, fish sauce and a pinch of salt, that she pounds with a large pestle, mulching and blending to distribute the palate invigorating ingredients. With the broth simmering gently, the cucumber salad plated, she turns her attention once more to the fish and the dish of *la pa*. As with the previous preparation, the cook is seeking the lip smacking balance of heat, sweet, sour and salty to determine the success of the recipe and as cooks are wont all over the world, the use of an additional ingredient to enhance the finished dish is slipped in for good measure. To begin, she blanches slices of the skin fish in boiling water for a few seconds, drains and allows to cool in a bowl to the side. Once it has cooled sufficiently, the indigenous South East Asian spice galangal is chopped finely, followed with micro-thin strips of lime leaf, shredded spring onion, lashings of lime juice, dried red chilli flakes, sieved fermented fish paste and a good lug of fish sauce. Her use of dried chilli contrasts with my two previous examples, that both utilised fresh chilli, which she insists is equally as effective in delivering the necessary heat, but she alters its profile slightly by incorporating the dried version. To finish, she pulls a glass jar from the cupboard that houses a nutty brown residue made by toasting and pounding sticky rice to a fine powder and delivers a heaped teaspoon to the bowl. I look across at my small black, shiny bugs and wonder how these will be cooked, as she boils the snails, painstakingly purged four times in water to remove any unsavoury grit. Next, she prepares an omelette with sliced white onion, tomato and spring onions and pounds young ginger root with red chilli, salt, sugar, lime juice and fish sauce to accompany the snails. The fate of the dung loving beetles is confirmed by the arrival of a wok, half-filled with oil that is now heating on the gas ring ready to deep fry this peculiar delicacy. The oil sizzles as the bugs are fried to the point of crispy incineration and drained onto paper before finding their way to join the assortment of mouth-watering food that adorns the table.

I quickly pick a hot, crispy morsel from the plate and while, still with thoughts of a crusting, squelching dark water buffalo dung entrenched in my brain, take a bite that delivers a brittle, dry texture not dissimilar in taste to the crab and chicken flavour of the tarantula but, and I tell no lie here, lingering back notes of buffalo muck!

The cucumber salad is a palate propelled grenade, the rip roaring chilli causes a near fiery inferno in my mouth as the lime juice zips through to clean and extinguish, fully supported by an inviting salty hit and the glutinous sticky rice that I dip in the excess liquid at the base. The contrasting, almost uninteresting omelette offers a welcome relief before I delve into the fish salad. The crumbled fish slices have absorbed the other ingredients but remain distinctly identifiable and create further blistering havoc in my ignited chops. After the relative mellow, soothing food in the Vietnamese Delta and the democracy of introducing your own heat to dishes in Cambodia, the sudden switch to the realities of the Lao cuisine is taking some adjusting to, but its bold, exciting flavours delivered with instinctive verve have introduced a pulsating beat as my journey up the Mekong enters its eighth week.

When I first visited Pakxe back in 2002, my stay was merely a transitory affair, a convenient stopping off point on the way to the capital Vientiane and I remember little of the food. My loss then has been my gain this time round as during my six days I have uncovered a superior cuisine. Every evening the inviting aroma of barbecues grilling meat, fish and vegetables captivate the warm, humid air along the banks of the Mekong and the Laotians, particularly the young, gather here in numbers to socialise and enjoy the smoky charcoaled offerings. On our arrival, Ariya had arranged to meet three ladies visiting from Vientiane and local friend named Thet. To a background of melodic Thai pop music and flickering candlelight, we enjoyed a moreish feast of food that arrived steadily at our low-slung table. The common theme that has reigned throughout my Mekong journey is that of communal eating and this occasion is no different. A steady flow of dishes arrives, beginning with salt-crusted grilled fish accompanied with a dip and garnish plate of banana flower, lettuce, mint, the green, sour leaves of *pak lleua* and *pak tua* leaves and a separate plate of cooked rice vermicelli noodles. Each of us picks meat from the fish and I watch as Ariya nestles a lettuce leaf in the palm of his left hand and proceeds to add the fish, garnish and noodle, before wrapping it, handing it to me and instructing me to dip it in a pineapple and chilli sauce. The dipping sauce is a mixture of classic sweet and sour, a far cry from the heavily starched nonsense that is administered from the average Chinese take-away back in the UK. Such a clean, fruity chilli taste, the perfect foil to coat the small lettuce wrapped parcel. An interesting plate of fried rice with finely shredded pork rind, roasted peanuts, lime juice and fermented fish paste is topped with fried crispy pieces of pork meat, an unexpected combination and enhanced by the pleasingly crunchy textures of peanuts. Finally, a heap of sticky satay meat skewers are demolished, the caramelised exterior of grilled beef, cooked quickly, contains juicy, succulent protein that is even more lip smacking when dipped in the accompanying sweet chilli sauce.

Pakxe also has specialised goat restaurants run by Vietnamese cooks and the best bowl of noodle soup since Anh Hong in Ben Tre. The small soup restaurant, shrouded by trees, sits on the bend opposite the confluence of the milky, chocolate waters of the Xedon and greener flow of the Mekong River and is a peaceful breakfast or lunchtime retreat that is an alluring way to spend an hour admiring the restful, charming vista. The Lao call their noodle soup *foe* and even though the subtle flavour of cinnamon, star anise and ginger were lacking, the richly flavoured beef broth with juicy sweet cabbage served to garnish, was still an excellent example and worth a special visit.

The passenger ferry service that has long since ceased to operate means I'm once again, for now, restricted to road travel for the onward passage to Vientiane, and so I book a ticket on a modern, brightly painted sleeper bus that departs Pakxe at 8.30pm. My previous travel experience of road transport in Laos has been colourful and above all grindingly slow, so my expectations of leaving and arriving on time are basically zero. The only thing that occurs with any pace in Laos are the rocket-tail speed boats that propel people up and down the extensive navigable river highways of this land locked country. The river has long been the lifeblood of its people but even here, the gradually improving road system, particularly in the lower southern regions, is placing less reliance on water borne travel. Before I leave, Ariya extends an invitation to join him at friends for a few beers and light food to send me on my way. He also informs me of one last culinary treat that his friend has prepared in my honour and after the dung loving beetles episode, I've now decided not to ask any questions as to the identity and habits of the food I may be challenged to eat.

Tucked down a scrubby dirt road, we find Mr Joe, a man of huge proportions sitting in a bulging plastic chair. The rolling flab from his stomach extends over his thick, black cotton shorts as he pours himself more Beer Laos from the familiar, brown bottle. He reaches out to greet me, and then disappears into the house, returning minutes later clasping a bottle of Black Label Johnnie Walker whiskey. Their insatiable appetite for all things whiskey holds no bounds and during my time here Ariya had shown himself a man that shared a passion for drinking the fiery home brew and imported spirit that often left me reeling just at his stamina. I sit in a rickety swing chair barely able to support my light frame, as a lady brings a blackened pot to rest on the square bamboo table outside. I lean over to inspect the content. Whatever is inside is as black as freshly laid tarmac, with the appeal of drinking a glassful of diesel fuel. I can just about make out the feet and head of a creature that reveal sharp razor teeth and claw like toes, but I am none the wiser. A mushy purée of aubergine, onion, garlic and chilli has all the smoky hallmarks of the Lebanese *baba ganoush* and while I contemplate the mysterious concoction, I dunk sticky rice into the soft dip. I still can't work it out, my dumbfounded efforts at guessing are useless, so I grab a chopped piece from the pot and pop it in my mouth. An intense hit of rich, malty taste with a sharp degree of bitterness sits uneasily, the tar like stickiness is not unpleasant but is unrecognisable. The actual flesh is hard to distinguish, its flavour masked so manifestly that I could say with no clarity at all what it could be considered similar to. Ariya, sensing my anxious curiosity, explains, as he has done for all the food, what the recipe contains. I've actually just eaten the flesh of a lizard simmered gently in Beer Laos with lemongrass, lime leaves, galangal, red chilli and garlic. It is an extraordinary conclusion to my time in Pakxe and as I bid Ariya a fond farewell at the bus terminus, I determine that missing out Si Phan Don was a stroke of fate that has led me to discover much in an area, which, according to general guidebooks, offers little to the modern day traveller.

On the Bend

The rains have been falling intermittently during the last four weeks, its effect on the Mekong so visible in Cambodia at Kratie, that my arrival in the Laos capital of Vientiane and the river's surprising barren appearance leaves me a little perplexed. Vientiane hugs an immense sweeping bend on the Mekong, which at this time is dominated by a wave of sandbars giving the illusion that one may easily wade to the other side. The Mekong, having escaped from the gorges upriver that during the height of the wet season flood to form hazardous rapids, appears to simply tiptoe through a narrow passage that clings to the opposite bank. It seems almost unimaginable, that in the coming months, a torrent of water will transform this arid corner completely, submerging and eventually, threatening its low level banks to burst.

Vientiane has had a turbulent history, from the economic crisis that swept Asia in the late 1990s (the kip lost ninety per cent of its value against the US dollar) to the devastation it suffered at the hands of the imperious and ruthless Siam Kingdom over two hundred years ago, whose troops sacked and razed Vientiane, leaving only eminent religious dwellings intact. Garnier, who had anticipated his expedition's arrival (forty years after its decimation in 1826) with quiet and hopeful pleasure was astonished by the severity of the ruins that greeted him but was equally amazed to find the royal remains of what is now Wat Sisaket in reasonable shape and the recently restored That Luang, the most famous monument in Vientiane and one of the most revered in all of the Laotian states. Founded in the late sixteenth century, the great Buddhist stupa had only just been restored when the explorers saw it and today this splendid pyramid, covered with gold leaf remains a potent symbol to the people of Laos and the Buddhist faith, and burns ever brighter in the land of a million elephants.

The expected tourism has arrived, Highway 13 (connecting the south with the north) is completed, the wats gleam with golden splendour, international cuisine has emerged and GDP is steadily, rising but despite tentative reforms, Laos still remains one of the world's poorest countries and is hugely reliant upon foreign aid and investment. The Communist Party, the only legal political force in the country, has ruled since overthrowing the monarchy in 1975 and although it has allowed liberal reform, this is strictly limited and it maintains an iron grip over the media. Any slandering of the state, distorting of party policies and spreading false rumours are all criminal offences. It is estimated that eighty per cent of the population survive by subsistence farming, although experts claim that less than five per cent of the land is suitable and its reliance on the Mekong to feed the fertile floodplains to produce the main crop of rice once again illustrates the river's influence through a country that has little industry. Its people may be embattled in the rigours of their daily struggles to eat and live, the infrastructure is cumbersome and electricity, basic sanitation and education a mere pipe dream for the majority of its citizens, despite all of this Laos offers the outsider a genuine warmth, still largely untainted by the imbalance of mass tourism.

Every evening here I would stroll down to an open air bar, stopping always to observe locals playing *boules*, a bowling game introduced by the French, which is every bit as prominent as their legacy of freshly baked baguettes, and watch women gather under a large shed to perform yoga to pumping Thai and western pop music. Hawkers ply the riverfront selling cigarettes, dried fish and fruit, as I watch ladies and children forage for snails and crabs in the forest of dry vegetation on the extensive sandbars, amidst a redundant back drop of activity on the water. Vientiane is a city with the feel of sprawling low level towns, cobbled together and cemented with village fibres that lack the intensity of Saigon and underbelly of notoriety that lend Phnom Penh its sometimes lurid reputation. The laid back ambience of this city can either be refreshingly understated if you have spent weeks in the jungles of Northern Laos or damn right boring if you dare to compare it with the bright lights of Bangkok or Kuala Lumpur. Daily life ebbs and flows, beginning with the early morning call to alms by monks enrobed with bright saffron coloured cloth and climaxing with the dramatic, pummelling orange sun disappearing in a hazy shroud of brilliance, while lanterns burn and flicker as the air lingers with the wafting charcoal smoke of the barbecue restaurants that line the river's banks.

I, like Garnier, although for reasons of culinary obsession, not for the practicalities that he so yearned for, was expectant of a fruitful stay. My fortune in meeting Ariya's friends in Pakxe boded well for delving under the skin of the capital's cuisine, the resulting food while perfectly satisfactory, offered for the most part, a disappointing instalment after the excellent food of Pakxe. Every day Ariya's friend Khamphaeng would drop by my river-fronted guesthouse and join me for lunch, while for dinner we would be accompanied by her friends. Having studied in Chiang Mai, in the Northern Highland's of Thailand, she returned last year to take up a post working within government and her grasp of English is exemplary, although bashfully at first, she seems apologetic if I don't understand her. Her intellect to me is obvious, as she also speaks fluent Thai, French and a not insignificant knowledge of the Japanese tongue.

On my first night we drive through the streets of Vientiane to one of the many night food markets that operate from the early evening. The light traffic on the roads, a tangible sign of a still weak economy, means driving is less frenetic than Phnom Penh or Saigon, although accidents happen with the same regular frequency. We park the bikes before a barrier, where for a small fee a man guards them, while we slip into the street market. Women grill chicken on bamboo skewers, fish threaded through sugar cane or lemongrass and marinated beef kebabs that scent the warm night air, as plumes of smoke drift from open charcoal barbecues. Vendors serve whole river fish in tomato and onion sauce from metal trays and sticky rice from traditional lidded wicker baskets, as I lick my lips in anticipation. Here there are no seating areas, as the food is served, packaged and eaten off the premises. We choose the fish in tomato and onion sauce, sticky pork ribs direct from the barbecue, sausage flavoured with lemongrass, garlic, chilli and galangal and a mashed stew of soft aubergine with tomato, herbs and chilli that is spooned into a thin clear plastic sack. Large, nutty brown, deep fried discs of shrimps, minced fermented fish with chilli, snails cooked in beer and a container of soft, creamy bamboo soup complete our spread as we fill the basket on the front of the Honda and drive back towards the river. All along the river, tables for dining form ready-made picnic areas where cutlery is available even if your food is purchased from elsewhere. The novelty of dining solely with ladies allows me much needed respite from the alcohol-fuelled banquets that have become far too regular when sparring with male dominated testosterone and its cultural boozy bonding process.

I dip in and out of the culinary scene in the four days I spend here, frequenting restaurants that serve me roasted beef tongue with soy, coriander and chilli dip, more versions of *lap* that by default, is now my most eaten dish since my journey commenced, a tasty deep fried frog dish stuffed with pounded pork, garlic, lime leaf and salt, grilled young beef, bacon and liver cooked at the table and dipped in a similar broth eaten in the Asia restaurant in Pakxe and the intricate web of complexity spun by the creation of *aw lam* with its spellbinding selection of ingredients, that originates from the northern reaches of Laos. While eating my first example of *aw lam* the inescapable prospect of transporting myself upriver to Luang Prabang proves overwhelming, as it has done since my arrival in Vientiane. Perhaps I am guilty of not immersing myself totally in this city's food offerings and without the distraction of what many term 'the jewel of the Mekong' perhaps my attention would have been plunged in with deeper concentration. In truth, Vientiane held me here as a convenient stopgap, before I moved upriver, through the higher ground and onto the ancient royal capital.

Higher Ground

My bleary eyes struggling to open, I stare blankly at the flickering TV screen. I'm still fully clothed and the lights are on in my hotel room; my miserable failure to remain awake to watch the

Champions League Final only registers when I look at my mobile phone: 4.55am.

After a couple more hours sleep, I'm showered, clothed and downstairs for breakfast ready for a miserable cup of instant coffee and a slice of aerated toast. The token breakfast on offer is made worse today, for it doesn't begin until 8am, so my sleep deprived mind and body is instantly forced into convulsions of rejection. Having enjoyed the rich coffee of the Bolevan Plateau, the dreary, insipid hot liquid contained within the single serving is a tragic disappointment. I check out and hail a tuk-tuk to take me to the Northern Bus terminus, where I have an acceptable bowl of *foe* and a glass of fresh strong coffee with condensed milk. The multi-coloured bus looks battle scarred, the reclining seats, complete with flower power headrest covers, operate at body mangling angles that seem sure to cause discomfort. Since I woke this morning, the whole left side of my upper body has been stricken with a thudding pain, that increases to discomforting proportions with any sharp movement. My self-administering of Tiger Balm and painkillers, offers only mild relief to the puzzling rasping agony, as I settle and watch Vientiane disappear in the blink of an eye.

The bus sluggishly negotiates the inclines of the increasingly rugged terrain, as the monotonous lowland yields to dominant, dramatic valleys of limestone karsts that rise spectacularly over the Nam Xong River. Having completed this journey five years ago, I had toyed with the idea of flying to Luang Prabang but as I admire the stunning landscape to a chorus of clanking gears and creaking suspension, the vindication for not all apparent. From Vientiane, the Mekong disappears, its upriver passage points directly east, before charting north-westerly through narrowing gorges that during the wet season produce a barrier of successive rapids. The French explorer Henri Mahout had expressed surprise, that these gorges were able to contain the river's torrential force. The traffic on Highway 13 is very light and over the years this route has suffered from the fear of banditry and reckless driving from over zealous tactics of overtaking on blind bends. Indeed, just prior to stopping for lunch in the town of Kasi, a group of local tribes people could be seen, surrounding a wreckage that had overturned, its roof completely crushed and if the passengers survived, it would only be due to not tumbling down the steep bank it now unceremoniously teeters on. A canteen style lunch of pork, green beans and stir-fried greens is acceptable and infinitely finer than the average dross served up in our own expansive network of roadside eateries, although having a pee next to a stocky man carrying a pump action rifle over his shoulder could be described as just a little disconcerting.

Limestone karsts give way to waves of peaked hills, split by expansive valleys, the evidence of deforestation displayed by virtue of the hard to kick habit of slash and burn. Steams trickle down, descending into cascading waterfalls as a network of woven narrow paths navigates below, interspersed with shelters that offer shade to farmers in the middle of the day. Sweetcorn, banana, orange and longon trees line the road, hugged in part, by wooden constructions built directly to the ground and surrounded by wild herbs and edible plants. The need for stilted houses, which are so dominant in the preceding lowlands for fear of flooding, now become a superfluous practicality.

The first signs of Luang Prabang appear when the café au lait flow of the Mekong re-emerges far below to my left, snaking its way upriver, as we descend once more to join the mighty river and for the third time in my life, I can once more take pleasure in one of Asia's most beguiling cities. The sacred steep, forested hill of Phou Si, crowned with a Buddhist stupa stands high above the city, a striking symbolic gesture, guiding you to this country's religious core and officially announcing my arrival.

Ant Eggs and Lizards

In John Keay's book, *Mad About The Mekong*, about his own journey retracing the epic expedition of the Mekong Exploration Commission, he writes glowingly of Luang Prabang and describes it as the one city that still offers the modern traveller a sense of perspective of what greeted these nineteenth century explorers in April 1867. At first this could be seen as an astonishing disclosure but seen from the river, the approach to Luang Prabang is shrouded in leafy secrecy, its steep banks shield the eye from the low level colonial buildings, shops and quiet roads that sit behind swaying palm trees. Motorised pirogues arc across the swift flow of the Mekong's water, delivering goods and passengers to Xiang Men on the opposite bank. The tiered pyramid red roof of Wat Mai, emblazoned with gold, looks just as it would have all those years ago, so to today's traveller, putting aside a few modern extravagances of cars for water buffalo, engines for paddles and electricity for power, the Luang Prabang that greeted the early explorers could still be imagined to this day.

Luang Prabang sits on the confluence of the Mekong and one of its tributaries, the Nam Khan River. Royalty and Buddhism have been intertwined here for centuries, a bond severed by the incoming Communist Party of 1975. Initially viewed with hostility, as in most communist states, the importance and strength of this religion brought about a restrained tolerance and allowed Buddhism to play an active role in Lao life. Today, Buddhism continues to grow and its effect on daily life is most clearly observed here in its natural epicentre. The official royal line of command may have been severed when King Sisavang Vatthana was forced to abdicate in 1975 but their long reign here (even during French control, Luang Prabang continued to direct its own affairs) left a lasting legacy, no less in its cuisine, which is considered the finest in all of Laos.

As morning breaks, I'm woken to the rhythmic banging of drums, and as I step onto my balcony and wipe the sleep from my red eyes, I watch the mist rising through the trees overhanging the Mekong. It is a little after 5.30am, the echoing thuds announce a procession of saffron robed monks silently parading through the streets, wooden bowls cradled in their palms as one by one they leave the confines of the monastery grounds. Slowly they glide through the cobbled streets accepting alms from women who kneel by the roadside, filling the monks' bowls with sticky rice from kettles and wicker baskets. Early rising tourists gather, mostly respectfully, except for a Japanese lady, who darts abruptly in front of a monk who recoils as the flash on her camera explodes. The morning ritual has changed little over the centuries, the monks certain that the devout people will provide for them, nurturing a simple, enduring bond between belief and daily life.

Mr Somneuk is the assistant manager of the Sala Prabang, the stylish boutique hotel where I have chosen to stay for the duration of my time here. Its position overlooking the Mekong is advantageous and a delightful reminder that it was here that the seeds of my journey to explore this great river were sown and the subsequent culinary adventures to date, only happened due to the mesmerising, tranquillity of the scene before me. Having checked in yesterday and subsequently explained the background and purpose of my journey, Mr Somneuk had warmly extended an invitation to join him, his wife and young child on a picnic, on the outskirts of the city. I enthusiastically accepted, if he would allow me to purchase all the food. Around 7.30am, we stroll along the river road, taking in the former Royal Palace, temples and stationary tuk-tuks, their drivers softly touting for business. The

Royal Palace, built by the French, is a fascinating fusion of French and Lao architecture and now preserves paraphernalia of its distinguished monarchy. Constructed in 1904, it now houses the *Pha Bang*, the most sacred Buddha image in all of Laos, which its people believe possesses miraculous powers which safeguard the country. Rumours abound as to the true authenticity of the statue and historical accounts concur that the original was cast in solid gold and not the gold, silver and bronze on display here.

Every morning a food market squeezes into life on a narrow cobbled street, over-spilling up towards the main drag of Xiang Thong that runs parallel to the Mekong. The laid-back vibe that hums through the streets, wrapped in the palm of Buddhism, evokes its sleepy charm as traders display fresh produce. The perfume of blossoming trees of white, purple and yellow flowers wafts in the breeze through the quaint streets and bolsters the idyllic shopping environment. The slamming of a cleaver, squawking of a chicken or the feint rustle of plastic as a sale is completed, occasionally breaks the quiet hush of activity as locals mill about discussing the topics of the day. The distinctly cooler breeze of the early dawn slowly fades, as the sun exerts its authority and radiates over the old royal city.

The mellow atmosphere generates a plethora of mind spanning produce that whets my appetite. Since I left England, the longing to return here has accelerated with each passing day and the need to further my limited knowledge of its proud cuisine, tinkering on obsession. Like many markets throughout the world, the importance of arriving early to select from the fullest quota is easily apparent here. I steal a glance over my shoulder at two creatures that I reckon I may already have sampled in Pakxe. The chopped up flesh of a lizard rests in a pile next to the blood stained frame of its yet to be dismembered companion, its taut primeval claws and stiff tail, one of the many bush items on display. Somneuk averts my attention from the lizard, guiding me over to a lone snake curled up in an aluminium bowl and urges me to negotiate a price with its trader. Memories of the darkened, underground room in Phnom Penh drown my brain, as I begrudgingly explain that snake has been banished from my wish list. The thought of gnawing through the paltry flesh of another snake leaves me cold and unexcited, so I spin away and fix my culinary sights on a far more tempting purchase.

A solitary leg of wild deer, hunted from the thick, surrounding forests that line the Mekong's path, rests on a blood-splattered table, the remainder of the animal long since sold. Flies hover over the deep, dark red meat, picking at its recently killed flesh, which I decide to purchase. Nearly ten weeks into my river journey and I've thus far escaped any food-related illnesses, a fact I'm very happy about and long may it continue. The meat is slung into a plastic bag, along with a bag of skin that I'm learning is very popular too. Stacked sheets of bottle green, dried riverweed with sesame seeds and compact bunches of peppery watercress, both specialities of the region, are added to my wares. The leaves are a degree smaller than our native variety, the flavour more subtle and may only be found in the Luang Prabang region of Laos, where it is harvested in great abundance. Long lengths of lemongrass, join spring onions, red tomatoes, garlic, galangal and two bunches of cress, as our shopping moves gently through the gears. Halfway down the narrow road opens out to the left, where traders display pork, beef and particularly fine chickens that look well reared by the tight formation of their bodies. Just to my right, a man slams a cleaver through a sizeable catfish, the razor sharp blade cuts through like a hot knife through butter. The Mekong has long harboured fish of gigantic proportions and is home to more species of massive fish than any river on earth, the giant catfish is a prime example. Due to the destruction of local habitats and the increased damming, notably in the upper reaches of the Yunnan Province, larger specimens are becoming a rare occurrence. However, in 2005, Thai fishermen netted a catfish as big as a grizzly bear that weighed an eye opening 646 pounds, a world record for the largest freshwater fish ever caught. Experts, who studied the fish, were astonished that in the present climate, it could survive in such hostile waters. Once examined, the fish was feasted on in a remote Thai village along the banks of the Mekong. The one in front of me now, while big, may only way up to forty pounds, a mere lightweight in comparison.

The fish trader's reluctance to sell me any of the catfish baffles me somewhat; mind you, my pigeon Laos, hand signs and weird expressions no doubt baffled him more. Somneuk intercedes, beginning a more thorough interrogation to secure us a section of this prime looking catch. The man is adamant that it cannot be sold, the same answer is offered for another fish, until he hovers over an already filleted fish, which he urges us to buy. I'm insistent that it is the catfish or nothing, so my latest culinary acquaintance moves in for one last attempt and is again greeted with a shrug of the shoulders. This is pure food frustration, the glistening white flesh, so excruciatingly tangible seems destined to never touch my lips, when an olive branch is offered. The trader now claims the fish has already been purchased but would renege on it for the highly inflated price of 70,000 kip per kilo, twice its original price. I'm flabbergasted, Somneuk is mildly offended and the mere thought of stealing another man's fish, along with the indecent price tag, is enough for me to drift away, disappointed but with a guilt free conscience.

Somneuk crouches down to inspect weird minuscule items laid out on white plastic mats, grasshoppers and silkworms briefly draw my attention away from the specks of white that are unidentifiable to me. 'These are my wife's favourite food and a true Lao delicacy' enthuses Somneuk. I feel I'm just about to have another dung loving beetle moment, as he proceeds to tell me that these are the larvae of ants. Embryo of fertilised duck, cobra snake, tarantulas, dung loving beetles and now ant eggs are added to a long list of peculiarities. Strange to me but here it represents another form of protein collected from the bush, that is as normal as eating chicken, fish or deer and what I will term 'insect caviar' for descriptive purposes. During economic hardship villagers would traditionally go to the bush, seek out an anthill and proceed to beat it with sticks to separate the eggs. It is another blunt advertisement for the creative force of foraging for foodstuffs that in the western world would be shunned as unnecessary madness, alongside eating road kill. For purposes of culinary pursuit, I buy some silkworms, with by now an unerring blast of calm assurance, delivered by my previous battling conquests.

A sense of normality is restored through bargaining for a bundle of sun dried buffalo skin, green papaya, four more bunches of watercress, an intriguing bark that I recognise from the *aw lam* in Vientiane and finely shredded, tender bamboo that a lady sitting cross-legged on the floor deftly shreds into a white bucket. Bamboo is now becoming more prominent, a fact not lost on me. It is the fastest growing and most widely used woody species in the world and in one way or another forms part of everyday life for many South East Asians. Approximately forty million hectares of the earth is covered with bamboo, mostly in Asia. About two hundred million tonnes are harvested annually, for building, papermaking, furniture making, food and a multitude of other uses. Bamboo is lightweight, hard, flexible and tough. It bends under heat and can be drilled using a steel bit, indeed weight for weight, bamboo is tougher than steel. For food lovers, it is the tender shoots that are the prize from this versatile member of the grass family. For centuries, people have been harvesting the young vitamin rich shoots just as they appear above the ground and cooking a variety of dishes from them. Significantly, and rather ironically, our final purchase is a live duck tethered at its webbed feet and caged in a cylindrical bamboo pen.

For breakfast we walk to Café Laos and enjoy a decent bowl of *foe* while watching the monks chopping grass with machetes opposite at Wat Heau Xieng or dislodging mangoes from the tall trees within its grounds. Firm pork dumplings float in the *foe* that we dip in a smooth peanut and chilli sauce and drop the peppery watercress into the steamy broth savouring its comforting familiar qualities, explaining to Somneuk that in England watercress has long been loved, it is one of the rare occasion throughout my journey that any such exacting comparison can be accredited. With all the ingredients for our afternoon picnic safely stored in Somneuk's white minivan, he drives to his home near the covered Phosy market, while I stroll to the tip of the old city. Outside Wat Mai, men are busy carefully laying a symmetrical red brick paving, as I divert to the inner road and past the Royal Palace gates.

Tourism has seen a dramatic increase in visitors, since foreign investment, restoration projects and a significant rise in the standard of accommodation has bought the old city to the attention of the outside world. Boutique gift shops, slick coffee houses, French restaurants, internet cafés and indulgent massage parlours cater to the modern traveller's every need. It shows no signs of abating, rumours abound that international hotel chains are scouting surrounding sites, ready to capitalise on this unique environment. Locals are justifiably uneasy about this, many having been squeezed out already by a crippling surge in property prices, in what citizens term, the 'gentrification' of the old city. Improving infrastructure, increased daily flights to the delightfully understated airport, have brought a wave of package tourism that brings a fistful of dollars, pounds, euros and baht to spray through its charming, compact streets. A brief pause to admire the commanding colonial architecture of the white-washed Villa Santi brings me to Wat Saen, where an ornate boat shed houses the monastery's two longboats, used in the annual boat race festival. Held at the end of the rainy season, the boat races bring a flurry of energised excitement to the Mekong and are believed to lure the city's guardian Naga back into the rivers after high waters and flooded rice paddies have allowed it to escape. Wedged between the Mekong and Nam Khan, is the Golden City Monastery, or Wat Xiang Thong, perhaps the city's most historic Buddhist monastery. Graceful lines curve and overlap extending to the ground, reminiscent of a bird with outstretched wings or 'a mother hen sheltering her brood', the symbolic description used by the locals. Built in 1560 by King Setthathilat, this sympathetically restored temple escaped unscathed when early Chinese marauders razed much of Luang Prabang and I can't help thinking that its significance may help this jewel of the Mekong to adopt a compassionate approach to tourism in the future. I ponder this as I meander back to my hotel, unable to shake off the feeling that this ancient gem balances precariously on the precipice of further change.

The bank is steep as we descend to the edge of the Nam Khan River. Trestle tables occupy a clearing in the dense vegetation that has been ripped away from the shoreline to create an ideal picnic area. Two women stand fishing in the shallows, their simple bamboo rods wavering in the breeze. The fast, clear running stream breaks over rocks with hypnotic, soothing frequency as the midday sun beats down, producing mini rainbow flashes in the water. Soon after leaving Luang Prabang, we had turned from the road that guides you to Louang Namtha and driven on the lumpy dirt track that winds eventually up to eco-style lodges, where the main draw is exploring the deep forests and riding elephants. Our main purpose is definitely to eat. Somneuk's wife, Hatsadome, has come laden with food, equipment and their two-year-old baby daughter. For me, it also offers the opportunity to visit the grave of the early French Explorer, Henri Mouhot.

Henri Mouhot's exploration of Thailand, Cambodia and Laos between 1858 and 1861 and his attempt to resolve many questions about the Mekong that puzzled the French in Saigon, were at the time, considered a failure. This may be so, but the significance of his efforts was considerable and more crucially, his description of the temples of Angkor in Cambodia revealed an unsurpassed level of detail and passion. His description was not the first to come before the European public but Mouhot laid greater emphasis to the magnificent temples in the deep forest. He has long since been credited as being the person that bought the wonders of Angkor to the attention of the Western World. It was on the banks of the Nam Khan, that the fever-racked Frenchman penned the last entry into his journal before slipping away in November of 1861. His servants and many who came in contact with him held Mouhot in high regard, this due in part to his love of all things living, which endeared him among its Buddhist faithful. Many maintain that this was the reason he was allowed any form of burial, as Buddhists believe that it offers an invitation to the spirit of the deceased to linger and make trouble, thus cremation is the norm here. For many years his grave and monument had been lost, swallowed up by the rampaging jungle. His natural empathy for its people went against a backdrop of hard, commercial imperialism that sought no compassionate liaison with its inhabitants, thereby making his successes all the more outstanding.

As I make my way back down, the feint smell of burning kindling and charcoal wafts towards me. Somneuk is crouched down, strengthening the wooden barbecue that is permanently fixed by stakes driven into the ground. Hatsadome shreds green papaya into a bowl, her condiments by her side in a semicircle of everyday familiarity, ready to blend and create. I grab the two fish by her side and find a perfectly flat rock to scale, gut and clean the fish on. The fish is threaded with a thick wooden skewer and clamped between a natural wooden brace to hold it during cooking. Overhead the clouds are darkening and a light wind now whips across us. The shredded green papaya is mixed with lime juice, pounded red chilli, garlic, chopped tomato, peanuts and fish sauce to make the classic fiery sour salad *tam mak hung*. Drizzle quickly explodes into torrential rain, forcing us to hastily gather everything up and walk up the now slippery, muddy bank to dine in a rickety bamboo shelter. Thankfully the fish has had time to cook, as the dampened fire splutters and begins smouldering, abandoned for another day.

The spread is laid out on the raised, alarmingly unstable, bamboo platform, as my damp clothes cause my body to shiver. The silkworms have been deep-fried; the rubbery mini tubes, like giant maggots have a toughened resistant skin, that once pierced is neither rubbery nor tough. I've come so accustomed to these experiences now, my immunity to any grub, bug or excrement from living things, is disturbingly high but each one does still captivate me, so when I bite through to its pus like core I'm intrigued but not overwhelmed. The loose grainy texture distinguished by black dots in the yellow mush seeps into my mouth with the distinction of nutty pork. Reared solely on mulberry leaves, their composition is not dissimilar to that of shrimps and these deep yellow worms are packed with protein. Hatsadome smiles gleefully, enjoying every morsel of her favourite delicacy. The prospect of the ant eggs is brashly enticing now, hell, bring it on, while I'm in the zone, the thought of a ten course 'insect feast' menu is actually rather appealing. The fried larvae have been cooked as one would for egg fried rice; mixed with beaten whole egg, chopped spring onions, liberal use of soy and fish sauce. The resulting dish is a triumphant revelation, the rich, savoury notes from the condiments deliver an infinitely scrumptious snack and would unwittingly mask anyone's preconceived ideas of chomping through as moreish a dish that I've tasted on my journey thus far.

My decision to abandon Vientiane earlier than I had anticipated is fully vindicated in the six days I spend here. Wave after wave of imaginative cooking, not restricted to the sideshows of ant eggs, silkworms, lizards, snakes and all manner of irregular items that tests the will of this Englishman's resolve, but also the likes of everyday food that have gone before in the Vietnamese Delta and Cambodia. With a few notable exceptions, to date, I've rigorously steered my course to the centre of the 'people's food', the food that touches many not just the few. Thus far, the ability of people, their passion, knowledge and skill have smashed through me like a tidal wave. Their open abandonment, freewheeling creativity with food holds no bounds and as I have moved upriver, the subtleties of change mirror the increasingly lofty landscape. Before long, the notorious Golden Triangle will wrap me in its cloak of deceit, then lead me into the new economic powerhouse of the Chinese Republic to explore one of its most ethnically diverse regions.

Luang Prabang is a place to linger; I remember my earlier longing to spend more time in Tra Vinh in the delta, times that by ten. That is not to say that I loved all the food I discovered here. One evening, Somneuk and I visited a traditional herbal sauna 4 km out of town. The Lao men and women frequently enjoy a long, therapeutic steam after work or at weekends in simple bamboo rooms fired by local wood scented with lemongrass, galangal and other health enhancing plants. The hot, intense steam soothes and cleanses, invigorating and revitalising aching bones and tired skin.

Men and women mix together in communal areas on wooden benches wrapped in traditional cotton cloth, covering their respective modesties and sip boiled natural earth water collected from a well situated to the rear of the building. Massages are administered; it has to be said with a varying degree of expertise, like a gardener waters the garden.

Having tried and failed in many establishments to find anyone still serving barbecued duck, we rather reluctantly accept defeat and end up in a dimly lit, scrub hole of a place in the back streets on the outskirts of the old city. The dusty, soulless room whirrs to the sound of an old ceiling fan, as an aluminium charcoal-burning vessel is placed on our table. The murky, deep dark liquid looks as appetising as crushed coal blended with starchy water. Inside, every last piece of a goat's anatomy has been braised, chopped up scrotum, lungs, heart, ears and blood congealing in the simmering broth. Somnuek tucks in, trickles of sweat run from his forehead as the blasting heat of chilli kicks in. He loves it, I loathe it, simple as that. The broth is as bitter as the charcoal that heated it; the acrid taste trashes the subtle lemongrass, lime leaf and galangal forcing them to surrender in a pitiful fight for supremacy. Luckily, the next ensemble, barbecue goat, is a good deal more appetising. We grill thin slices of goat meat and wrap them in raw cabbage leaves, herbs and the snaky green yard beans, before dipping in a concoction of smooth pureed goats liver mixed with coconut milk, chopped peanuts, spring onions, red chilli and a hit of fermented fish paste.

Perhaps the most extraordinary example of cooking is the intricately woven ensemble of *aw lam*. Hatsadome lovingly prepared this in the small home they share near the large central market, where I ate on three separate occasions. The district of Ban Nong Kham is a far cry from the splendour of the old city; shacks for homes, and many that double as shops, music bars or seedy brothels flank the dark, shabby square. Their abode is a mishmash of stock for their shop, a simple bed, bare concrete floors and walls that lead to the cooking area. To the rear, the sanitary conditions are bleak; a foul festering pit toilet emits a polluted stench, the meagre space doubles as a bathing area, where a cold water bucket shower is the extent of the bathroom. It also functions as an occasional food preparation zone, a place to wash vegetables, kill and clean chickens or ducks, the waste dumped in a bucket adds to the potent odour. Somneuk's job brings him into daily contact with individuals, here to soak up the beauty of the old city, enjoying the hotels clean, swish rooms complete with designer bathrooms, air conditioning and beautifully crafted furniture. It is a stark reminder of the poverty that co-exists with the rich vein of tourism and owes my hedonist food journey a blunt reality check.

Aw Lam is a bubbling stew; traditionally made with beef or buffalo meat, the slowly braised succulent meat is joined by a speculative array of ingredients. Dry buffalo skin, crispy deep fried pork skin (like pork scratchings) meld with garlic, galangal, lemongrass, red chilli and onion and crunchy pea aubergines, *pak ason* (a slimy green bitter leaf), strips of wood ear mushroom, a dose of fish sauce and the mystifying addition of chopped dill. His wife also favours adding ping pong ball sized green aubergines and soaked sticky rice, to produce a thicker, richer sauce. It is a sophisticated, novel preparation, both challenging and beguiling, each flavour striking a chord before joining in orchestral harmony and exploding in a triumphant finale. The food she produces in the confined space is nothing short of miraculous. Fleshy, creamy bamboo soup, turned a nuclear green by leaves of a wild vegetable is light and clean; barbecued deer meat marinated with garlic, oyster sauce, salt and sugar grilled over charcoal; grilled deer skin marinated in fermented fish paste; delightful broth flavoured with deer meat, green chilli, galangal and sour green leaves; duck broth with bunches of chopped watercress; duck stew with coriander root; the flesh of chopped raw duck dressed in its own blood, an alternative example of *lap*.

To add to the amazingly rich vein of food, the famous crimson sausages of Luang Prabang, traditionally dried in the sun, along the main through fare of Xieng Thong, hang from plinths in the street. Wafer thin sheets of sun-dried river weed, crisp and delicate, studded with garlic and chilli; young bamboo shoots flavoured with garlic, red chilli and lemongrass wrapped in the citrus leaves of the Bai Champa tree; fish steamed with lemongrass and slices of lime smothered in a tangy sour tamarind sauce; *praneng kai,* a velvety coconut soup with lemongrass, lime leaf, chilli, galangal and fish sauce containing pulled chicken, minced pork balls and strips of moistened fried buffalo skin; pounded frog flesh in creamy, soft aubergine with hits of holy basil, red chilli and salty fish sauce; *sun doot,* chewy strips of sun dried buffalo meat, a Lao version of jerky, the deep coloured meat offers light salty notes to balance the caramelised protein. The jewel of the Mekong has delivered a succession of tremendous fayre, surpassing the excellent food of Pakxe and overcoming the variable efforts of Vientiane. In the hearts and minds of its people, its superiority still reigns supreme.

Two Speeds to Xieng Kok

Phet arrives with minutes to spare. The old customised barge remains tied to its post, as I peer down the steep bank from my vantage point near the navigation ticket office. I'm perturbed by his late arrival, our arrangement was set for 7.30am and the time now is 8.30am and the boat is loaded, passengers aboard and ready to leave without us. Driving here, he had been apprehended by the police. His initial offence, driving up the street in the wrong direction, led to his failure to produce a valid licence for his motorbike and resulted in him losing his temper and planting a right hand to the temple of the charging officer. The imposed hefty fine, nearly $45, is just shy of his monthly wage and the regret in his face lends him a sad crestfallen look. We hurry down the bank, balance carefully along the gangplank and board the boat. I'm still attempting to gain a level of comfort on the crude, wooden hard backed bench seat, as Luang Prabang gradually disappears and we steam upriver.

Travel-weary backpackers recuperated from days of meandering, sipping cappuccinos, temple viewing and gorging on pastries, now head upriver to cross into Thailand. Returning native Lao, laden with goods, head back to their respective remote jungle villages, the front of the barge heaving with sacks of rice, other provisions and clothes.

The muddy silted waters of the Mekong flows against us, tiny rapids, swirling whirlpools and protruding rocks require an experienced skipper. The scene on the river remarkably unchanged from yesteryear, amazingly unperturbed by the incursions of modernity that plague the lower reaches, in the polluted south of the Vietnamese Delta. Limestone karsts rise from the dense jungle forest, the blanket of dripping green halted by the river as it squeezes through. Water buffalo frolic in the shallows, goats nimbly cling to clearings on the bank and vegetated terraces flourish from the rich river waters. Punctuated limestone caves, used for centuries as a repository for old and unwanted Buddha images, emerge where the Nam Ou River flows forth and into the Mekong. Occasionally the impenetrable forest clears, revealing age-old wooden huts, tiny hamlets of human life cast in an undisturbed time warp, their man-powered pirogues lashed to the banks. The peaceful, eternity of our ascent is broken only by longtail rocket boats, their ear–piercing engines create an unerring din, as they skim through the water. Tiring of the rudimentary, uncomfortable bench seats, I follow the lead of a Lao man and nestle my appreciative body on the comfort of rice sacks. I doze in and out of sleep all the way to the riverfront town of Pakbeng.

After a fitful night's sleep, the dawn of a misty, damp morning brings another day. After a breakfast of fried fish and black sticky rice, we buy a few provisions and clamber back on the boat, for the journey to Houayxai. Thankfully, Phet's mood has lifted, his depressive outlook of yesterday traded for a cordial manner that I hope will continue as we head into the Golden Triangle. The day drifts by in a haze of picturesque splendour, as we steam upriver, through a series of more forceful rapids and extensive waves of pristine crystal white sand, that extend from the lower level. As we edge into mid-afternoon, the skipper and his crew bust open a bottle of lao-lao, in anticipation of our imminent arrival. Everything seems in order, before the engine suddenly splutters and dies, forcing us to drift and come to rest against a rocky island. All of us foreigners look at each other in bewildered silence; many of them wish to cross the border to Thailand this evening and too much of a delay will scupper their plans. Phet leans over and whispers that this is the reason for the mysterious breakdown, to force a further nights stay on Laos soil and bolster the coffers of their hotels and restaurants. Hours later, the sun slides behind a blanket of orange cloud, as dusk greets our arrival in Houayxai.

The morning brings a complication to our ascent to the heart of the Golden Triangle. Phet informs me that if I wish to travel by boat to Xieng Kok, we must first go by road to Ban Mom, 27 km north of town. He also warns me that the cost of hiring a boat from there is likely to be prohibitive, so, with a dwindling supply of cash, I beat a retreat to the bank to arrange sufficient funds. After an hour in a pick up, we are dropped at a solitary bamboo shelter, peering across the wide breadth of the Mekong at a cluster of white pagodas in the golden land of Burma.

The Golden Triangle is synonymous with the opium trade. The illicit business once dominated the infamous area formed by the meeting of Laos, Thailand and Burma. From the early colonial rule of the British, opium flourished, controlled at differing times by colonial powers, the CIA and a colourful collection of drug warlords who built an extensive network that spanned the rugged interior. The Burmese opium warlord Khun Sa, a native of Burma, is identifiable as having had a significant impact in the battle for dominant supremacy. At the height of his notoriety, Khun Sa presided over a veritable narcotics empire, leading a 20,000-member private militia called the Shan United Army in Burma's north-eastern Shan state. His sophisticated empire included satellite television, schools and surface to air missiles that aided his operations carved out of the jungle valleys. By the early 1960s he had become a major player in the Golden Triangle, the world's major source of opium and its derivative heroin. In July 1967, Khun Sa tried to ship sixteen tonnes of opium on a three hundred mule caravan to the tiny village of Ban Khwan. This episode nearly crucified his operation. News had spread of this audacious shipment, the Chinese Nationalist Fifth Army set about hijacking the opium but it was troops of the Laotian army who stormed in from the south and east to snatch the heroin. Khun Sa's soldiers fought off the Chinese with machine guns and carbines but were no match for the hundreds of Lao paratroopers and dive bombing T-38 propeller planes. After that he retreated to a less hostile environment in Thailand, where he continued to run his operations from a hilltop base, until he was driven out by Thai forces in 1982.

The Golden Triangle has long since lost its sway in the opium market. The Taliban-free Golden Crescent (Afghanistan) has regained total supremacy of the world market and a world drug report issued in June 2007, suggested that the Golden Triangle contributed less than five per cent of global opium production. The

Laos government now believes the country to be virtually opium free. In Thailand the penalties are severe if caught and sustained campaigns have all but eradicated any poppy field. Officially only in Burma does opium grow in any quantity, but due to the inhospitable terrain, this must surely be hard to quantify with any certainty.

After filling our stomachs with stir-fried eggplant, tender bamboo and strips of sun-dried pork, negotiations begin for the journey upriver. Negotiating in these situations is damn difficult, as I have little bargaining power because there is only one available longtail and I'm the only customer. Being so close to Thailand, the captain's preferred currency is Thai baht or failing that the equivalent in US dollars. Pre-warned I had come armed with Thai currency, ready to battle for a decent price. For twenty arduous minutes the price is cemented at 3500 baht, his tough exterior suggests I'm losing the battle and at this moment I'm close to biting the bullet and agreeing to the price. Then, without further prompting, he agrees to drop the price to my preferred 2500 baht, if I would allow a novice and elder monk to be dropped halfway upriver. With a potentially precarious journey ahead, the inclusion of two monks is very welcome indeed.

The national flag of Laos flaps in the breeze as we pull gently away into mid-stream, seconds later the rip of the engine shrills into life and catapults us up river. The inclusion of thick red life jackets and sturdy crash helmets are both reassuring and disconcerting. We hurtle along avoiding protruding rocks, riding rapids that thud against the hull, as he steers straight towards a solid rock island, imminent carnage is assured as I utter my last rights, before he flings the boat to the left, avoiding contact with the red painted hull by a hair's breadth. Accidents on this stretch of river are a common occurrence, last week a ferry carrying Burmese passengers downriver sunk when it struck an obstructing obstacle.

Everyone on board perished but due to the lack of information in this remote area, only local people discover the distressing truth. After an ear-numbing, adrenalin-pumping two hours of threading our way through the dense jungle, we round a corner and the sleepy border town of Xieng Kok comes into view, my racing heart and shredded nerves relax enough to soak up my jungle surroundings.

Eating with Akha

I feel like I've been transported to another world, a hidden pocket of co-existence lodged in the secretive jungle of Laos, a world of underworld seclusion, smuggling and of tribes rarely seen along the more prolific stretches of the Mekong. Hundreds of hunted pangolin forced into white crates, their thick scaled bodies curled into a ball, as bare chested Chinese traders openly haggle with Akha tribesmen for these scaly anteaters that resemble walking pinecones. Illegal animal smuggling is rife, fuelled by Chinese demand for exotic species, the pangolin has been virtually hunted to extinction in the surrounding Lao forests, so now the Akha resort to raiding the forests just across the river in neighbouring Burma. According to wildlife groups, China is the main market for illegally traded exotic species, which are eaten or used in traditional medicines. Pangolins are in high demand because their meat is considered a delicacy and their scales are thought to help mothers' breastfeed new born babies. It is a highly lucrative business; the Chinese are prepared to pay huge premiums and today the price is an eye-watering 2000 Thai baht or 58 US dollars per kilo. Trade is booming, border controls are lax, bribery endemic and even if fines are imposed, these are normally lower than the potential rewards. The bush traders follow us, as we disappear into the inner sanctum of a large bamboo slatted building, the furious tapping of calculators accompany our meal of crispy fried fish with soy sauce, garlic and chilli, and bowls of steaming fluffy rice.

My much improved relationship with Phet begins to bear fruit in Xieng Kok, the pressure of the hefty fine imposed in Luang Prabang for now stored in a numb section of his brain, as together we explore the rugged, hilly streets in search of a local guide to accompany us to a remote Akha village. I rather like it here, the town itself is a little dilapidated but it maintains a peaceful charm, the ebbing and flowing around the boat landing area adds vibrancy, as Chinese cargo boats load and unload merchandise, before heading up or downriver. Colourful Akha men wander the streets wearing traditional headgear of disc shaped red turbans or tall hats festooned with seed beeds, while cows snooze at intersections and women return from the rice fields, baskets strapped to their heads. A young boy struggles up the hill, dragging a trailer laden with water in buckets, the sheer exertion extolling all his energy, so I rush down to assist him, he beams an excited smile of enthusiastic gratitude.

As the sound of generators whirr into action, in the fading evening light, we walk the tarmac road to Phet's friends who live 1 km from the main town. A group of men swigging lao-lao huddled under a bamboo shelter, beckon us over and thrust deep fried pig skin at us which we dip in a bowl of syrupy blood and pounded ginger. Before the potent moonshine bottle is offered, we wander off and continue on our way. His friends greet him with excitement, the clattering of pans in the background ceases, as a lady abandons the food preparation to join in the jubilation. He has not seen these people in over three years, the show of open affection is touching, bottles of Beer Laos, lao-lao and Johnnie Walker are opened to compliment our own offerings we bought in town from a humble bamboo store.

To the rear of the two-roomed concrete dwelling, a large

decorative mat is spread over the distressed concrete floor, through the middle a length of blue plastic is positioned as a makeshift tablecloth. Plates of minced duck dressed in its own blood and mixed with mint, coriander, spring onion and chilli conjure up a reminder of a similar dish in Luang Prabang. A soothing broth flavoured with duck, galangal, garlic, chilli and fish sauce is spooned into bowls, and crispy fried fish dipped in salt and chilli are all fine examples. Having seen the plight of the hundreds of pangolin, the speciality of the evening at first seems a little surprising. Bush animals have always been enjoyed in these societies. The Akha are prolific hunters and highly skilled, their techniques honed over many centuries but due to damaging logging, slash and burn and hunting for commercial exploitation, the pickings have been greatly diminished. Among many others, it is home to a very small bear, that Phet's friends now only eat if one is accidentally knocked over by a motor vehicle, preferring not to encourage their exploitation for purposes of the pot. The grilled pieces of bear meat are spiked with pounded wild juniper berries and black pepper, the indelibly rich, gamy meat is soft and feathery, disintegrating in my mouth like edible cotton wool. The evening drifts into the pitch of darkness, old friends reacquainted, we take our leave and wander down the hill and return to our bamboo-stilted hut overlooking the hushed bend of the Mekong.

In the morning, our trek to the village of Muang Kan begins early, the light damp chill still clinging to the moistened air. The rogue traders from yesterday have left a void of innocence, no doubt already well into Chinese territory and planning the sale of their illicit bush goods. We join the road that leads to the old opium weighing station town of Muang Sing, before branching off and heading into the hilly interior, where I haphazardly slip on a rock while crossing a knee high stream and plunge to an early morning bath.

We follow a series of muddy paths, the forest highway of the Akha, and rise gradually until eventually I can turn to view the widespread devastation brought to the forest by the abrasive methods of slash and burn and glimpse the distant waters of the Mekong as it snakes through the jungle.

The link between poverty and stripping the environment is clearly defined. Formerly people earned money from growing opium, the void it has left to the income of the very poor, has brought about survival wholly dependent on the sticky rice they grow on the cleared slopes and whatever they can find or kill in the jungle. It is a situation that many in the western world simply can't fathom or excuse, preferring to condone these primitive measures through blinkers and neither understanding nor sympathising with the plight of everyday people. Whereas people bemoaned the plague of poppy fields, their attentions are now firmly fixed on environmental sustainability, but the choice for the locals caught in the crossfire is quite straightforward: to feed their families.

In the next three hours, we move in and out of the deep forest canopy, crossing log bridges that span narrow streams, resting in permanent bamboo shelters and picking wild chillies, pellet size green aubergines and wild herbs. The paths are very steep and in places where no sunlight reaches, very muddy, making conditions under foot extremely testing. Sweat drips from every pore in my body, drenched from the intense humidity and the heart-pumping ascent to our destination. Phet is very slow, the guide and I pound through the bush leaving my wispy moustached companion trailing in our wake.

We enter the village through a tunnel of vegetation, children freeze with unknowing anxiety, before darting for cover in their wooden stilted homes or maintaining a wary distance from this foreign intruder. The village opens out, hugging a steep sweeping incline that falls away and drops into the wide valley beneath.

Sturdy teak wooden houses, many with tin roofs, mingle with less elaborate bamboo structures, all of which are defined by fences that distinguish each family's territory. Pigs, emblazoned with a patchwork of black, brown and camel, snort and roll their fit bodies in the sandy earth. These mountain pigs reared by the Akha produce pork of enviable quality and the killing of a pig is a major event. The Akha take great pride in dividing up the animal, the entire beast is cut up and distributed in equal proportions, to include the hide, fat, meat, bones, blood and an equal share of the organs. Slaughtering the pig is performed with time-honoured continuity. The pig is tied up and sprinkled with ceremonial water before its heart is pierced with a knife and the blood drained into a bowl with water and salt. Once dead, it is set over a fire to remove its hair and any parasites, and then cut open and the intestines cleaned and divided, as these are considered a particular delicacy.

The Akha began migrating south from China's Yunnan Province in the mid-nineteenth century, bringing the tongue of Tibeto-Burman language with them and the animist belief that relies on a village shaman to help solve problems of health, fertility or protection against malevolent spirits. These tribal villages are distinguished by an arched wooden 'spirit gate' hung with bamboo 'stars' that bring good luck and block evil spirits. The end of the harvest is celebrated with a festival, when the villagers offer food to the spirits by way of further protection and a fruitful harvest for the coming year. A feast of chickens, pigs, vegetables and rice are eaten in the ensuing celebrations that involve hefty drinking and joyful dancing.

The heat of the midday sun blasts down as we clamber up and down nifty wooden planks. Deliberately positioned wooden steps allow our feet to steady as we enter the village chief's encampment. The zip on my Cambodian trousers that I purchased in Kratie snapped clean off last night and my dignity is now held gingerly together by a safety pin. The darkened room offers a cool retreat; a gentle breeze floats though the swinging shutter doors, as I rest against a soft cushion. Clothes, hats and catapults line the walls, above my head handmade tools and a saw balance on planks of wood, as the chief chops tobacco on a thick cylindrical log and rolls a cornet in banana leaf. After a lunch of fried fish stuffed with ginger, chilli and garlic, accompanied with glutinous sticky rice, the chief brings beer and lao-lao. The rice whiskey is as potent as I've experienced and consumed much earlier than I would rather, and sends my head into a spinning haze and rasps the back of my throat. As we are staying the night, the subject of dinner is broached, which throws up an interesting choice of protein, namely chicken or dog, which rolls of the tongue like beef or lamb slips from ours. The prospect of eating dog is not that appealing, especially as there is a choice. I'll admit at this juncture to having already dined on canine flesh, the image flashes before me and I sense it like it were yesterday. Six years ago, while pottering about in the northern hill tops of north western Vietnam, I chanced upon a family about to celebrate an occasion by cooking a whole dog. I can still vividly picture the dead dog, upside down hovering over a burning fire, its legs taut to the sky and blank bulging eyes seared from the heat. Dog is very popular in Northern Vietnam, particularly in the colder months and while people from our background may struggle with the idea, dogs are reared specifically for meat just like cows, sheep and pigs. They, like us, have dogs as pets but would never dream of killing it for the pot. I remember them serving every little scrap, grilled, stewed, fried and boiled, accompanied by a dip comprising its fresh warm blood, chopped ginger and spring onions. Imagine if you will, a slice from the well hung area of a dog's wedding tackle and you may empathise with my dilemma. In the end, my decision is neither moral nor due to taste (dog is actually rather tasty), it is much simpler: I fancy a bit of chicken.

By late evening a steady procession of women begin returning from a hard day's work on the arduous slopes, blue headdresses adorned with jangling silver coins, deep bamboo baskets strapped to their forehead, as they trudge home and begin the task of cooking dinner. Coming from England, where society has embraced the idea of equal opportunities and sexual equality, it still amazes me that the women do nearly all the work here. True, the men hunt, perform in the bedroom and deal with local politics but the hard labour is still distributed in the same fashion as when they first settled on these slopes. In the concentration of women, a slim tall man wearing an old green army jacket and grubby blue baseball cap steps forth carrying a live lizard by its tail in one hand and a long, slim rifle in the other. Officially, guns for the purpose of hunting have been banned for a number of years in the northern reaches of Laos, in practice it is very difficult to enforce and the Akha, who generally work in harmony with the land, continue to hunt for good eating animals, in much the same way we hunt rabbits, shoot grouse or hook a wild salmon.

The appearance of the lizard introduces a last minute change to the menu, the chicken is banished from the board to join the dog in an instinctive switch of allegiance and tonight we dine on the flesh of this primeval reptile. The chief instructs a man to clean the lizard. To my amazement he trudges over to the open-air enclosure where the women are bathing and kills, guts and cleans it without a care in the world and delivers it back. The unfazed women show more concern at my presence, than the blood splattering demise of the lizard. Phet, eager to impress with his cooking knowledge, impressively begins issuing specific instructions as to how it should be prepared and cooked. Evening turns to night, a single generator clatters to life in a neighbouring house, as the rest of the village descends into restful darkness, the faint light of kerosene lamps flicker and the chopping of the lizard commences.

Working by candlelight, the chopped lizard sizzles in the pan for five minutes followed by slice unpeeled galangal, ginger, bashed stalks of lemongrass, shredded lime leaf, sliced red chilli, garlic, spring onions, a sprinkling of salt and a splash of water. The scented firewood burns brightly, as a lid is slammed on the pot, the lizard left to cook for forty five minutes. The meat is decanted to battered tin bowls and brought to the room on an oval flowery red and white tin tray. The soft meat is a pleasant surprise. I remember the beer cooked version in Pakxe being a little tough, this is sweet malleable and exceedingly delicious. The fragrance of the lemongrass, combined heat of the ginger and chilli deliver a heady concoction of tribal delight. A few glasses of lao-lao later, the windows are secured to ward off evil spirits, the flickering lights extinguished and I drift off to sleep for what is my final night in Laos.

Yunnan Province

Dai Power

The Mekong hugs the border of Laos, slipping briefly into Burmese territory as its upriver north-eastern trajectory straightens, angles abruptly east, before doubling back on itself and leading me north-westerly into the burgeoning, economic territory of an exploding China, where it is called the Lancang River. The remote, backward, sleepy jungle towns of Laos feel like a wonderful distant memory. Whirring generators dumped in favour of electric cables, ignite the Yunnan Province. The palm tree lined streets of Jinghong ring to modern urban traffic, broad avenues entertain sparkling new hotels, locals shop in department stores, hail taxis and dine in the plethora of restaurants that demonstrate my upheaval from mellow backwater, to the booming commerciality of China's breakneck advance and the contemporary trappings of materialism.

The sudden change of pace throws me briefly into a whirlpool of blind panic. Only ten years ago, Jinghong was an undeveloped, exotic jungle city dominated by the traditional Dai culture, of stilted thatched houses with roofs that tuck sharply in at the ends before splaying out again in the classic South East Asian style. Almost overnight, roads were ripped up, widened and resurfaced, the encroaching jungle cleared away and the city's population lived in a choking smog of dusty concrete. The new economic prospects brought the inevitable wave of Han Chinese who poured into the city, engulfing the Dai population in a ferocious tidal wave that threatened their unique position in the society. Thankfully their influence hasn't been completely swamped, due in part to their unified commitment to protect their lifestyle, ability to adapt and the unusual softening tolerance of the Chinese regime.

The morning after my arrival I meet with Li, a twenty-one year old student, part-time guide and a fluent speaker of Thai, Japanese, English and local Dai dialect, that makes my inability at foreign languages all the more palpable. With breakfast as our priority, the early morning rush hour traffic, flanked by wide cycle lanes, hums through the gears, as we search out the traditional Dai fuel that propels them into a new day. The atmosphere on the clean streets is easy-going, creatively landscaped roundabouts circled with fluorescent coloured lamps create smart intersections and lines of gem traders glitter in the morning sun, the city's close proximity to Burma and its famed jade, rubies and sapphire make this a hotbed of activity.

We halt outside an undistinguished whitewashed concrete building with four low-slung tables outside on the irregular pavement, where people squat on plastic stools and slurp broth from their bowls. Through the open passage to the rear, men jet-wash cars, the powerful water sprays shiny vehicles, throwing damp mist through an open window. Inside two tables line the simple tiled walls with bowls of condiments and chopsticks in steaming water laid out for customers to help themselves. Behind the counter, a lady dips noodles into boiling water, while her other hand lifts the lid from a deep pot, a plume of steamy vapour rises to her face, as she ladles the clear liquid into a dish over the noodles. *Mi xian mi gan* is to the Dai what pho is to the Vietnamese; a soulful bowl of hydrating liquid, filling carbohydrate and piggy protein, but it would be immensely unfair to compare them. Here the broth is produced with pork bones, simmered overnight with hints of garlic, ginger and salt; the lighter, less rich liquid leans towards the Dai love of pigs. She spoons minced cooked pork, an oily mixture of crushed peanuts and dried red chilli flakes, garnishing the top with chopped spring onion and baby leeks. A slick of red grease floats to the top, Li adds an ambitious addition of dried red chilli, before we sit down and tuck in. I blend the chill oil into the broth; it clings to the noodles, soaking into the white strands, before the excess gradually rises back to the surface. Unfair it may be, but my mind shoots back down the Mekong evoking memories of Ben Tre and the excellent pho I enjoyed there. The cloying oil clings to my tongue like chewing gum sticks to the sole of a shoe, not offensive but drives an inferno of dried red chill, clearing my sinuses in seconds.

In Laos you seldom experience any hustle and bustle, the food and general markets are marked by their human restraint. One foot into the main food market in Jinghong and I'm thrust headlong into a hive of fervent activity. A real sense of urgency is felt, as animated traders are locked in combat with tough negotiating punters and the shrill of tethered chickens compete with squealing pigs, squawking ducks and sizzling woks. Dai women chew on beetlenuts, their teeth blemished with dramatic orange and red stains, crouched down over baskets of fish, encouraging buyers to pause and ponder a purchase. Li is calm and restrained, I'm champing at the bit, escaped from soothing Laotian meditation, everywhere I look signs of shifting culinary influence meld with the staples of my journey thus far. Crusted, cured legs of pork, similar to Parma, Serrano or Carmarthen ham share a table space with bellies, loins, shoulders and trotters. The deep, dark pink flesh is exciting, as I imagine it thinly sliced and falling into my mouth. Slabs of silken white tofu, trays of cinnamon, star anise, fennel seeds, peppers and juicy round peaches continue the assault. Steaming black mountain chickens intrigue me, Peking style ducks, their beaks almost touching the grubby market surface, hang lined up in a parade of dark glossy familiarity. One stall along a lady bashes the head of an eel, before hooking its head onto a sharp nail and slitting its belly, sending a sea of blood all over her already ravished jacket. And this is just the periphery of the market. Last night, I enjoyed a supreme example of roasted duck, the bird fed entirely on a diet of rice and vegetables came with micro thin crispy skin, succulent, soft flesh and not a hint of the grease that bog standard Chinese restaurants in the UK achieve with blatant regularity.

Further in, shackled dogs bark loudly before whimpering into resigned contemplation of their fate. Bowls of blackened tomatoes, charred red chillies, ginger, garlic and salt are pounded into a Yunnan style salsa, and I stop and stare in bewilderment, eventually trudging off, scratching my head. I'm still pondering the origin of the salsa, as I'm confronted with heaps of wild mushrooms, bulging deep chestnut fungi draw my eyes like a bee to a hive, as I enthusiastically shout 'porcini'. I stand and meticulously count the total number of varieties and even with my limited mathematical dexterity I reach fifteen, quite astonishing and a delightful addition to an ever-increasing list of mouth-watering produce.

That evening, the market's produce vividly etched in my brain, Li continues my Dai culinary exploration with a visit to what he himself terms 'a culinary institution'. Gou Man Dai, translated as 'crossing slowly', is reached via a labyrinth of back street alleys. The old style Dai houses in need of some repair offer a taste of yesteryear against the backdrop of a new economic dawn.

The Dai are an ancient people. The first recorded contact with Han Chinese occurred in 109BC when the Emperor Wu Di set up the Yizhou Prefecture in south-western Yi (the name for the minority regions of Yunnan, Sichuan and Guizhou provinces). History, as recorded in Dai scripts, dates their culture to over a thousand years ago. The Dai, roughly translating as 'freedom-and-peace-loving people' number over a million, mostly inhabiting the plains, river and lake shores of Xishuangbanna and Dehong Prefecture, but also in Lincang, Honghe, Yuxi, Simao and elsewhere. Far from the main centres of Chinese authority, the Dai have exercised significant freedom over the centuries and even today, like many other minorities in the rich, diverse region of Yunnan, practise a casual disregard for the concept of borders and passports.

Like their ethnic cousins in Thailand and Laos, the Dai are Theravada Buddhists. A Dai landscape is easily recognisable not only due to its stilted houses and fruit orchards, but also its many temples and pagodas. Their sophisticated culture includes intricate musical genres, such as the well known narrative operas called *zhang khap*, solo performances in which singers are accompanied by the Dai flute. In April, their most important festival is held, the Water Splashing Festival – a week of unbridled hedonism which seems like an unrestrained carnival – which actually originated as a solemn Brahmanist rite. In the Dai culture, water symbolises emotion and wisdom and during the festival it follows that drenching people is a token of goodwill. Even though the government has now limited these celebrations to one week, the Dai continue to congregate in huge numbers, in what is one of the biggest ethnic gatherings in the whole of Yunnan.

The restaurant looks more like an undersized storage space, opening into a cavern of rooms. A wooden staircase leads to the solitude of an upstairs area, the traditional living space for the Dai. A long cylindrical bamboo cage, normally for the purpose of housing live chickens, dangles from wire on the ceiling, thankfully empty. The canopy of a stubby tree brushes against the tin roof. The time is 8.30pm, the restaurant is totally empty but a confident Li announces that soon it will be packed, brushing my concern aside. Still perplexed by the lack of people, the food comes to my aid. These venues are entirely given over to grilling by barbecue, the impressive display of food in front of me offers a mix of skewered meats, fish, vegetables and parcels from threaded river prawns all the way through to webbed chickens feet, flattened frog and wriggling worms. Neat banana leaf parcels tied with strips of bamboo, precede vibrant fresh bowls of leaves and herbs, while whole skewered, cooked waxy potatoes are a curious offering, as, until now this tuber has played a non-existent role in my auditorium of culinary treasures.

The drill is simple here, choose any amount of items you like, tell one of the friendly waitresses who writes your order on paper fastened to a clip board, sit down and enjoy the enticing smells that drift in the evening air. Having left the ordering to Li, the role call of food just keeps coming; when it is ready, it is delivered to your table, not in any specific order but in a steady flow of excellence.

Interestingly, the sticky rice of Laos is also a mainstay of the Dai diet. I'd been expecting fluffy white grains to be served but I soon get over it and begin picking at grilled fish. In total we devour thirteen items; beef, hanged and dried over the fire for four days, is pulled and shredded like fine horse hair; chopped up pigs head flavoured with red chilli, garlic, lemongrass and ginger is packed into banana leaf and tied with the tops of lemongrass; a slab of fried tofu is stuffed with pounded pork, garlic, pepper and spring onion before being grilled over the coals; fried flat rice noodles with pork and chilli; fish stuffed with ginger and lemongrass; grilled beef dipped in pepper and salt; the intriguing Chinese tomato salsa that had so amazed me in the market and an abundance of prawns, beef, pork and chicken all grilled to perfection. By the time we leave, it's 10.30pm, the expected influx of people has arrived and the old rickety place is heaving.

Huge Dividends

The Yunnan is China's melting pot of ethnic diversity. It harbours half of the officially recognised minorities in its stunningly varied landscapes. The great rivers of the Yangtze, Mekong and Pearl flow through its mountains, plains and plateaus, crashing through deep gorges, dissecting semi-tropical jungle and the teeming rainforests that protect the greatest density of flora and fauna in mainland China. It is a cultural epicentre, feeding from bordering Burma in the west, Laos and Vietnam in the south and the Tibetan highland in its north-western corner. Unlike the other provinces in China and even though it is geographically aligned within the economic power base in Beijing, it throws a protective shield around its borders and continues to boldly live a unique existence, beyond the jurisdiction of the swarming Han Chinese.

In the remote south-west of the province, the ancient forests hold the key to one of its most highly prized assets, a familiar world commodity, but taken to another sphere on the shrouded slopes of this wealthy corner. My whirlwind education begins on the streets of Jinghong. Li, proving an invaluable ally in opening the door of opportunity, introduces me to the rich pickings of the regions famed tea.

Tea has for centuries been an important trading commodity for the Chinese and here in Yunnan the tea trail extends north, into Tibet where the quality of tea is especially revered. For thousands of years, an ancient network treaded by human feet and mules transported tea, bridging the Chinese Yunnan and the Qinghai-

Tibet Plateau. Along often rugged, unpaved roads, the trail traversed forests and a series of towering mountains, forging links with other ethnic groups. Tea and other commodities like salt and sugar flowed into Tibet, bartered for horses, cows, furs and musk, which came back the other way. Dubbed the *Ancient Tea-Horse Road*, its origins can be traced to the Tang Dynasty (618-907) and lasted until the 1960s, when the construction of Tibetan highways bought about its sudden demise, much the same as the dawn of modern civilisation did for the Silk Road.

To many, China is accredited as the birthplace of tea and the Yunnan is also reputed to be the home of its most prized variety Puer, the ancient colossus of the tea world. To find out more, an instantaneous trip to seek out the fabled trees would be necessary. Due to prior commitments, Li would be unable to come, but furnishes me with detailed instructions and promises a visit to his sister's tea shop when I return to Jinghong.

The next day, I board a bus heading to Menghai, the centre of Puer cultivation and an excellent springboard to its surrounding hills and mountains. Away from the centre of Jinghong, the bus gradually climbs the perfect tarmac road, the early morning mist clings to the hills interceded by rubber tree plantations, sloping terraces of tea and rice fields in its basin. A chance meeting with friends of Li, travelling back to visit their families, provides intelligent company during the short journey. Menghai is a functional, dusty town, the approach into the new bus station, an encapsulating glimpse of the clash of new and old, as gleaming blocks of flats rise above the feathery rice fields that languish opposite, their demise surely already ascertained. At the station, the recent departure of a bus to Xiding is an unwelcome hitch to my plan. It also happens to be the second and final bus to depart there, so I turn to Li's friend for nuggets of wisdom to help with my problem. He suggests the only practical choice is to hire a private car, so he guides me up to the corner of the road and engages a man wearing a red Manchester United shirt. An amicable agreement is quickly thrashed out on my behalf, sparing the driver and me from my bumbling pigeon Chinese.

I find an enjoyable lunch near the main market, in a canteen style restaurant that delivered lightning fast food of discerning excellence. A delicious salad of shredded chicken bursting with chilli heat, zinging sour lime juice and crunchy peanuts (a lean towards neighbouring South East Asia), while a simple chicken broth accentuates a steer to central China by virtue of star anise. I return to the bus station, throw my rucksack in the boot of my driver's vehicle and begin the two hour drive to Xiding. We pass through the town of Mengzhe, noticeable for its cantankerous use of speed humps and blanket covering sandy rice husks strewn over the side streets, and soon the terrain is littered with boulders and potholes, making the final thirty minutes tedious and uncomfortable.

Xiding is a village perched on the hilly slopes, a collection of traditional thatched roof Dai houses, a dilapidated market area and the over indulgent Chinese authority's, semi-circular, freshly painted white headquarters with its sweeping presidential drive and beautifully manicured gardens. A group of women huddle on a quiet bend, selling scantily displayed tomatoes, cabbages, gourds, mangoes and lychees. My driver helps arrange a bed for the night in a barely functional truck drivers dosshouse. The owner is quite taken aback by my foreign features and doesn't converse in Mandarin Chinese but local Dai. The single storey building consists of seven three-bedded rooms and she saunters off and brings the key for room three. The damp, dingy room is dark, ripped lino partially covers the floor, crude concrete walls of distressed grey paint meet a ceiling of woven cobwebs and groovy plastic panda curtains. A rusting tin washing bowl, an old toothbrush decaying in its basin, compete with a bashed up black desk near the window for furnished bragging rights. A grimy, ineffective mosquito net dangles from the ceiling in a pathetic bid to cover the slim single bed that it services. After I arrange a few necessary items, a torch, candles and wash kit, I step into the early evening to explore the fascinating tea plantations just yards from my sleeping area.

Recent rains have made the slopes very slippery. An amphitheatre of stubby green bush trees, sprinkled with grander, older masters, form neat rows on the inclined terraces. Crouched ladies wearing conical bamboo woven hats, pick the dark green leaves and fling them in baskets that are secured to their heads. Although its botanical origins are the same as other teas, the climate and geographical conditions that exist in the seven pockets of the Yunnan allow these trees to undergo natural mutations that give the leaves the necessary attributes for producing Puer. In accordance with an ancient Dai document of Xishuanbanna, Yunnan had tea trees here some 1700 years ago. In 1961 in the primeval forest on Dahei Mountain, a large wild tree was discovered that rose to 32.1m with a diameter of 1.03m. Miraculously, this verdant specimen can still yield quality tea leaves. Yunnan's favourable conditions are suitable for the cultivation of large-leaf trees, which feature early budding, strong buds, long growth period and tender leaf texture. The region's mild climate, frost-free winter and spring, abundant rainfall, nebulous ambience and fertile soil align to provide the ultimate tea growing conditions.

It is the age of the tree, long fermentation method and longevity of its storage that contribute to its fame. In China's swelling middle classes, the scramble for wealth is being sought through its booming stock market, buoyant property market and speculative business activities driven by a burgeoning mass of entrepreneurs. However, the alternative choice for many wise, informed souls is the potential golden rewards to be reaped in investing in tea and in particular Puer. Back in January 2007, at an auction in Guangzhou's Fang Cun market, a pressed brick of raw Puer tea sold for the staggering amount of $39,000 and the quantity only weighed 500 gm. For someone used to brewing tea from the neat perforated tea bags that line our supermarket shelves, this revelation is quite astonishing. The Chinese speculate on top quality Puer tea, like wine connoisseurs drool over the market value of Chateau Petrus or the sweet wine of Chateau d'Yquem. The finest leaves from the oldest trees, matured and stored for long periods reap the greatest rewards. The stampede for the humble leaves, has seen prices rise by over 50 per cent in the last year and instead of drinking it, millions of astute Chinese are hoarding it, creating a shortage of available tea, sending prices rocketing. For the farmers that grow and rely on it for their income, the rampant demand has swelled their coffers significantly. A monthly income of 3000RMB or the equivalent of $400 is quite normal now, a figure that is significantly more than many urbanites, let alone the habitually poorer rural folk.

I sit for a while, in a deliberate clearing, surrounded by these modest trees and gaze at the fruitful simplicity of the natural scene. Women continue picking through the red brick soil channels, as the sun begins dipping over the rice basin in the valley below and I wander down the slope, back to the winding road. With the evening sun disappearing, the air takes on a chilly note, the elevated altitude, in excess of 1200m, dictates a rapid decline in temperature.

A heavy downpour ensues, the deafening silence interrupted by a litter of black pigs foraging through refuse in ditches and two men freewheeling on bicycles in the pitch dark. Earlier I'd sought advice from the hostel owner as to my dining options, to which a pointing finger directed me to the only place in town open and serving food. It is every bit as inspiring as my digs, two failing candles flicker in the entrance, where two men sit in hushed silence and quickly scoff noodles from their bowls. I grab for my notebook, reel off a flurry of food items and attempt to order food that contains pork. The proprietor's negative response is followed by similar answers to beef, chicken or anything else that constitutes meat and my feeble, hopeful stab at ordering fish is met with a resounding no. Hopelessly out of my depth, I resign myself to her helpful, fully logical solution of eating the same food as the other diners. The unexciting soup, a vegetable stock with strips of green squash, sliced tomatoes and coagulated beaten egg is insipid but a crispy potato cake, with golden exterior and soft centre is actually rather good. The strands of fine potato are luxuriating in their unrestrained familiarity and remind me of a rosti cake.

That night, I huddle under a thin damp duvet, cover myself with a thick blanket and drift to sleep riddled with irony; outside I'm surrounded by the most valuable product, a commodity weight for weight more expensive than gold, yet my lodgings are of the most basic I've paid for.

I rise early in the morning, the outside air is thick with mist, and the surrounding hills drenched in a blanket of moisture, as goose bumps appear on my sleeveless arms. The bus heading back to Menghai is parked outside my room. Tickets are sold from a kiosk occupied by the guesthouse owner and a little after 7am, the full vehicle trundles out of Xiding. The driver flicks on the radio, activates the television screen and we descend to the blaring din of Chinese pop music.

Li's promise to visit his sister's teashop in the centre of Jinghong is fulfilled later that afternoon. The shelves of the compact shop are stacked with oval bricks of pressed tea, beautifully wrapped and displayed. A middle-aged gentleman sits behind a thick wooden table and pours tea into miniature glasses. The preparation of Puer is a ceremonial passage towards the abyss of tea heaven and the precise method is performed in defining stages. In front of the man is a dark brown grooved wooden tray and four figurines in the right corner positioned as appeasing offerings to the spirits. He picks up a pair of tiny tongs, breaks up the brownish red tea from a pressed brick and drops it in minuscule fine china pot. Next, hot water is poured in to cleanse both the pot and the leaves, eliminating any loitering flavours from previous tastings. This initial cleansing process is then repeated in a decanting jug and all the cups, the latter as petit as the china pot. This water is discarded in the draining grooves beneath and a round-ended brush is used to sweep it away. Now the drinking can officially commence. Hot water is added to infuse the leaves and using the tongs, he delicately wipes the bottom of the cup with a small towel to dry it before handing it to us. The tea is offered at the optimum temperature, each cup is no more than a single mouthful and I'm expected to finish each one before I'm served anymore. The golden amber liquid is smooth, defies any bitterness and imparts delicious honeyed sweetness quite unlike any tea I am used to. The leaves continue to be infused and incessant refills follow, each time adhering to the same time honoured etiquette that ensures the drink you receive is served at its best.

The leaves of Puer mature and develop over time due to a unique natural, bacterial fermenting process that enriches the leaves and over time deepens the colour and flavour. The Chinese have long extolled its virtues of both taste and life-enhancing qualities, which clinical studies have proved lowers cholesterol, cures lipema, aids digestion, dispels alcoholic toxins and is effective in fighting dysentery. In summary, this is a commodity that brings wealth, phenomenal flavour and helps individuals in the battle to lose weight. The ancient practice of tea cultivation affords Yunnan, the title of 'Kingdom of Tea' and the ageing property of Puer reigns from its lofty throne.

Hunting and Foraging

In the coming days I travel parallel to the river, shadowing the Mekong by road to Lancang, Lincang and Baoshan before traversing the great river and driving west to Xiaguan and north to the old town of Dali. The journey by bus to Lancang was fairly routine, although at times the road degenerated to a sloppy bog in the Puer growing town of Jing Mai and hulking blue tipper trucks, laden with coal, dredged through the quagmire. I'm enthralled at the sight of ethnic ladies that line the roadside, fresh from the forest and laden with baskets of wild mushrooms. I dream of a pan sizzling with meaty fungi, garlic, leeks and shredded ginger, the gently caramelised mushrooms, a decadent treat at any time of the day. I eat a decent whole fish for dinner in Lancang but a dire mushroom broth that was insipid and had an abundance of raw wild mushrooms did no justice to their superlative qualities.

The road to Lincang heads north before turning west and added up to a marathon, beginning in the thick morning mist and driving on a road under heavy construction. Frequent stops to allow workmen to shovel huge boulders and rubble, delay our bumpy progress. A stop for lunch in the scrum of a truckers' eating-house was marred by, of all things, undercooked rice! A young boy, no more than nine years of age pushes his paltry, crunchy starch grains to one side in disgust and joins the heated protest aimed at the retreating cooks. I knew there would be many suprises on this trip but poorly prepared rice was the last thing I had expected to be commenting on. I share my lunch of fatty broth with my momentary young ally, he reciprocated by offering a plate of fried wild mushrooms. Neither of us speaks a word: spoken language exchanged with the quintessential silence of sharing food with a stranger. A brief stop at the intersection with the road from Burma; this is a heavily patrolled border, a notorious route for smugglers and my bags and the entire bus are thoroughly searched before our laboured journey can continue. In Lincang, I check into the plush Wasai Hotel and enjoy an excellent leg of black mountain chicken, steamed and flavoured with star anise, the twist of aniseed a subtle triumph. Like Lancang, this town is one continuous building site. Gleaming new office blocks, hotels and shopping malls line sweeping wide boulevards, only in back street alleys may one still wander past traditional buildings.

The sound of our driver's deep throat spitting tarnishes a pleasant journey to western Yunnan's industrial and transportation hub, the city of Baoshan. A slapstick kung fu movie, a chuckling piece of cinema in the vein of Laurel and Hardy, once again illustrates the Chinese people's love of blaring audio entertainment. A change of bus here allowed me to chance upon a scrumptious street snack, served with gracious aplomb by a lady with a gleaming infectious smile, the wide rimmed silk hat upon her head, more suitable for Royal Ascot than the street corner she occupies. She filled squares of cooked rice noodle sheets with juicy bean sprouts, crunchy chopped peanuts, sliced spring onion and dresses the parcel with soy sauce and vibrant spicy red pepper oil. I enjoy them sitting in front of the expansive curved frontage of the central bus station, overlooked by the golden dragons of the grand monument behind me. They are that good I wander back and buy two more of these local specialities.

A brand new super highway fast tracks us through to Xiaguan, via long tunnels carved through the mountains, a 435m bridge that spans the Mekong (I only know this because each new bridge displays a sign with its length) and the bizarre sight of a farmer herding water buffalo down the highway like it was developed for this purpose. The bulldozing speed of change in China is so rampant that some are merely crushed in the rush for world economic domination. For many, it is a frightening prospect.

The ancient city of Dali, with its old stone cobbled streets, ox-blood coloured shops and the traditional curved tiled roofs of Bai houses, nestles between the sacred waters of Erhai Lake and the imposing marbled, Cangshan Mountains that harbour an immense variety of wildlife and flora within its eighteen granite peaks and feed the green, verdant fields from its tumbling streams. The Bai, who dominate the region, are the most prolific of all the ethnic minorities in Yunnan and their ancestors lived around the Erhai Lake area 4000 years ago, cultivating rice and other crops. Erhai Lake is a vital daily focal point for the Bai, offering a deeply spiritual power and supplementing their diet with an abundance of fresh water fish. In relation to my specific journey, it is also an important drainage system for the Mekong River, being fed directly from the Xier River whose waters are swelled by the melting snow and glaciers of the Qinghai-Tibetan Plateau. Erhai Lake would feature prominently in my stay here, but for now my journey would take me south, first to the market of Wei-San and its surrounding area.

Xiao He is a twenty-two year old Bai woman, whose shy demeanour conceals a well-educated mind and openly caring attitude towards the minorities of the Yunnan. Our small van seems inconsequential as we wind our way up the mountain road. Rain has been steadily falling all morning, the lamentable track is awash with slicks of mud and visibility is at best five metres. A trickle of Yi, Miao, Hui and Lizhu tribes head down from the hills to attend the market. Many trek on foot and rise at 4am for the long, arduous walk down the mountain. Our driver, apparently misunderstanding our request to drop us at the market, completes a precarious U-turn and follows the procession of tribal folk to Wei-San market.

The entrance is congested by a various supply of horse drawn passenger carriages, the downtrodden animals pitying themselves in the foul conditions. Just inside, large bamboo baskets filled with marijuana seeds prove a popular choice for the colourfully adorned Yi, as an elderly lady pops a few into her mouth. The floor is a mud bath, the dismal weather is filthy and attendance is sharply down due to this. A compact crowd, jostling vigorously imploring the traders' eyes to fix upon them, draws my attention. Passionate tones ring out, the occasional argument flares as heated negotiations ensue as I struggle to view the object of their fascination. Expecting my next excursion to the underbelly of the weird and wonderful, I'm pleasantly surprised to find the relatively normal spectacle of pig meat. Business is brisk, the excellent quality of the mountain pigs' deep coloured meat and hard, dry skin create a mild frenzy among the crowd, their glowing awareness of natural, well reared livestock is openly appreciated by me. Xiao ushers me away, towards traders selling tiny red berries, their fragrant, intoxicating aroma is accentuated when I'm allowed to scoop some up and breathe in their sweet, fruity qualities. Hot mountain pepper grows prolifically in these regions and their characteristics form the foundational seasoning for much of the cooking here. The cuisine of South East Asia, its influence still pervading in Jinghong, is finally flushed away, the citrus of lemongrass is no more, and a different food style is now patently in force.

The rear of the market is given over to trading of livestock, enclosures full of bulking water buffaloes, horses, bulls and calves being inspected and negotiated for, share the floor with herds of goats in the far left corner, huddled nervously against a wall.

Turning away and back to the entrance, three men sit under a bulging canopy, with buckets of clear liquid containing corn fermented liquor. Their vacant, glazed eyes awash with tales of potent liquor fix annoyingly on me but to be civil I buy a cup and instantly regret it. The harsh brew rasps the back of my throat, inflaming my mouth and leaving a lingering corn flavoured taint as punishment. A few stalls along, I collide with another home brew, this time fermented with rice and papaya, it too is strong but has developed softer tones, incorporating a sweet honey finish, that alleviates any unpleasant after-burn. Before we depart I buy loose tea, dark conical mounds of sugar, fresh bundles of tobacco leaf, half a kilo of mountain pepper and a box of cigarettes.

The weather and visibility gradually improve as we once more wind up the mountain road, the hilly terrain occasionally illuminated by flashes of sunlight. Near the tiny hamlet of Wu Miao Lin, our driver halts, we alight and bid him farewell and he soon disappears on his way back to Dali. We negotiate the remaining 1 km on foot, climbing up a steady incline that delivers us to a remote Miao village. An elderly woman, wearing a thick black headdress, welcomes us, remembering Xiao fondly from her previous visits and directs us to another dwelling across the way. The steep slopes are heavily vegetated with corn, as we traverse along a narrow path, brushing by apple, pear, plum and walnut trees that leave me pining for the rolling hills of England. Loud, violent barking from an aggressive dog sends a shiver down my spine but mercifully a young boy tugs at its mane and restrains it. A man modestly greets us on the muddy flat forecourt and brings stools, tightly woven from straw, that are exceedingly comfortable. Having released the dog, his son now tears around teasing young chicks, the scurrying birds squawk as he gleefully mocks them. Down in the valley, construction workers toil in the midday sun, creating a brand new highway to connect the growing ambitions of the regime. Up here, the story is very different; their new unfinished home is constructed from a mixture of red mud, stones and straw. Wooden pillars support the thick exterior walls; the interior walls have yet to be added, so temporary, rickety bamboo fencing cordons off their sleeping quarters for now. They have no sanitation, no electricity, limited education and scarcely any money, their very livelihoods rely on subsistence farming, hunting and foraging in the surrounding forests. In the new cut-throat Chinese society, these are the poorest people I have yet to meet on my journey up the Mekong.

A small fire is lit in the early evening, the man sits crafting a new catapult for his son, who casts an admiring eye over his father's shoulder and when it is ready they playfully sling stones into trees hoping to knock out small birds. An hour later, the boy's mother and sister return laden with carrier bags bursting with green leaves and promptly disappear to begin cooking supper. Xiao had forewarned me that their diet was essentially monotonous, dull and nutritionally poorly balanced, so that night dinner is a watery soup made from the green bitter leaves, cold steamed rice flour buns, bulked up with steamed rice. Meat is rarely eaten, a lavish treat, generally only afforded for special occasions or when a hunting trip yields bush deer or game birds. A pounded paste made from mountain pepper offers the only salvation, a beacon of light in an otherwise dark narrow tunnel. On occasions when vegetables are scarce, a meal might just consist of rice and a few steamed buns. Even tea seems to be an exorbitant luxury, so the tea I have brought brings real joy.

In the morning, the torrential rain of last night subsides. I'm out of bed by 6am, as the day begins early here. Today I'm joining them on a hunting and foraging trip and after a paltry breakfast of greasy fried shredded potato, steamed rice and leftover soup from the night before, we set off after 7am. The young boy skips off in front, carrying a wooden bow, a tube of sharp pointed bamboo arrows and two catapults. We descend into the valley and cross a low bridge, flank the construction site, where guard dogs bark furiously and the kid hurls stones at the roped restrained animals. The scent of pine permeates the air, as we ascend through the forest along well-trodden paths. The boy's earlier exuberance has now faded to a disgruntled childish rant, throwing a tantrum before flinging all the tools on the floor and stomping off down the slope.

After an hour's solid walking, we enter a compound, where we are greeted by the brother of the man who is guiding us. Consisting of two buildings, the lower levels housing pigs, the upper for feed, wood and other essentials. His brother, whom I'm guessing is a little younger, is a more muscular, fuller faced individual than his slighter framed sibling, but maintains a similar diffidence in his outlook. His wife mixes the feed for the animals with her left hand, her right is missing three digits, lost due to an accident while chopping wood, leaves only her thumb and forth finger intact. His brother brings toasted sunflower seeds, weak green tea and a host of orchard fruit; green plums, tiny cherry apples, flat oval peaches and apples. The tough skinned cherry apples are good, the peaches bland, crisp and lacking any punch.

His brother joins our group and as we sweep along the side of the valley, the cooler mountain air dampens my clothes and causes me to shiver, as we move through isolated valleys, thick bush trails and cross streams of bubbling fresh water. At a clearing, we scurry down from our defined path to pick fat, white skinned mushrooms. In a little over five minutes our plastic carrier bags are full to bursting. To the experienced eye this forest offers a cornucopia of incredible food opportunities, but to the untrained it is a blanket of blind alleys, a network of concealed treasure hidden in the dense forest. Their observation skills are phenomenal, with eyes like hawks; they frequently disappear, returning clutching wild herbs, fruit or plants harbouring medicinal qualities. They collect threads of riverweed, thumb sized blackberries from thorny bushes, a herb that looks and smells of oregano and a zingy, sour marble sized fruit with clear white flesh that explodes in my mouth like a sherbet dip. The daughter, already a prolific forager at the age of ten, busies herself in thick green bushes, picking eight pronged reddish green goodies, that happen to be wild star anise. Wild mushrooms are inspected closely, the poisonous ones glaringly obvious to the experts are left in place.

With our significant bounty of wild food, their attention turns to the subject of protein, the hunt for bush meat could amount to a feast of flesh if successful but nowadays, with the encroachment of modernity these forests have suffered and catching an animal is now much harder. Ten minutes later, there's an almighty commotion in the depths of the bush, and a sudden eruption of activity as his brother snuck steadily through the trees and spooked a bush deer from it sleep. Seconds from success, the deer sprung up and scurried to safety in the nick of time. A nonchalant shrug of the shoulders, the only admission to the one that got away and we troop off empty handed. All the way they continue to take opportune pot shots at the canopies of tall trees. To me their catapults seem primitive and success is a highly speculative gamble of pure chance. At times they are powering stones a distance of one hundred metres, aiming at birds no bigger than a sparrow. I'm not at all convinced we have any decent chance of success, when they nimbly manoeuvre through patches of violet and yellow wild flowers to inspect a possible target. Edging closer to thick scrubby bush, the older brother pulls an arrow from the tube, loads it into place and draws back the bow. He crouches, slowly creeping closer to his edible objective but just as he is about to release, two colourful pheasants flap, take flight and distressfully race from view along the valley. After six hours, we head back to his brother's and console ourselves with warm green tea.

The disappointment at the lack of meat for supper is only partially satisfied by the prospect of fried wild mushrooms, so I offer to buy one of his chickens for us all to eat for supper. The bird is selected, its throat slit over a bowl and the warm flowing blood reserved. It is plucked, cleaned and chopped into pieces, all but the excrement is utilised and thrown into a heavily blackened pot to fry in corn oil. He decants the meat, tosses in a handful of red chillies and allows them to blacken, before adding water, ground wild star anise, slithers of garlic and salt. The cauldron of bubbling chicken is cooked over a fierce flame for one hour, after which the blood is poured in and removed from the fire to serve. Meanwhile, his wife fries potatoes with hot mountain pepper and concocts a soup with the wild mushrooms, which she enhances with air dried pieces of pork rind that I can see hanging on a metal hook from the underside of the roof. It is redeemably fine, honest fayre, the intensely flavoured chicken meat is packed with chilli heat and subtle notes of aniseed from the star anise, the richness from the blood is a little overwhelming for me but that would be a minor grumble. The hot mountain pepper energises the fried potatoes, enticing the humble spud with a fruity piquancy.

When we arrive back at base, the sun is fading over the valley below. The boy is rejuvenated and larks about the raised forecourt. By his side, a small bird, no bigger than an average sized quail, flounders by the side of a catapult.

The Lake

After two broken nights sleep in the mountains, I wake refreshed, draw the curtains and focus my eyes towards the Cangshan Mountains. The yellow cross of a Catholic Church towers above the curved roofs of the old city, while the domed crowns of its mosques symbolise the diversity of the Yunnan region. While the Bai dominate this area, significant other ethnic groups play an important role in everyday life. My delightful guesthouse is owned by Hui Muslims, the majority of whom reside in Dali Prefecture and moved to the Yunnan around 1200 years ago. They descended from the Arab and Iranian traders and soldiers who travelled to China during the Tang Dynasty era but suffered terrible reprisals between 1855-1873 when most of the population was wiped out after rebelling against a dispute over gold and silver mines. Their culinary influence is felt through their penchant for grilled kebabs, flatbreads and hand pulled wheat noodles, the dexterity of skill in the latter, always an impressive display. The wife of the owner of my guesthouse is a cook of some distinction and is supported by her daughter. Every morning for breakfast, a steaming bowl of beefy broth packed with squares of wheat pasta, chilli and herbs brings replenishment and substance to start the day. Lunch and dinner are equally impressive, notably a brilliant dish that she regularly prepares with goat meat. Chopped pieces of meat left on the bone are coated in a spicy crumb before being gently steamed and garnished with chopped spring onions. I'd never dream of steaming anything crumbed but here the result is meltingly soft meat with a spicy flavour that delivers a warming level of intrigue. She fries wild mushrooms, meaty morsels that are the equal of porcini, bursting with earthiness, sautéed with strips of green chilli, slithers of garlic and chopped spring onion. The Yunnan has already demonstrated its unparallel diversity, the unique traits of its colourful ethnic inhabitants, emulated in fascinating interwoven food experiences that have the ability to change with every footstep.

Away from the delightful, if a little saturated, touristy streets of the ancient city, Xiao and I travel 20 km north to the town of Xizhou, en-route to her father's home on the banks of Erhai Lake. Having woken in the confines of an Islamic house, my cultural allegiance shifts to the region's ethnic Bai power base, as Xiao guides me through Bai customs, its cultural heritage and systematically inflicts its delicious food upon me.

The Bai were among the original people to settle in the Yunnan and are considered the most successful ethnic group in the entire province. The fertile land they occupy has proved invaluable and the cornerstone of their economic achievements have been shaped by farming and fishing, but it is their ability to forge lasting relationships with the Han and Yi populations and their tremendous skill in woodcarving, stonework and marble quarrying that has cemented their enviable position. The Bai peoples' architecture is unique and admired by many for its timeless, classic design. The typical style of three houses on three sides and on the other a decorative screen wall to reflect the sunlight to the house, is known as *san fang yi zhao bi. Si he wu tian jing* describes a house with a major courtyard and four small ones that flank it at each corner. The majority of Bai houses are decorated with stone and woodcarvings, in recognition of their esteemed heritage.

Xiao leads me to view the sacred trees that are a feature of every town or village. Birds nestle in their sacrosanct branches, above the base of the trunk, which displays spiritual offerings amongst a hotchpotch of bamboo frames in a sign of lasting respect to the deceased.

Along the main thoroughfare, a line of food sellers cram the wide pavement area, with curious sight of old rusting electric fans, gnarling and turning to blow air over wide, thick black pans that rest on stubby legs. A lady appears from an opened shop front carrying a flour dusted tray with four fermented doughy rounds and slides them into the dry heat of the pan. A hot charcoal tray lid is then placed on the top, allowing the fan to ignite the coals to power the fire with consistent red-hot heat. In the small shop front the lady produces a steady flow of these specialities called *po zhu* here but named *baba* when referred to by the Naxi in Lijiang. In a wide aluminium bowl, the blistering, bubbling dough has been allowed to rise overnight, developing the natural yeast enzymes that create air within the wheat flour and water mixture. The soft, pliable dough is then kneaded in small pieces, before incorporating minced pork, chopped spring onions, salt and red chilli paste and folding the dough to conceal the filling. She flattens it slightly before placing it on a wooden board and gently running a rolling pin over it to correct the shape. The final touch is to spread a generous quantity of pork grease on top, to moisten during the cooking process. The cooked lightly browned savoury pastries are cloyingly fatty from the excess oil and sit heavily on my stomach but the addition of wheat to my diet offers a glimpse of things to come.

We cross the road, entering the narrow concrete streets that lead into the old village; the crooked pathways chronicle a thousand tales of historical woes, and triumphs and creative artisanship. The faded ox blood houses hold their dignity against a tide of modern intrusion, many traditions holding sway over escalating mechanised industry. Four long, double length thin poles, the exact colour of the solid wooden doors that form the doorways to the houses, are wrapped with the creamy elasticity of the region's thin cheese, that twirls to the top and props against the wall outside in a timeless scene of symmetrical synergy. A Muslim lady donned with a white flannel cap brings more to dry, Xiao politely asks if we may step inside to observe its production and we are ushered in to observe an elderly gentleman shredding starchy potato. The workroom is dimly lit, poky and leads onto a tiny bedroom. Many of the clothes, shoes and other everyday items spill into her tight working space. The untidy area contrasts with the slick, silkiness with which she works, beginning with fresh cows milk. A deep oval, wok shaped pan sits over a funnel of simmering water ready to receive the milk, which coagulates as it hits the pan. She stirs it with a wooden spoon, lifting it gently up and down, tilting it occasionally to maximise the drainage of any excess liquid. The warm mixture is then worked vigorously in her hands, to enhance its suppleness, before she manipulates it round a thick cylindrical wooden tool and begins deftly spiralling pliable strands around the twin pole to form a wafer thin coil of wet cheese. In the space of ten minutes, wheat has been joined by dairy as a new example of foodstuff.

Back on the street, a cobbler is busy searing a sole to the base of a defunct shoe and a distinguished, bespectacled gentleman is a picture of deft concentration as he etches a marble slab with precise calligraphy, while ash drops from the cigarette in his left hand. The main market is slowing to a trickle as we pass briefly through and begin the walk to her father's house. The sun has burnt off the misty rain of the morning. Flat emerald green rice fields sweep to the base of the Cangshan Mountains, as horse drawn carriages trot by taking people home along the cobbled roads and narrow streets.

Xiao's sister greets us warmly, as she appears from the separate building where she is busy preparing lunch. Xiao has not been home in many months and sadly her mother recently passed away after a long illness. Her sense of loss is tangible, the grief has yet to subside fully and the gap left in the family will never be replaced. Inside the house, a permanent vase of pink flowers is replenished every day in their mother's memory. Her sister produces platefuls of delicious food for lunch: fried fish in a sweet and sour soup is a lip smacking effort showing exuberant use of hot mountain pepper, sour plums, dried papaya, tomatoes and spring onion. The fish, caught that morning in the lake, retains all its subtle character but the explosion of hot, sweet and sour ignites my palate to leave it performing cartwheels all afternoon. Throughout my journey I've eaten a significant quantity of what we in the West perceive as 'oddities', food beyond our normal jurisdiction and our conservative palates. I've yet to be offered, until now that is, an example of raw meat, that I've just brushed away a festering fly from. For the Bai, it is an extremely popular choice but one that must insist upon the best, top quality meat and is a good barometer by which to judge a cook's eye for suitable produce. A plate bristling with slithers of translucent pork loin, shredded rind and slices of liver, temporarily reminds me of the well known travel parable 'if it is not thoroughly cooked to within an inch of destruction, do not touch with a bargepole.' Sound advice for the masses but not for an Englishman bent on eating all before him. The quality of the meat is indeed of acceptable freshness and quality and is really rather good dipped in a whacking sauce of chilli powder, hot mountain pepper, toasted sesame seeds, ground peanuts, a splash of sour plum liquor and a sprinkling of salt. Thick slices of sweet local ham, crispy local fried cheese, fried pork with blackened chillies, flowering chives and spring onion, fried corn kernels with green soy beans and red pepper and a soothing, cooling broth with chunks of white gourd, complete a ringing endorsement for Bai cuisine and her sister's natural verve with the ingredients.

A thirty-second walk from the house brings us to the meaningful shores of Erhai Lake, China's seventh largest freshwater lake and considered a sign of real providence to the Bai. For centuries they have fished these deep well-stocked waters, foraged for edible foods and lived in harmony alongside it. Xiao's father, a quiet, considered man, scans the water as he tells me worryingly that the lake is now under pressure, as the blue waters of yesteryear have become heavily polluted. He recalls a time when you could drink this water directly from your hand. He is fearful for its future prosperity in the current unrelenting world that plunders life's riches with little care for the consequences of its actions. It is a sentiment shared by many elders and respected environmentalists who study the health of the lake. Minutes later his brother saunters down, puffing on a tobacco pipe, carrying a long bamboo pole on his shoulder, draped with a blanket. A powerful bull, lashed to a tree struts about, snorting in disgust and thrashing wildly in a vain attempt to unleash itself, as his brother washes the blanket in the shallows. In the village of Jin Guisi, artisan craftsmen have been producing blankets for centuries, a tradition that still flourishes to this day, washing them in the holy waters of the lake, a vital step in the process.

I follow her uncle back to his house, past the gut-wrenching stench of the communal toilets, where a man relieves himself in the pit beneath him, and into the open courtyard where he hangs the just washed sodden blankets to dry. He prepares tea, draws knowingly on his pipe, and then disappears up a ladder, coming back down seconds later with a rolled blanket and a bag of sheep wool, which he empties to the concrete floor. The blanket is unrolled onto a bamboo mat that covers the crude floor, as he sets to work chopping the soft wool through a long bow like tool. His action is much like using a pair of garden shears to trim thick grass, the clumps of wool dropping to the ground in ever finer clumps, making the fibres softer and cleaner. Having removed his green wellington boots, he now moves steadily about, wearing only a white plimsoll on his left foot, distributing the prepared wool in patches that he identifies as needing to be strengthened. He brings a blackened kettle with boiling water, and using a splayed bamboo brush, gradually walks around the edge trickling water and flicking it with the brush to send an even spray over the blanket. Next he moves to the back wall, tucking in the end of the blanket, a motion he repeats several times to manipulate the finished shape, then centrally positioned, he draws the bamboo mat up and rolls it firmly and tightly with his bare right foot. His foot rocks gently back and forth, working different sections until he is satisfied with the result. He repeats this several times, paying extra attention to the edges, a procedure that ensures the correct size, thickness and quality is achieved. There is something truly wonderful about watching craftsmen absorbed in the act of creation and as he once again hoists the bamboo pole upon his shoulder for the well trodden walk to the lake, he knows in his heart that he has achieved something of meaningful quality.

In the morning the crow from a cockerel hastens my eyes to open, the time is an uncomfortable 5.30am. I shift on the sofa and doze for thirty minutes, before getting dressed and welcoming the dawn of a new day. Outside, a strong breeze cools me as I wash my face with water, then stroll to the lake's edge, where the breaking light over the hills strikes the tips of the waves, as scores of fishing boats struggle in the rougher conditions. A couple heading for deeper water use enormous energy to propel forward, their small square paddles no match for an engine. Back at the house, Xiao's father is lighting pink incense sticks that protrude from the exterior wall.

After breakfast, I visit the local market with Xiao and her sister, which acts as a prelude to the much better, more diverse market in Xizhou. The limited produce hastens our decision to hail a waiting horse carriage to trot us into town. When we arrive, her sister leaves us to attend a hospital appointment but before she departs issues Xiao with specific instructions of what we should purchase and the items she prefers to buy herself. The market is thronging with activity, a colourful display of ethnic pride, traditionally dressed Bai ladies wearing red headdresses mingle with other ethnic minorities and Han Chinese, primarily dressed in western attire. An intense buzz rings through the air as early morning shoppers secure the best of the produce. Xiao notices a huddle of women in the far corner and leads us over, revealing a bowl of translucent fish, the size of tiny whitebait with bulging black eyes. Apparently this variety can only be caught in the middle of the night (the locals say 1am) when the fish are most active. Xiao quizzes the trader, who much to her disappointment announces that her small haul has already been sold. These diminutive creatures are becoming increasingly rare but are much sought after by the Bai, as are any fish from the lake, so farmed varieties are becoming increasingly more prevalent.

At the beginning of my journey, it was easy to be shocked, dumbstruck or completely overwhelmed by novel produce such as live headless frogs, snakes, the putrid smells of animals innards, tarantulas, ant eggs and a whole host of other oddities, but now I feel a cast iron immunity to almost anything that beams into focus. I wander this market with all my usual curiosity, still excited by any new wonderful produce but it genuinely feels good to be at ease, and here, it is the simple sight of trucks laden with humble potatoes, enormous gourds the size of rugby balls or a decent loin of beef that motivate my culinary urges. I'm surprised to see crayfish in buckets, yard long purple snake beans, women frying pancakes and pastel coloured duck eggs displayed adjacent to the much larger ones from geese. A group of ladies crouching on stools, oblivious to the food and garbage gathering at their feet, as they enjoy a morning snack of rice porridge drizzled with deep caramel sugar syrup. This is a place to socialise, catch up on the gossip and bemoan the intrinsic challenges of modern day China.

One hour after we have returned to the house, Xiao's sister arrives clutching plastic sacks of minuscule lake shrimps, a block of soft, silky tofu and dark brown wild mushrooms. She instructs her sister and I to peel bulbs of garlic and remove the heads from the shrimps, while she sets to work in the kitchen. Her cooking area is a semblance of practicality and good organisation. Neat rows of spices in containers, bottles of cooking oil, soy sauce and other kitchen essentials, line shelves above a cupboard brimming with stacked plates. Her chopping block, clear of any clutter, resides adjacent to a wood burning fire, upon which rests a snug fitting wok. She fries the shrimps briskly over a fierce flame, the translucent shellfish change quickly to a light orange, pinkie colour, before she adds whole beaten chicken eggs, hot mountain pepper and salt. A heap of washed, sliced wild mushrooms, sautéed with finely shredded green chilli and pieces of local cured ham. Tiny eels, in total, fried three times, are simmered in water, chilli powder, diced tofu, and crispy pork skin and scattered with spring onions before serving. Her style of cooking is seamless; her effortless, instinctive ability to marry her ingredients produces a myriad of wonderful food. Before I leave, I'm entertained by a colourful show of traditional Bai costumes and friends of the family and their siblings take it in turns to be photographed for family albums. All I must contribute is to shoot pictures from my digital SLR camera and marvel at their show of ethnic pride and how they are embracing their future around the focal point of their lake.

Drama, Confusion and Changing Topography

From Dali I head north to the Naxi stronghold of Lijiang and spend a few days recuperating in the old city, before contemplating the journey ahead and rejoining the Mekong's path up into the north of Yunnan and through Tibet. The city of Lijiang, once an important staging post on the ancient Tea-Horse Road, is divided between the historical element and the bustling commerce of modern China. The ancient town, once a sleepy thoroughfare of cobblestone lanes, canals of melted snow and charming Tibetan architecture, now feels like a miniature world of make-believe.

Hordes of domestic tourists invade its delightful, narrow undulating streets, following flag waving tour guides like sheep obeying the commands of a shepherd. At times, the intolerable strain of its current predicament overwhelms this area, as convoys of Chinese tour buses crush through the labyrinth of souvenir shops, cafés and block the quaint bridges that negotiate the rhythmic flow of water, symbolic of the stunning backdrop of the Jade Dragon Snow Mountain range. That said, at the crack of dawn, it is still just about possible to indulge the fantasy of yesteryear. Elderly Naxi women sit eating bowls of *liang feng*, a thick porridge made by soaking yellow beans overnight, then grinding to a fine powder and boiling with water. The grey plaster coloured slop is placed in bowls and sprinkled with a mixture of salt, black pepper and hot mountain pepper. I did, under some duress, eventually force a bowlful into the pits of my complaining stomach but it is about as appealing as chewing on a piece of chalk. The predominance of wheat, the increase in dairy and traditionally dressed Naxi women hawking baskets of juicy strawberries and traders in the well stocked market grilling rounds of black pudding, is still enough to excite a palate that has been richly rewarded by bountiful feasts of food.

It is now ten days since my last glimpse of the Mekong River and the time spent in Lijiang has left me hankering to rejoin it. Today my aim is to reach the town of Weixi, so I board the solitary bus to leave for this destination, from the new, well-marshalled bus station. The smooth road journeys through landscape categorised by forested hills, rolling wheat and rice fields, corn and streams that tumble from the mountains and feed another of China's great rivers. Like the Mekong, the Yangtze River begins its epic journey from the glaciers of the Qinghai-Tibetan Plateau and as it comes into view on my right hand side, it is but a fraction along its titanic journey and has yet to establish its true course through the heartland of China. The world's third longest river is the beating pulse, the main artery and symbolic master that cuts through a range of diverse energising landscapes. Nearby are the thundering Tiger Leaping Gorge, the dramatic Three Gorges Valley and the equally impressive, yet more tranquil Little Gorges. Through the searing heat, smog and densely populated commercial hub of Chonqqing, downriver to the controversial dam at Wishan (a brilliant piece of engineering and said to be the brainchild of Mao-Tse-Tong, which created the world's greatest shifts of population in the history of the world). Continuing on its north-easterly trajectory all the way to the ultra modern, gleaming skyscraper city of Shanghai, where it dumps into the East China Sea. Unlike the Mekong, the Yangtze has long been utilised as a commercial gateway and it has always been a huge focal point for the Chinese population.

Entering a wide flat valley, our lunch stop is the epitome of tranquillity. Picturesque hills sweep down to emerald green rice fields that cover the entire basin. The solitary modern building, with flourishes of ancient style, blends effortlessly into the environment. At the rear, a series of low-slung tables are positioned in front of a pond ringed by a colourful spray of flowers. It is about as magical a location that I have seen since I left England and the food doesn't disappoint either. In Lijiang I had purchased a hi-tech, hand-held Chinese translation computer, in anticipation of my future remote journeys and I use it to good effect here. From the annexed kitchen, I order an excellent broth highly flavoured with ginger, containing tender pieces of chicken and a plate of expertly fanned, cold sliced pork accompanied by a heap of dried chilli, hot mountain pepper and soy sauce. Delicate sprigs of coriander garnish the meat that is kept succulent by a pleasing ring of fat and sparkles in my mouth when dipped in the chilli, pepper and soy sauce.

After lunch, the Yangtze edges away from us, heading first north towards Sichuan before making a dramatic U-turn near its border and heading south through Lugu Lake and eventually travelling on a north-easterly path along the perimeter of Sichuan Province.

After seven hours, the bus pulls into the ragged bus station in the county town of Weixi. On first sight it seems rather a shabby place to end such an enduring journey and the hotel I hastily check into on the opposite side of the road, is a disgusting, flee ridden cesspit with damp sheets, faulty electrics and unhelpful, abrasive staff. I dump my rucksack and stroll through the unimpressive streets. Hopeful punters spill onto the pavement from the lottery stores, many stagger due to an excessive alcohol intake, in fact there appears to be a host of inebriated men, although, not in anyway threatening to myself. Dilapidated Naxi architecture breaks up modern soulless shells and one building in particular stands alone for its unique style. The wooden construction curves serenely around a sloped bend with a set of neat railings halfway up, lining a balcony and decorative doors that enter the upper house. The fading façade of golden wood, patchy and distressed, doesn't hide the expertly crafted doors that lead into a dimly lit restaurant on its ground floor. Further up the hill, a brand new street of retail outlets blend with hotel blocks and restaurants. I walk the short distance to the food market, which is all but closed when I arrive. Most of the traders are playing cards or engrossed in *ma jiang* – the omnipresent chess game favoured by the men of Yunnan. There may not be much activity, but on display here are some of the finest examples of cured meat products I have seen in the province. Cured ducks, sausages, aged legs and shoulders of pork, their crusted exteriors cage fine dark flesh and trotters, loins and slabs of belly pork that offer the distinction between plain good and damn excellent produce. I'm constantly stared at in the market; one lady stops dead on the spot and examines my features at close quarters. Is she struck by my handsome face or fascinated by my large nose? This I will never know but at times, it felt quite uncomfortable being the subject of such scrutiny. In the evening I wander back to the old house on the corner and enjoy a plate of stir fried pork with green and red chillies spiked with a fruity mountain pepper. This time I'm the individual mesmerised by another's features. A Pumi lady dressed in a blue, green and white long sleeved jacket, embroidered belt and silver bracelets and earrings, sits perfectly poised, her headscarf shrouding her hair, plaited with silk threads and yak-tail hair. The Pumi are one of the smallest minorities in Southwest China. They are traditionally mountain people, descended from a Tibetan race and legend claims their ancestors were a nomadic tribe that roamed the Qinghai-Tibetan Plateau.

Upon arrival yesterday I had secured a ticket for the onward journey to Deqin in the far north-west of the Yunnan, so in the morning I arrive at 7.10am and I'm mystifyingly shown to the exact bus that I had arrived on yesterday. Far from heading north, the driver is returning to Lijiang and I discover the bus to Deqin has already left and it is the only one of the day. I remonstrate with the lady behind the counter who had sold me the ticket but am greeted with a frosty glare and derided with a flurry of vocal abuse. A young English-speaking woman fortuitously leaps to my rescue, just prior to me considering a counter assault of my own. I'm in luck, there is a bus that will leave shortly for Yanmen, a considerable distance on the road to Deqin. I thank my new ally and hop on the bus.

The dank morning is dark and grey with a light blanket of drizzle as we join the road to Yanmen. The driver is careful on the slick potholed asphalt surface as we motor gently through the valley. We track the glistening flow of a clear water river, the shallow stream harmonises over rocks and boulders, before crashing into the swollen red silt mass of the Mekong, which swallows up the minor channel as it surges downriver. Old style chain bridges span the river, festival flags stretch over its breadth, houses perch high on the slopes and pagodas nestle in the trees, as the mighty river unleashes its full power in a show of brutal authority. At one stage, its descent is accentuated causing a torrent of white foam to crash into the cliff face, furiously rampaging against the battered rock and thunderously hurling it back into the swirling mass midstream. Fierce white water rapids, swirling whirlpools enhance the Mekong's personality. Gradually the scenery is becoming more dramatic as our altitude increases.

At a compact town, we drive headlong into market day, dominated by the Lisu ethnic minority. The scenes are chaotic, the main square alive with colour, noise and grilling food that make my stomach rumble in tormented agony. My confusing beginning to the morning had meant I missed the opportunity to have breakfast and with no opportunity to alight here, for fear of being left behind, it will be prolonged until we reach Yanmen. Lorries and vans struggle through the mass of human and animal bodies, herds of brown goats and saddled horses meander in the melee along the single file street. Our near empty bus is soon heaving with the rich, smelling bodies of Lisu, every inch of space is filled, baskets of live chickens rest on laps, through the aisles or wedged under seats. For the remainder of the journey to Yanmen, I sit squeezed tight against the window, admiring the Mekong and bedazzled by a pink emblazoned guesthouse that hugs a precarious bend nestled by the side of the road.

Alighting at Yanmen, I'm fully expecting to spend the night here and am not overly concerned at doing so. It feels like a pleasant enough town, occupies a favourable location by the river and will allow me to eat a belated lunch and rest before moving onto Deqin in the morning. The driver of my bus though, aware of my intentions, as the lady in Weixi had explained my final destination, introduces me to a shabbily dressed man wearing a grimy green cap, who leads me to a yellow bus that is leaving immediately for Deqin. The bus is already full, only a few positions in the aisle remain, so my rucksack is hoisted up onto the roof and I scamper quickly off to relieve myself in the public communal toilets. Nearly all towns have some kind of facilities, no matter how primitive and one becomes immune from the gassy odours that emit from the lack of any real sanitation. With no time to explore any decent food options I hastily buy soft drinks, cakes and biscuits, and hurry back to board the bus.

As we leave Yanmen, I'm sitting crouched on a low wooden bench that I share with a tall, slender Tibetan man and his young son dressed in commando green uniform. The atmosphere on board is jovial and communal but much more restrained than on the previous Yunnan bus journeys. The absence of tinny, blaring music and ridiculous videos is a welcome relief, the driver's bus is blessed with good luck charms that dangle from the rear view mirror. The changing topography enters a new, even more spectacular phase, the winding road climbs unnervingly, and the narrow track blown and carved from the cliffs offers a jaw dropping descent if any error of judgement is forthcoming. Great limestone karsts and dramatic cliffs drop directly to the floor of the Mekong as it crashes through the narrow gorges deep below us. The land slowly becomes more barren, less populated and our driver occasionally stops to step from his cabin to remove obstructive boulders from a primarily tarmac surface. Landslides form part of the everyday treacherous nature of driving along these high mountain roads and I was just about to find out the hard way.

The bus gradually came to a halt, the scene in front of us is neither an exciting prospect nor given the width of the track, a particularly easy one to traverse with any degree of safety. A landslide has caused the muddy track to be partially blocked; looking above us the cracked slope seems less than stable. This whole stretch of road is surrounded by unstable landmass, brought about by exploding dynamite to construct the crucial roads that connect these remote areas of the Yunnan. A slanted pile of heavy rocks and one significant boulder to the right have left, by my calculations, just enough room for the bus to squeeze through but that is not taking into account the slick, slippery mud bath and the sheer vertical drop to a certain death, due to there being no form of barrier to prevent any slight slip. All the passengers have disembarked and walked to the safety of the other side, while the driver and many of the men assess the uncertain outlook. A steady persistent rain begins to fall, as volunteers get to work to shift some of the rubble with pick axes and their bare hands. The main problem is the gigantic boulder, so men commence to dig under each side and then use long poles to act as leverage to dislodge the obstructing object. Any progress is checked, with a rock to prevent it slipping back, great roars of human emotive effort reverberate through the valley, as the chanting men join in collective raw power. It is a painstakingly slow, tedious process but not without rewards and after two long hours, the offending boulder is sent smashing down the vertical rocky slope and crashing into the wild waters of the Mekong. The driver jumps back in the cabin, reverses fifty metres or so and drives quickly and incisively and although it is wider now, any slip at this speed could be catastrophic. The front wheels hit the mud, nervously progressing but when the back wheels connect the vehicle slides dangerously, shifting violently from side to side, any attempt to gain any grip just sinks further into the mire. The bus is stuck, the driver gingerly climbs out of the stricken vehicle, picks up his mobile phone and rings for emergency help.

Two hours later, the cavalry arrives, as a large road cleaner has come to our rescue. Two hundred metres behind us the broken remains of another lays in ruins, its work life long since given up. An industrial, steel towline is fixed to the front of our bus and it is ripped from the bog, dragging it clear and to the joy of everyone, we load back onto the bus and continue on our way. Our disrupted ascent continues, as we steadily climb higher, the cloud level is breached on numerous occasions and the river now permanently squeezing through deep, towering gorges exalts an uneasy magical aura as this inhospitable terrain both inspires and leaves my nerves ripped into fine shreds of panic. Tiredness, hunger and a sore backside have long since aggravated as the light begins to fade. Half the passengers are asleep in various contorted positions, several are throwing up and the remainder sit in observed silence willing the journey to end. Many enter these journeys as strangers, even for me as the token foreigner, you soon become immersed in a communal unit, a travelling family whose conclusion is never ascertained. Bonding of this nature transcends any cultural barriers and is one of travel's inescapable, rewarding and compelling experiences that for me stand above all else. Twenty minutes later, the glimmering lights of Deqin appear as we descend to our journey's end and a little after 9pm we stagger into the bus yard, tired, hungry and extremely thankful.

In the Midst of Meili

The appreciation of last night's safe arrival, a hot bath and a decent nights sleep, allow me to channel my thoughts to the challenges ahead. The mystifying land of Tibet is in touching distance. Thus far, my journey's main agenda has been dominated by the exploration of the cuisine along the Mekong, which henceforth will share equal billing with my quest to reach the source of what the

Chinese call 'The Turbulent River.' Travel through Tibet is still in theory forbidden for single foreigners, the Chinese authorities' accentuated scepticism towards 'wayward souls' is a point of huge international attention and the persecution of the Tibetan race by the communist regime continues against a wave of fierce resistance from Tibetans and the international community at large. My own secretive paranoia of the current situation has led me to maintain a profound silence regarding my plans, even my girlfriend Alison believes I will take the alternative and legal route through Sichuan Province, but to do so would be to omit a significant section of the Mekong River and in my heart and mind this would be simply unacceptable. The coming week will be spent securing a driver prepared to in effect 'smuggle' me safely through to Zadoi, the gateway to the headwaters in the Qinghai Province and one of China's most wild and remote regions. Judging by the Chinese dominated concrete structures of Deqin, this grotty, chaotic town is not the place to begin my enquiries. Patience will be my main tool, so I decide to head for the tiny hamlet of Mingyong, an hour's drive from here.

My taxi motors north along the winding mountain road, leaving Deqin behind, where farmers tend to partially harvested wheat crops and groups of Tibetans gather at the sacred Felai Si Temple, opposite a growing number of guesthouses strategically positioned to view Meili Mountain. The hidden peaks of the immense Kawa Karpo range, blocked from view by a sea of fluffy clouds, their true magnificence obscured. This gigantic range of mountains consists of thirteen peaks, all of which exceed 6000m, including the soaring Mt Kagebo, Yunnan's highest peak at 6740m and unconquered by a succession of climbers, a quite astounding fact that makes it one of the world's remaining challenges for leading mountaineers. Kagebo is considered the first of eight sacred mountains in the Tibetan region of Yunnan and is one of the most important pilgrimage sites in Tibet. Natives believe that Kagebo represents the mind emanation of the Lord Buddha, whereas Mount Kailash in western Tibet represents the body and Ne Tsari in central Tibet signifies the speech. Every autumn, people flood from all over Tibet, Sichuan, Qinghai and Gansu to circumnavigate the mountain, absorb its spiritual atmosphere and pay homage to the mountain God for a week. It is a gruelling mission that requires enormous discipline but it is a pilgrimage every Tibetan endeavours to accomplish at least once in their lives, as it allows them to free the soul of sin and prepare oneself for the ascent into paradise.

Down in the valley floor, a man with impeccable flawless English points across the Mekong and informs me that the road is blocked from a hefty landslide and the only way to Mingyong is to walk the remaining 6 km. A little deflated but undeterred my taxi driver crosses the bridge and drops me to the other side at the heap of fallen rocks and boulders. The sun has ripped away the clouds, the early morning damp mountain chill traded for brilliant sunshine, as I rest on a sturdy boulder. A voice from below, adjacent to where I sit, issues instructions and more rocks are sent tumbling from above by two diminutive looking youngsters. After twenty minutes the falling debris comes to a halt, a signal is given for me to cross and I quickly scramble over, looking up nervously for any unexpected flying objects from above. I settle into a steady march on the snaking uphill trek to Mingyong, resting briefly on a small bridge where a rocky river runs beneath me, its cement coloured water rushing down to feed the great river. Herds of saddled ponies meander downhill, their owners dawdling behind, as I pass by traditional Tibetan houses and walnut trees, their round green shells ready for picking. Plum trees and rows of corn on neat terraced land, mingle with sunflowers and the surprising spectacle of orderly vines packed with dark purple grapes that trigger a yearning for a glass of fruity red wine.

By the time I reach Mingyong, I'm a hot, sweaty but contented Englishman. Greeted by the melodic, therapeutic sound of jangling bells, worn by the horses who return from ferrying domestic tourists to view the glacier, and the hypnotic flow of the teeming river that encapsulates the alpine scenery. I check into the first hotel, a modern, functional construction with flourishes of time honoured Tibetan architecture, run by a family that at first seem a trite lazy but whose idiosyncrasies grow on me daily and who show considered patience as I communicate the whole time through my new best friend – the hand held translation computer.

I spend my days here relaxing, enjoying a ride to the foot of Kagebo to view the glacier that spreads from it and eating food from the hotel kitchen. Since I left Dali and Lijiang, the variety of food has dwindled, the creative force of central and southern Yunnan partially flushed away, as the ingredients to hand are not so prolific and repetition is a common theme. Breakfast, lunch and dinner follows a similar routine throughout, where I appear requesting food, am ushered into the kitchen and pick from trays of ingredients that more often than not get stir-fried. One notable inclusion is the meat from the hybrid male yak and cow known as *dzo* or female yak and bull cross called *pien*. It may be repetitive but it is certainly not without merit. Actually the owner, a young, gentile man is quite an accomplished cook producing deep-fried dzo cooked with copious amounts of red chilli and sprinkled with sesame seeds; fried egg with strands of cucumber; dzo fried with pieces of cured ham, green chilli, green pepper and spring onions; fried eggplant with slices of garlic cut from a bulb the size of a button onion, spring onions, green chilli and green pepper; stir-fried wild mushrooms with cured ham, garlic and green chillies and my particular favourite a dish of fried pork with mustard leaves, shredded green chilli, coriander and mint leaves, a dish of some aplomb in its own right. For breakfast they make fresh flat wheat noodles that are the same width as linguine from Italy, blanch them in boiling water and add them to fried pieces of cured ham, before moistening with water and adding sliced tomato, spring onions and a little salt. A final flourish of dried red chilli is added at the table. Not an outstanding soup, considering the superlative broths that have gone before but soothingly pleasing in a kind of rural sustenance fashion.

While I was pony trekking to the foot of Kagebo, I had enquired of my local guide if he would accompany me to the Tibetan border that is reached by following the Mekong upriver. Two days later Hua, a very fit, dark skinned man in his late thirties arrives at my hotel, dressed in an excellent fur lined hooded green baseball jacket and dark blue waterproof trousers and, only with a few necessary provisions we head down the valley, across the bridge I rested at days before and begin trekking the dusty, rocky path high above the Mekong. At times the landscape capitulates into a dry, arid terra firma, occasional green shrubs cling to the lifeless slopes, as preying birds sweep high over the valley and the only noise comes from the jingle of the pony's bell, the distant reverberating hum of the river and my feet dragging on the floor. We pass a dead goat, its body slowly decaying in the heat, swarms of flies scavenge on its fetid flesh as up ahead a herd of more fortunate wild goats scurry across a rocky bridge and nimbly climb a ridiculously steep rugged face. Across the valley, convoys of trucks laden with goods destined for Tibet, line the treacherous, painstakingly slow mountain road. Just after 1pm, the sun beating down on our heads, the first village appears like a fertile terraced oasis, it seems hardly plausible but as we cross a bridge over a ravine of water, the careful innovative approach to growing vegetables and staples like corn and barley leaves quite an impression on me. Prior to entering the tiny settlement, stonewalled areas hug the side of precipitous slopes, inside chillies, gourds and corn grow healthily but it is the sight of black skinned avocados hanging from trees that most surprises me and leaves me scrambling for my computerised translator in order to confirm this with Hua. A group of elderly women sit, huddled under a tree idly chatting in the cool shade, one staggers to her feet to greet us, her wispy silvery hair protruding from a thick maroon headscarf. The welcoming demeanour that exudes from her, as she leads us to her family home is gut wrenchingly warming but the gnarling, gnashing of teeth from a leashed dog will become a familiar if unwelcome addition as I travel in Tibetan environs.

We are led into a lounge area, the walls fitted with bench like seats, covered with comfortable long brown and cream cushions. Her daughter appears carrying hunks of juicy watermelon on a plate, the watery sweetness parches my dry throat and soothes my stomach; plates of roasted sunflower seeds and weak tea follow as I gaze around the room. When lunch is ready we are ushered into another room, much larger with ornately carved fitted wooden shelves, a cooking area that extends one-third into the room and decorative carved beams that decorate the ceiling. A well-worn silver teapot is positioned with a mat on the low-slung table and small china bowls distributed in preparation for my official introduction to true Tibetan life. The light brown, creamy liquid is poured to the rim of my cup; a greasy film floats on the top and emits a saltiness that is moderately off-putting. Butter tea is the indispensable drink of choice for Tibetans and every family will keep a slim wooden cylinder, which is used for churning up tea. A wooden piston is used to push and pull inside the barrel where yak butter, salt and freshly brewed brick tea are mixed. After a minute or two it is poured into a kettle, so that it can be kept warm over a fire, and be ready for serving at any time. I might still officially be in the Yunnan but the spirit is indelibly Tibetan and when the hot liquid touches my mouth I feel a new threshold has been crossed. The fatty, salty brew is certainly not pleasant but the Tibetans take their tea very seriously and to decline would be tantamount to cultural suicide. Lunch is a basic stew of coagulated rubbery egg, mixed with tomatoes and capsicums, with only the addition of fruity hot mountain pepper bringing any sense of vigour. Sour, pure white yak cheese, crumbly like feta but with a drier texture, is mildly appetising but I would prefer it crumbled over the acidity of sliced tomatoes, not plunged into butter tea as is demonstrated by all those present around the table. It seems total madness to add more saltiness to the tea, maybe they will pluck it out when the dry texture is moistened somewhat but they don't and it bobs gaily in the warm buttery fluid and is left untouched in the bowl.

The next village is approximately 5 km further on, so we decline their kind offer to spend the night here and bid them farewell. As the next, more substantial village looms into view, a loud crashing explosion rings through the valley, the blast of dynamite spooks the pony who bolts down the hill, over a bridge and up the other side before warily coming to a standstill on the other side of the ravine. To my right, a waterfall cascades from the brown rocky cliff face dropping gracefully to the turbulent rushing waters of the Mekong, sending a fine spray into direct contact with the sun's rays, that produces a colourful, brilliant rainbow. It is just after 4pm when we enter the village; a group of kids play under a tree, as Hua questions an elderly lady about the possibility of spending the night. She leads us through a series of rough, bumpy alleys and deposits us outside a house. A slim, elderly man appears extending the invitation and the pony is led to a stabling area down to the side alley beneath the open first floor terrace. Even someone with my lack of centimetres is forced to crouch through the ox-blood swinging doors, happy to avoid once again the fierce attack by a tightly leashed dog.

The smooth concrete terrace affords commanding views over the river below, the barren hills and a glimpse of the Kawa Karpo range. A light breeze cools my sweating body, as I free my burning, aching feet from my restrictive walking boots that have caused me discomfort due to the swelling of my feet. The wall to the fore is lined with potted plants, flowers and herbs; golden marigolds and purple flowers do battle for colour supremacy. The elderly man's grandson, at first shy and nervous, is a hyperactive ball of energy, and scurries about on a restrictive wooden scooter. His wife, laden with a heavy basket of grass for the animals, returns an hour after our arrival and brings bowls of washed purple grapes, sun-dried yak cheese, round flatbreads and the ubiquitous butter tea. The tiny grapes are exceptionally sour, the skins tough and housing a high ratio of pips but the overall flavour is concentrated and a welcome initial diversion from the delights of the tea.

Traditional Tibetan houses have a real sense of order, style and sound methodical planning. The foundations and walls, now normally constructed with concrete, are complimented sympathetically by wooden doors, windows and intricately crafted exterior and interior features. Downstairs is given over to everyday living, kitchen to the side, living room to the back and underneath the house is the area for livestock, and here they keep black pigs, chickens and rabbits. A further kitchen is situated to the side, through another tiny entrance and upstairs are three well-proportioned bedrooms that lead onto a balcony with light blue railings.

To a backdrop of silhouetted hills and mountains and a chorus of floating Tibetan violins, dinner is served on the darkening terrace. Fried silken tofu with chilli and spring onions; stir-fried dzo with shredded green capsicum and dried red chilli taste adequate, except the strips of meat are as tough as the leathery skin of a Kalahari nomad from Southern Africa. A simple soup with green leaves is at best clean and refreshing and a pan of steaming rice fills my belly with sufficient carbohydrate but I am quickly realising why the Tibetans are not renowned for their widespread culinary arts. No matter, this must be one of the most pleasing locations I have been privileged to stay in, the clear sky now sparkles with a blanket of brilliant stars, as I tap probing questions into my hand held computer. The elder is concerned at the aggressive dynamiting of the area, fearing for the unique wildlife of the region, including one of the world's most elusive creatures, the revered snow leopard, as well as clouded leopards, Asiatic black bears and red pandas.

In the morning, after a breakfast of last night's rice, fried with egg and the remainders of yesterday's supper, we head down the bank to cross the river. The pony is nervous, refusing many times to be cajoled to cross the swaying chain bridge, so is left behind to be collected on our way back. The landscape continues unchanged, we stop for lunch halfway and have a very good plate of fried pork (its flavour exceptional) with wild mushrooms, green capsicum and mountain pepper. By the time we reach the dusty, unkempt border town, we have walked 25 km, my feet are blistered but I'm exhilarated to be standing on the cusp of Tibet. Also, Hua knows of a man that may be willing to drive me through to Zadoi, this I'm thrilled about and as I drift to sleep that night, my dream of following the Mekong's path through to Tibet is given a confident boost.

Tibet and Qinghai Province

Transit Through Tibet

Immediately after my return from my three-day trip upriver, discussions and negotiations begin for a successful passage through Tibet. I spend my time studying maps with the guesthouse owner, Hua, my intended driver and a host of knowledgeable locals. I work out my budgetary requirements, not just for the trip to Zadoi but beyond to the source and to deliver me to Xining, the capital of Qinghai Province. There would seem little or no opportunity to change money until I reach Xining and the bad news is that no bank in Deqin will change foreign currency, so I'm left with a financial dilemma. The only guaranteed place to exchange foreign currency is in Zhongdian, a journey of over six hours by car, so with little choice I hire a private taxi to drive me there and bring me back to Mingyong the following day. So far as inconvenient journeys go, this one ranks among the most spectacular, certainly of my entire trip, if not of anywhere I've ever been. High mountain passes that rise to over 4000m, winding through magnificent steep gorges, valleys, rice and wheat terraces, ravines and limestone rock faces and on the return leg, blue skies that clear all before me and offer truly awe-inspiring views of the colossal Kawa Karpo range in all its raw intensity and splendour. I return with pockets full of money, thrilling memories and a second hand Nokia mobile phone.

Dainzin arrives early on the morning of departure, his thick cropped hair perfectly flat across the top, a dark lean face, wispy extended goatie beard and wearing a long saffron robe with dark blue trousers. My gut instinct when I first met him was one of quiet, solid trustworthiness, understated humbleness and harbouring good knowledge of the route. One major downside to this new relationship would inevitably be communication. During my early negotiations, it soon became apparent that while he spoke both Chinese and Tibetan dialect, he could only read the latter, thus making personable sentences from my technological gadget completely null and void. The planned duration for the entire trip is estimated at seven days, the enforced silencer on my own voice may well be difficult for me to bare but the language barrier and its daily frustrations will pail into insignificance if we make it through to Zadoi without too many problems. I've made it very clear that I do not have any specific documentation, except for my passport containing my Chinese visa and although travel permits inside Tibet are in theory useless and a way of lining officials' pockets, they still prefer you to travel in organised tours, chaperoned by a recognised Chinese guide who carefully manipulates the route and limits any contact with real Tibetans to the bare minimum. I would rather not speak for seven days and experience Tibet as it touches me and in any case the route I travel in the east of the country may well harbour deep suspicions of my intentions. Since I arrived here, I've ceased to tell anyone of my motives, I'm no longer a travel-writing chef, just a plain old humble cook transiting the region. Any mention of writer, journalist, businessman, radio producer or TV assistant would definitely see me dismissed from the region or at the very least observed at very close quarters. In Burma, I once met a guy who was mystified how officials, hotel owners and tour operators had knowledge of his every move, his mistake upon entering the country was to scribble 'journalist' on his landing form. He had a very restricted visit thanks to the oppressive regime overseen by the military junta. My plan is a simple one; if I can get halfway through, I stand a sporting chance of being thrown out in the direction I'm heading. It is the only solace I cling to as I bid farewell to Mingyong and motor towards Tibet.

Tibet has a long, rich and proud history dating back two thousand years but its recent record is mired in Chinese attempts to suppress Tibetan culture and exercise its own oppressive control over a region it claims is inherently Chinese. The Tibet Autonomous Region is the only area officially recognised by the Chinese Communist Regime to fall within Tibet but the 'real' Tibet is a designated area of twice this and comprises the northern reaches of Yunnan, western Sichuan and the entire Qinghai Province. In 1903 the British invaded Tibet, in a dual attempt to open up trade links and to halt suspicions of Russian influence in the territory, it proved fruitless and within two months they had gone, failing to exercise any authority, thus concluding one of Tibet's most bizarre episodes. Eight years later, with the Chinese locked in the grips of civil war, the Tibetans formally proclaimed independence, expelling any Chinese from its soil. It tightly controlled its own affairs, patrolled its borders, raised its own flag, issued currency, passports and stamps and signed treaties with its neighbours. Independence was short-lived, the forces of Mao Zedong, victorious in the long running civil war, invaded Tibet from the east in 1950 in what was termed the 'return of Tibet to the embrace of the Motherland.'

The Chinese, in principle, agreed to allow the Dalai Lama to remain as head of government but would control all military matters and other key features. The Dalai Lama, a title bestowed by the Mongolian leader Altan Khan on Sonam Gyatso, the sixteenth century leader of the Geluk or Yellow Hat sect, had been at the forefront of Tibetan politics since 1642, and the fifth Dalai

Lama managed to reunify Tibet and extend its influence to the fringes of Tibetan territory. Monasteries were erected all over Tibet and during his reign Tibetan culture flourished. Unusually, the Dalai Lama ruled through a theocratic style of government, whereby the spiritual leader is also a king figure and combines religious and political responsibilities in his mandate. Tibet was ruled in this fashion for over three hundred years but following the invasion by the Chinese his political powers were quickly suppressed and in 1959, he fled on horseback to north-east India and Lhasa descended into chaos. The ensuing uprising left tens of thousands of Tibetans dead. The Dalai Lama has been in exile ever since, fighting the Tibetan cause on an international stage but little direct dialogue has taken place between his exiled government and the Chinese regime. The resistance of the Tibetan people remains steadfast but the Chinese rule with an iron grip, putting down sporadic protests mainly led by monks loyal to the Dalai Lama and the freedom of Tibetan culture. In 1996, the Chinese, afraid of the powerful influence of the Tibetan spiritual leader, banned anyone from owning or displaying any image of the Dalai Lama. Images may be banned in a formal sense but just prior to departing Mingyong, Dainzin had proudly flourished a card with his image, before gesturing me to secrecy and slipping it into a pocket within the sun visor of his jeep.

Dainzin's durable four-wheel drive Mitsubishi jeep bounds along the bumpy unpaved roads and within the hour we have shot through into Tibet. The dozing guards at the border I had visited on my recce ignore us and allow us through with no sign of confrontation. The road runs low through the valley, just beyond the border two monks prepare to attach themselves to a sling and hurtle themselves high above the wild Mekong by way of a pulley bridge. Before bridges, this was the only feasible option of crossing from one bank to another, the rampaging channel beneath too brutal to entertain boat crossings. It is a petrifying spectacle, requiring a massive act of faith and huge courage; the drop below would most certainly lead to a gruesome death. The heavily constructed road brings us to the town of Yanjing, perched high above the river and featuring the prominence of a catholic church blending with tiny monasteries. After a ghastly, greasy bowl of broth with wheat noodles and goat, we head away and the road begins to rapidly deteriorate, the smooth tarmac of a brand new bridge offers brief respite and the glimpse of new improved infrastructure. Our progress may have become muted, the speed dial only touching 30 km per hour but I'm lost in a sea of beguiled fantasy at my surroundings that within minutes is ripped from me and transplanted with problematic reality up ahead.

The driver of the bus leans from his window, conversing in Tibetan with Dainzin, who turns to me, his shoulders slumped in a tangible sign of resignation and with his hands, performs an act of tumbling rocks. He motions for us to go back, I insist we go forward. I mean how bad can it be, the answer as we were about to find out was extremely bad. Stationary trucks, lorries, motorbikes and cars lay dormant to the side of the high mountain road, as we both jump from the jeep and walk towards the sharp right hand bend fifty metres away. The scene as we round the corner is a landslide of epic proportions, a mountain of huge boulders, rocks and rubble with a gigantic slab of cliff suspended in the middle reaches to the sky in numb crunching fashion. At its peak, it is the height of a juggernaut lorry. Men in yellow bash hats perch on rocks conveying possible solutions and bewildered truck drivers march back to their cabins scratching their heads. The time is now 1.30pm; any hopes of reaching Markham tonight decrease with every passing hour. Organised tour groups travelling to Lhasa and beyond to Everest Base Camp wait patiently, and pepper their guides with hopeful questions of a possible departure time. As the hours frustratingly drift by, an exasperated Dutch lady insists their particular group turns around and spends the night in Yanjing, a suggestion that is met with mixed views and one of consternation by their guide. He diplomatically insists that to turn around would be foolish, as any progress already made may be stumped by new landslides further down the valley.

Successive attempts at dynamiting the obstructive area fails to prove worthwhile, as everyone ran for cover to prevent being hit by flying debris. A few men even try chipping away at the mighty rock with pneumatic drills, a plucky but pointless exercise that at the very least makes me chuckle. I while away the hours by reading, eating and talking with a fluent English speaking Tibetan guy who assisted Michael Palin when he visited Everest Base Camp for a TV series and worked for six months in a Tibetan restaurant in the quintessential English city of Oxford. The sun is beginning to dip behind the snowy peaks of the opposite valley, when the light rumble of a mechanical digger can be heard edging its way up the valley. It takes about an hour of persistent work to dislodge the hefty slab but just after 8.30pm it smashes down the slope and work begins to clear a suitable path to skirt round the remaining mound of rocks. The all clear is given just after 10.30pm, engines begin to purr into life and a succession of vehicles file carefully around the cleared route and drive in convoy through tight passes, ditches, streams and muddy roads all the way to Markham. My mobile phone registers 2.30am as we roll down the main drag, red lights of illicit buildings and a surprising number of restaurants are still open. Persistent banging on the door of a guesthouse raises a sleeping night porter and we secure a room and join the drivers of the Dutch party for dinner. Glasses of potent local whiskey are knocked back with pangs of relief and hungry stomachs are filled with fried cured ham with green pepper and spring onions, stir-fried cabbage with blackened red chillies and fried egg, tomato and spring onions. I'm that tired I barely recall eating it.

The morning brings glorious clear blue skies. Ambling herds of yak mingle with the light hum of traffic along the main thoroughfare. Smooth tarmac roads lead us away from the town, through low lying hills, pastured valleys and stone walled fields of grazing yak and sheep, bundles of wheat drying on the roofs of houses and a blanket of yellow blossom and wild herbs. All day we rise up and down through pine forests, descending into rich meadows and wide expansive valleys where black yak woven tents provide my first glimpse of nomadic life. We stop for lunch by a sparkling alpine stream, at a tiny restaurant busy catering to raucous Chinese businessmen drinking whiskey and gambling heavily in a heated match of *ma jiao*. To my surprise the food is excellent; delicious fish, fried and steamed with ginger, garlic and spring onion is the first I've eaten since Lijiang and I devour like it may be the last. It is rare for Tibetans to eat fish, reminding me of Mongolians who despite having vast rivers, lakes and streams largely ignore this form of protein. Well flavoured pork fried with an abundance of shredded green chilli; tiny leaves that taste like spinach but have a slimy quality to their texture, fried with garlic and ginger; a clean, refreshing broth with stimulating hits of ginger and juicy slices of courgette, all washed down with plenty of smoky aromatic hot tea. We spend the night in the town of Zong Gou, sleeping in a basic guesthouse where to reach the toilet I had to balance across a plank, over a flea ridden pit and relieve myself staring down into a squalid quagmire of nauseating muck, while carefully balancing to prevent an unthinkable accident. I'm strongly advised not to wander about in the town, especially at night, as the authorities here can be volatile towards foreigners. Given my predicament, frustratingly, it is information I accept, so after a hearty bowl of soup and more tea I retire early to my room. I enjoy the broth, the pork flavoured stock lightly thickened by starch released from chunks of potato with juicy kernels of corn and salty notes from local ham are indicative of the chowders of San Francisco.

The drive through to Chamdo the following day leads us through the dusty juncture of Bangda. The long easterly road points to Lhasa but ours continues directly to the north. Bangda, at an elevation of 4334m, is home to the highest commercial airport in the world and may also unofficially be home to the tallest outdoor pool hall. We rise to 4572m, the thinning air causing me to breathe shorter and sharper, eagles swoop high over the breathtaking pass and there before me are a series of pool tables lined up and fully occupied.

Chamdo, once an important trading post and crossroads of two principal caravan routes in eastern Tibet is now a bustling Chinese dominated city. The concentration of Han Chinese is astounding; Sichuan restaurants line the streets, gleaming brand new apartment blocks and shops piled with technological commerce. Many, and I include myself, find the domination of the Chinese in Tibet deeply worrying but from a pure food perspective one can't argue that their influence brings wider variety to the region. The Mekong, out of view for much of the journey, glides serenely through mating with the Ngomchu, a small tributary. Prior to entering the city, we had a nervy moment at a checkpoint and Dainzin was quizzed extensively, while I was asked to produce my passport. While they talked, I avoided eye contact, staring to my right seeking solidarity from the river I had followed all the way from the Vietnamese Delta. When we are eventually waved through, we look at each other with sighs of relief and more importantly have breached the halfway point to Zadoi.

From Chamdo we drive westerly, away from the Mekong and then northerly through to Chongku. After our brush with the authorities yesterday, the checkpoint here, the last before leaving TAR, is a lot less forgiving. My passport is taken from me and studied by three officials, who unhappy that I have no official documentation send me back into town to the main customs office. Although it would now be churlish to send me back from whence I came, I'm still anxious as a lady ushers us into an office. Dainzin, nervous himself, sits quietly in a chair as the young woman flicks through my passport. There is little I can do but feign innocence, act unconcerned and hope her day has been a good one. The official is warm, clearly blessed with human kindness, issues me with no more than a proverbial slap of the wrist and hands my passport back. Back at the checkpoint, the barrier is raised, clear of bureaucratic meddling and forward into Qinghai. We have made it.

Dainzin and I both visibly relax once fully in Qinghai and over the next few days we spend time with his city dwelling family and, intriguingly for me, go back to his nomadic roots. We spend the night in Nangqen, a dust ridden low rise town, where his brother lives, tucked in from the main drag, in slum like retreats, grubby wasteland with pockets of lifeless concrete. The prelude to his nomadic heritage, for me is best observed by their eating habits. His brother rips raw yak flesh from a carcass, mixes *tsampa* with his right hand and gulps yoghurt from a china bowl, clearly old habits from their former existence are difficult to shift.

Nomadic populations throughout the world are under intense pressure; in Asia the last remaining pastoral nomads include the Mongols (primarily in outer Mongolia) and the Turkic tribes of north-west China, such as the Kazaks. Mine would not strictly be a baptism of fire, for I had spent time in 2002 riding horses in Mongolia, thus engaging with nomadic folk but time marches on quickly and here China's deep suspicion of those on the move has manifested a less than sympathetic approach to the situation. The nomadic people of this region are hardy, surviving winters in their thick yak woven tents in temperatures that in winter can plummet as far as -40°C. Their whole life revolves around livestock and in particular the Rolls Royce of the plateau – the ever dependable yak. From its wool they make clothes, boots, blankets and ropes; milk is siphoned to make yoghurt, cream, butter and cheese as the Tibetan nomads rely heavily on dairy products in their diet. Vegetables are seldom grown, the high altitude and harsh weather conditions make this unfeasible, and therefore meat is a total necessity in daily life. Their fires are fuelled by dried yak dung, the lack of trees on the plateau make this the main source of fuel.

Galup hugs a picturesque bend of the Mekong, the tiny hamlet dominated by monasteries, is far from the main road and we reach it along bumpy tracks. Scurrying marmots disappear to the refuge of their burrows, as a monk trundles along on a motorbike and opposite erected festival tents prepare for a religious gathering. Old friends greet Dainzin with immense warmth, often affirmed by a gentle knocking together of foreheads. The Chinese influence may be spreading but here it is untainted by outsiders, miles from prying eyes, with the luxury of free expression, with little fear of reprisal. His two brothers have driven from their nomadic dwellings and meet us in the friendly restaurant we sit in. I'm stared at, not with suspicion but with genuine curiosity, they as interested in me as I am in them. I enjoy a substantial bowl of deep flavoured yak stock, that is packed with mini squares of wheat pasta floating in the rich liquor with dried yak meat, leek, celery, cabbage and garlic and smile outwardly to the lady who cooked it. Back in Chongku, I had enjoyed a comparable dish, this time flavoured with sheep meat and cooked by wonderfully adept Muslim cooks, who rolled dough through a hand powered machine and left me pondering the origins of an Italian staple. If only I could speak directly with them, it is the only extended period I have spent without a translator and I'm afraid my hand held technological version is utterly worthless.

Motorbikes, trucks and jeeps have revolutionised the lives of nomadic people, where once horses and yaks would be their sole means of transport, the last ten years has seen one of their most dramatic lifestyle changes. The increased speed of transport has not affected their daily routine of subsistence, herding yak, sheep and goats is still fundamental to their daily existence, but does enable them to travel greater distances in much less time, increasing their social mobility and interacting more regularly with other clans. To reach their camp the jeep would have to be sacrificed, so we hop onto the back of his brothers' motorbikes, cross the bridge and motor into the interior. As we bump along the hilly terrain, I turn and marvel at the Mekong as it glides blissfully through, unperturbed by human encroachment, its raw state is masterful and dignified. After an hour we breach the top of a hill and descend to a valley sprinkled with black tents, plumes of smoke drift up from chimneys and swooping birds of prey target darting marmots in the undergrowth.

Take the motorbikes, sunglasses and North Face fleece jackets out of the equation and you could be stepping back five hundred years, transported to a world that knew only the pastures and mountain passes they roamed. Ferocious black dogs, snapping at their extended leashes, flash their bloodthirsty teeth, barking relentlessly and make me shudder at the consequences of them breaking free towards me. Inside the tent, a lady, her bushy black hair tied in a bun, shapes pliable dough with a rolling pin and bakes the unleavened flatbreads in a heavily blackened pan, fired by dried yak dung. The heap of fuel is stacked in the corner behind her, not such a romantic picture of neatly arranged logs but every bit as fruitful. Their very existence is built on necessary practicalities, variety as we know isn't important and their philosophy on culinary matters is such that food is for fuel not for any desiring pleasure; it is this most requisite style that underpins everyday life on the plateau.

A single white tent has been pitched for Dainzin and I to sleep in for the few days of our stay. Pitched bare to the ground, it is supported by a crooked wooden pole up through its centre and secured through the ground with hefty pegs. A basic thin floral mattress offers scant protection from the damp of an evening, covered with quilts and blankets to ward off the dipping temperatures of mountain nights. This camp is at an altitude of 4000m, during the summer the days are warm and pleasant, today the sun beats down and I relax in its warmth. Come the winter, the realities are severe; my idyllic snug surroundings turn to harsh winter snow, with temperatures plummeting to −20°C and beyond. It is difficult to comprehend how they survive in such conditions, their protection seems minimal to the elements, roaring winds that whip through the valleys, bone chilling nights and the drudgery of everyday tasks that become fundamental to their survival.

During the day us men sit around, drinking tea, eating unleavened bread, gulping down yoghurt and mixing tsampa with butter and hot water. The women not out herding busy themselves weaving yak wool, making yoghurt, churning butter and laying cheese to dry in the sun. The women are the backbone of everyday life on the plateau, they make the clothes, milk the yaks, churn the cream, care for the children, organise breakfast, lunch and dinner and repair necessary everyday items. Inside their tents they store yoghurt in wooden barrels, fine barley or wheat flour, sacks of brittle dried cheese, dried yak and sheep meat, creamy yellow butter and a stack of dried yak dung for fuelling the fire. From the long, mud brick cooking range inside, they boil, bake, fry and simmer all they need to survive. Indeed the only food items they purchase are wheat or barley powder, it is not possible to successfully grow this at such altitude, and sometimes onions, garlic and vegetables but very rarely will this occur. Their style of preparing food is primitive but let it never be said that the natural state of the food they produce is not exceptional. The tsampa, I find difficult to stomach, the fine barley flour served in a bowl with hot water (sometimes weak tea) and a good knob of butter is painfully dire and if offered I steer towards the yoghurt. Tsampa is traditionally made by roasting barley and grinding it to a fine powder and although tasteless, is a highly sustaining form of sustenance for the Tibetan, who actively enjoy it on an everyday basis and look stunned when visitors don't feel the same way. Their dairy products are quite simply exceptional, back in the UK we are bombarded with the benefits of organic food, and here the rich untainted grazing land produces milk of the purest quality. The yoghurt made from it, is thick, creamy and blows away any I have ever tasted, sprinkled with a little sugar to counterbalance the sour notes, it is a culinary treat of considerable status.

As the evening draws in, the animals are bought down from the higher slopes; the family's young daughter and her brother cajole herds of yak, flocks of sheep and goats down through the valley. Stray yaks from other families' stock are chased away by young kids who throw rocks toward them. The children mock the goats, picking up the younger ones and shunting them into position to be tethered for the night. It is nightfall before the livestock is arranged as they would like but still the woman must serve the dinner. A tasteless rice porridge, given no seasoning but a little salt, has been bubbling away for the last three hours, slopped into bowls and scoffed in minutes by the hungry family. A steaming pan of boiled lamb is hacked at with knifes, the blubbering fat is pushed toward me in a sign of befuddling respect. To a Tibetan, the fat is the most prized of the animal, in the winter it is this that provides warmth in the long hard winter but it is completely lost on me, as I eye the hunks of meat before me. The meat, when it is offered, is a little tough due to unsympathetic boiling but its flavour is rich and sweet, the prolific grazing pasture producing meat of exceptional quality. The dogs have gone quiet now, the still night air twinkles with stars, as the livestock scratch about and I head to my sleeping quarters. Dainzin joins me minutes later, the whiff of his unwashed body melds with rich dung from the animals, as a chill breeze wafts through the tent and I drift to sleep, thoughts of reaching the river's source etched in my brain.

The Source

Seven days after we left Mingyong in the upper reaches of Yunnan, we roll into the dust driven Tibetan backwater of Zadoi, where Dainzin and I part company. I'm sad to see him go. During the short time I spent with him and even though we never uttered a communicable word together, he has been all I first thought of him plus more. Zadoi is the gateway to the remote source of the Mekong, the town itself has a wild west feel to it and its guesthouse accommodation is basic and lacking any worthwhile facilities. The room I take is functional, the electricity is intermittent and every time I come and go the porter has to open and lock the door for me. The toilets are pit-dug affairs at the end of the corridor, there are no washing facilities, so, to shower here you have to use communal facilities a five-minute walk away and powered by a spluttering old generator. Having not had a thorough body wash since Mingyong, the feel of tumbling hot water on my skin is heavenly, foamy soap cleans the grimy crust from my body and cheap shampoo extracts the dirt from my balding head.

The source of the Mekong was and maybe still is, a topic of much-disputed intrigue and debate among scholars and explorers who claim to have discovered it. In 1884 two Frenchmen claimed to be the first Europeans to have discovered the geographic source above a pass at Lungmug spring. One hundred years later another Frenchmen, Michel Peissel, asserted the springs below Rup-sa pass were the source, a fact endorsed at the time by the Royal Geographical Society who reported it in The Geographical Journal of July 1995. This was discredited by the China Academy of Sciences who did not accept Piessel's claim. At the same time a Japanese-Chinese team of the Exploration Club of Tokyo University of Agriculture and the aforementioned Chinese Academy recorded the source as emerging from a glacier at the Guosongmucha Mountain at 5160m. In 1999 a team from the Chinese Academy of Sciences identified the source on the same mountain but declared the geographical point to be 360m upstream and 57m higher than the source identified by Kitamura, the leader of the Japanese team. In September 2003, the explorer John Pilkington became the first British man to journey to the source and with vital knowledge gleaned from him prior to leaving England I would hopefully become the second. Through my email correspondence with John, he had confirmed that I should venture to the most recent source, this being the one he himself had reached. He provided me with vital information, including a map, the name and contact details of a local man he had used, the costs incurred and during my trip offered great support and inspiration. He warned me of fierce dogs, deep river crossings, poor food and potential blizzards but most of all he wished me good luck.

Soon after my arrival I had made contact with 'Duojie' who immediately arranged to visit me at my hotel to discuss plans for my trip. I had been corresponding with him via a friend ever since I entered Yunnan and now here he was in the flesh. He is an impressive, well built man, harbouring a sense of urgency and greets me with a firm handshake. His shoes are highly polished, the dark blue suit he wears over a dark grey sweater lends him an air of dignified nobility. His English, while not polished is of a good enough standard, but he brings along a friend who is exceptionally fluent. My relief at conversing through spoken language is torched by the rapidity of the words that leap from my mouth. John had given me a complete breakdown of his daily costs and based on these I had budgeted accordingly, allowing room enough for manoeuvre and sufficient funds to travel to Xining upon my return from the source. I was prepared to pay more but early negotiations stall when Duojie rockets the price by nearly fifty per cent causing me to dig deep and patiently bring him down to a more palatable level. One of the stumbling blocks is his insistence that his friend be allowed to come, ensuring a proper level of communication but as I tell him later over dinner, his English is good enough, plus he reads Chinese, so I can always fall back on dialogue from my hand held translator. In two days time we would depart, the realisation that I may reach the very beginning of the mighty river is for the first time tangible.

A blanket of grey, misty drizzle greets our morning of departure, the quiet streets of Zadoi play host to dogs harassing nervous stray yaks and the odd hum of a motorbike break the inactive silence. Yesterday Duojie and I spent buying provisions, even though we intended to stay at various nomadic camps along the way, the remoteness to which we were going and the rugged terrain means a fully stocked quota of food, drink, fuel, tents, bedding and clothing are mandatory requirements. Much to Doujie's amusement, I also procured a heavy, solid baseball like wooden instrument, to which I fastened a vicious weighty chain and would be used to defend myself against possible attacks by snarling dogs. It raised several wry smiles as I marched through the streets like some mad gung-ho mercenary intent on battering all before him. Food, the binding theme of my trip, descends into a frenzy of convenience foods, for so much of this trip food has driven me forward and left me, on numerous occasions, spellbound by its breadth of creative, raw energy. Now, bags of freeze dried noodles, soups, biscuits, crisps, peanuts, fizzy drinks, chocolate bars, tea, sachets of 3-in-1 coffee and dried fruits suggest the final hurrah will not be marked with any huge significance but wholesale practicality and survival. Out come my bulky North Face Gore-Tex jacket, waterproof bottoms, fleece jacket and Mongolian woven woolly hat in preparation for the open elements of the plateau. At least half the planned trip will be spent on horseback, something I have been eagerly anticipating since I left England back in April and in years gone by would most likely have formed the entire transport from Zadoi to the area of the source.

Duojie drops by my guesthouse, as planned, just before 7.30am and we drive to his brother's house 400m away to complete loading the Toyota pick up he has borrowed from a friend. Waiting at the house is a friend of his visiting from Shanghai, dressed in jeans, a green sweatshirt and sun visor hat, Li is a surprise and not altogether welcome addition to our expedition to the source. I question Duojie about her inclusion, suitability and ability to cope in uncertain conditions, especially given that she only seems equipped for the pampered perils of a reality TV show. He insists she will be fine, so I determine not to push him any further on the subject but tell him she is his total responsibility and she is in no way to jeopardise our quest to reach the source. Duojie tells me not to worry, that she will be fine and he will take personal care of her. I'm not wholly convinced by his assurance but as the plastic sheeting is secured over the rear of the truck, I keep any further despondency to myself. One other, very important member is picked up on the outskirts of town, our guide and nomadic beacon, a man called Busrr and to whom John referred to in his correspondence with me.

A little out of the town, the tarmac surface runs out, replaced by a bumpy track that ascends up through the valley, occasionally becoming rocky and even slippery due to mud slicks that dip deep into the red earth. To begin with we traverse small streams that cause little problem and our progress is markedly quicker than I had anticipated, the track seemingly in better state than when John had followed the same route. We pause for lunch at his uncles camp nestled in the valley; the sun has burst through now and inside the black tent, the combined heat of the omnipresent fire and warmth of the day combine to make me sweat a little. One of the ladies makes yak cheese and offers us warm flatbread, tsampa, buttery tea and bowls of yoghurt, the latter is my favourite and neatly avoids confronting another bowl of toasted barley flour.

After lunch, the terrain continues unchanged, Li sits contented in the back and due to her decent command of English, I gradually warm to her and in the course of the next few hours my annoyance of her presence subsides to a tone of simple toleration. I force myself to remember that, to her, this is a massive opportunity to discover how nomadic people live on the complete opposite side of this colossal country and in a totally alien manner to which she is accustomed, as she is from the slick modern, skyscraper city of Shanghai in the powerhouse of the east. At times the panorama is simply breathtaking, a full circle of rolling snow peaked mountains, long sweeping valleys, deep basins and teeming streams and rivers, that cause me to gaze at its beautiful, isolated state. A wider river, its depth uncertain in places, provides our first significant obstacle and Duojie cuts the engine to investigate options with Busrr. They look and ponder, launching stones in an attempt to seek shallow areas to cross the pristine rocky waters and after much deliberation they hop back in and drive headlong into the rushing river. We drive aggressively through the water, dropping occasionally as Duojie grits his teeth and fights for supremacy with the wheel, urging it through, concentration etched on his face and to the delight of us all we successfully reach the other side. The next river is even wider, the challenge more substantial and as stones are thrown, it becomes clear that it has much deeper spots than the previous one.

With a few moments of anxiety, we eventually struggle through but at times the gushing water pours through the doors of our truck, as we sink deeper into the middle and get a little lucky when the failing grip of the wheels reasserts itself and brings us into shallower water. We drive along the waters edge, brushing through boggy areas, a seemingly major obstruction crossed from out list, when Duojie, for no apparent reason attempts to drive into the river and endeavours to cross back to the other side. This time no amount of willing persistence, gritty determination or pure luck comes to our aid and as the wheels spin furiously for any grip, the truck steadily sinks down into the sandy floor and water gushes in, forcing us to leap into the icy glacier fed river and clamber to a protruding grassy island. An annoyed Duojie, clearly mad with himself for such an error, offers me an apology, before carrying Li to the security of the grass and returning to contemplate a solution. From where we stand, a solitary abandoned red mud built dwelling can be clearly seen, it is only 400m from where our helpless vehicle lies motionless in the water. The time is 4pm, the sun still shines but ominous clouds are looming in the distance.

Before we attempt to free the Toyota, the men remove our shoes and socks and roll up our trousers and step back into the water and carry the food, bedding and other necessities to a drier spot and cover it with the tarpaulin sheet. The bone chilling water numbs my feet immediately and at times reaches above my knee, the soiled floor beneath sifts through my toes and confirms the main reason for our present predicament, as the teeming water rushes through the high plateau. First we try with ropes, pulling from the front while Doujie powers the engine in forward gear and then attempting in reverse as Busrr and I strain every sinewy muscle in our bodies. With every attempt, the truck sinks further into the mud and now slopes heavily down to its right, the water now filling up the open back of the vehicle. With the shovels that we brought along, we dig underneath the front and rear wheels, then using long poles that Doujie found up at the house, we try to lever under the carriage using brute force to at least dislodge it. With admirable persistence, Doujie and Busrr continue working out ways to release the wheels from the river floor but each time the outcome is a demoralising defeat and our options are swiftly running out. A light rain has now engulfed the surrounding area, dark gloomy clouds loom above us, as a pair of geese flies gracefully overhead. We continue until the light begins to fade, the glorious sunny isolation of earlier, replaced by winds that whip up from nowhere, roaring across the unprotected space, which bring rapidly decreasing temperatures and alter my whole perception from comfortable to lonely obscurity in a microsecond of nature's control on this remote, inhospitable landscape.

Quite implausibly Doujie and Busrr seem reluctant to give up but I've had enough for one day, the odds of us shifting it now are slimmer than when we started and the dogged and defeated pair finally call it a day as the clock ticks past 9pm and we trudge up the hill to the protected walls of the house. My feet are so numb that the stiff needle like grass causes me little irritation, my toes are purple from the icy waters and my body shivers from the harsh chill wind. In between attempts to move our stricken truck, we had carried all our gear up to the house and instructed Li to prepare a fire from the pile of yak dung we discovered and to lay out the bedding for us to sleep on. Much to my surprise she has gone about her task industriously and the smouldering glow from the fire throws out sufficient heat to counterbalance the huge drafts that rip through the old, delapidated windows as we strip down and change into drier clothing.

Inside, the house is littered with old beds, sofas, horse saddles, tables, broken chairs and crushed tins, remnants from previous inhabitants. I settle into a battered armchair, add boiling water to a box of flavoured noodles and mull over the events of the day. I feel like I am millions of miles from anywhere and I might as well be, I have no mobile phone reception, no transport, no clue how we will shift it and no idea if I will be able to push through to the source. The one glimmer of hope that I cling to is that Busrr is inherently nomadic and Doujie, although more a town dweller, seems like a guy who doesn't accept failure too easily. For me it is difficult to comprehend but to the nomads that inhabit the plateau every blade of grass offers a map to which they refer to and the rivers and peaks guide them to a destination. Tomorrow they will go for help; tonight I lay awake for hours wondering who they will find and how long it will be before they come back.

At daybreak, Doujie and Busrr march away from the house, up a hill and disappear down the other side, as I stand in the damp chill of the morning and ponder how long it will be before they return. The wind has settled to a stiff breeze, the surrounding landscape cloaked in a blanket of mist hanging over the plateau, as I look down towards the river and make out the lop-sided white Toyota. My muscles ache from the physical exertion of yesterday's efforts, as I grab out my wind up radio and optimistically try and tune into the BBC World Service. Amazingly, even in such a remote location, the familiar signature tune floats through the airwaves with crystal clear reception and I listen intently to the latest world news. Heavy losses on world stock markets, as US cuts interest rates by half a point, in an attempt to stave off an impending crisis in the housing market; in the aftermath of the Peruvian earthquake, the president appeals for calm; US threatens Eritrea, accusing it of supplying weapons to Islamic extremists in Somalia. All over the world now, people from every corner of the globe are listening to this broadcast. To me, out here its significance is hard to quantify, for in these nomadic lands it carries little meaning. I pull back the ring on a tin of fried dace with black beans and fork the salty, savoury fish into my mouth and wash it down with a glug of hot Lipton tea.

The hours in limbo drift by. Li walks away from the house to the brow of the hill, I can just make her out as she stands, peering out across the vast landscape, hoping to spot signs of human life and with it help to release us from the grip of uncertainty. Just before 12 noon, I spot a vehicle breaching the brow of a hill, bumping its way towards the river and following it along its edge and I race down in expectation of greeting the returning duo. To my utter dismay, it is not them but a lone man in a Cherokee jeep who looks flabbergasted and bewildered at seeing me rushing towards him. I gesture a finger at the stranded jeep, he looks and shakes his head. I'm not actually sure if this means he doesn't care or more likely I don't understand his outward expression. I run back up to get Li, who scampers down the hill and enters into Chinese dialogue, which fortunately he understands clearly. Ten minutes later, another truck appears from the same direction, seven hours after they left this morning, Doujie and Busrr arrive riding pillion in a battered Soviet style jeep, like valiant knights returning from a successful reconnaissance mission. Within minutes our truck is wrenched out from the river, the quest to the source is back on and a broad grin is etched all over my face.

Just when I thought that we could load up and be on our way again, the driver of the Cherokee that preceded their arrival, sends a shrilling call from downriver and we immediately decamp to investigate. Bang, smack in the middle of the river, the half submerged jeep makes for a depressing spectacle, its driver wades across to the shoreline and his bewildered expression tells the full story. Crossing these rivers, as I have found out, is often a game of chance, even the most experienced heads can get stuck here and on this occasion, being dragged out may take some time. The jeep that pulled us clear, is employed to drag it from the river but successive attempts end up in failure and to heap misery upon misery, the poor Soviet style jeep also gets trapped and then to add insult to injury, we try and shift it and get stuck also. I don't know whether to laugh or cry, the comical but serious turn of events has once again left us held hostage by the river I have been following for the last four and a half months. Fortunately, we manage to struggle clear, eventually pulling the jeep free but leaving the Cherokee stranded and the decision is taken to leave it where it is for a more heavy-duty truck to drag it out the next day. We drive on for just over an hour, arriving a little after 5pm to a nomadic settlement, a classic sweeping basin of grazing yak, sheep, goats and horses make for a timeless portrait.

A heavy-duty truck departs at dawn to rescue the stranded Cherokee from its unfortunate position, for us the slower but more reliable horse now substitutes transportation by motorcar. It is a crisp, bright morning, the woes of the previous two days now behind us, and the sight of horses being rounded up brings renewed vigour. A bulking mastiff dog, a showboating red collar around its neck, lay menacingly on the ground. All the men admire it, the nomadic Tibetans are passionate about everything to do with dogs and this they all agree is a top class specimen. After a warming broth of dried yak and fresh noodles, we climb aboard the horses and walk away to a chorus of barking dogs. A young foal, unwilling to be separated from its mother runs freely beside us, as we head down and through the valley.

My horsemanship can best be described as 'cavalier'. I'm not a particularly gifted technical rider but having learnt to ride five years ago in northern Mongolia, at least I am familiar with the style of trekking. Tibetan horsemen, like their central Asian cousins are brilliant riders, their natural empathy born from centuries of association is impressively apparent by the poise with which they ride. Their horses are small, no bigger than a pony, but they are strong, surefooted and blessed with resolute stamina, that until recently provided the only way for the nomads to travel long distances. In Mongolia, I heard stories of horsemen riding 150 km a day, roaring across the open steppes, bedding down with fellow nomadic families and carrying on in the same vein the next day. Even though the car, motorbike and truck have bought greater range to the people who live in these remote areas, their natural bonding with horses remain undiminished and their talents aboard them are truly, still one of the most enduring sights for any visitor.

After two and half hours of glorious trekking through the valley, we come to another camp, where we stop for lunch and wait for another set of horses to carry us to the next settlement, to continue our quest for the source. It is some two hours before the horses arrive, so we relax and enjoy the hospitality of our hosts. The generosity of these overtly warm friendly people seems limitless, always amiable and welcoming, their openness to strangers is beautifully pleasing and nothing is too much trouble. The horse that delivered me here was a willing partner; the one I ride away on is anything but. When I first clapped eyes on the chestnut animal, it appeared to be moody and lazy. It throws its head up high, doesn't look where it is going and shortly after entering into a strong gallop its left hoof stumbles down a hole and flings me out the side door, dragging me momentarily across the bumpy ground. In truth it was all over in a few seconds but travelling at speed, I am lucky not to have severely injured myself and fortunately all that is hurt is my pride. A little shaken but unperturbed I remount, give the lazy horse a couple of sharp reminders and walk on. After that it gives me little cause for concern. Doujie's, a black brute of a horse, is a handful, pulling double and wanting to gallop at all times, proving difficult to restrain and Doujie constantly fights to keep him on a tight reign. At times we speed across the open grasslands in exhilarating fashion, maintaining a strong gallop until my legs begin burning and I settle into a gentle walk. We cross a wide river, the horses making light work of the underfoot conditions and ultimately more reliable than a jeep, plus horses are strong swimmers if the need arises.

The glorious sunshine of the early morning has gradually faded through the day and as we reach the next camp, a heavy cloud cover has stifled its rays and a light rain begins to fall. We unload the packhorse, remove saddles, secure the horses and scamper into the tent before a torrent of rain is unleashed that pounds the yak woven material. It persists for about an hour, then subsides, clearing away the gloomy outlook, to leave the basin covered in sparkling sunshine. I go with Doujie to visit a family; there are four that occupy this picturesque location, bordered as it is by snowy peaked mountain-tops and rivers. The family, reached by crossing a stream, are as welcoming as one has come accustomed on the plateau but they harbour a deep sense of loss. The children lost their mother and father two years ago, so have been forced to survive without any direct elders to guide them in life. They have no livestock, a vital prerequisite for survival in nomadic life and one of the brothers, only fourteen years old, has a disfiguring disability and needs urgent treatment from a doctor. With no livestock, comes no money and with no money comes deprivation on a colossal scale and in this unforgiving terrain, their sense of isolation humbles me to my very core. Doujie impresses me with his kindness, the depth of his humane approach to life holds no bounds and he promises to help them seek a solution.

That night the rains come again, this time even heavier and more persistent. It is a discouraging sign now as I have come this far and I can only hope for improvement during the night and into the next morning. For supper, a lady rolls unleavened breads but instead of baking them, plunges them into sizzling hot fat, producing crispy aerated chapatti like breads, that we eat with chewy lamb, that I rip from the bone and work through my teeth. A little after 10.30pm I slip under a quilted blanket, dampened by drips of water penetrating through holes in the tent, that drop annoyingly onto my exposed forehead, causing me to duck completely under the cover. I lay awake for what seems like hours, begging the rain to stop but it doesn't and I eventually drift to sleep with the sound of pummelling rain ringing in my ears.

Mercifully the torrents from the sky relented during the night and come daybreak, the sun is shining and as I step from the sodden tent, my dampened clothed body is warmed by the glow of its rays and my spirit lifted into youthful gusto. In one hour we will leave for the source, my beaming face energised by the prospect, is joined by my intense desire to witness the very beginning of this great river. After two bowls of delicious yoghurt, the horses are prepared and we depart just shy of 7.30am. Li now riding, immediately lags behind and has to be chaperoned by Busrr who cajoles her less than willing horse. Clear of the settlement we rise gradually, Doujie excitingly points across the river at a black bear loping in the shallows and I reciprocate by giving him the thumbs up but I'm quite glad it is some distance away, as a confrontation with this predator would be distressingly worrying. I now know what the true purpose of the dogs is; to defend the nomad's livestock against threats from bears and the many wolves that patrol the plateau. The terrain does not allow for much cantering or galloping, indeed we frequently find ourselves dismounting to lead the horses up boggy inclines that are too precarious to carry both our weights up. Even on flatter areas, the ground underfoot is a waterlogged marsh, so our progress is agonisingly slow. At this point, I remember John telling me that on his mission to the source Doujie and Busrr had led him initially to the wrong source, so I continually pepper Doujie with questions of the authenticity of our route. He smiles wryly, with the sense of a man that has made the error once and is not about to repeat it this time.

To the Tibetans who inhabit the plateau the source of the Mekong is a sacred place, an area that breathes life into their everyday existence and every year many pilgrims make the journey here to pay their respects. As we descend into the Lasagongma Valley, a wave of reflective emotion overwhelms me, as suddenly I awake to the realisation that I'm going to travel all the way to this river's source. The low lying fertile maze of the Vietnamese Delta seems like another planet, a distant place, unrecognisable from where this river originates from, as memories of its busy networks flood my mind and the bustling food markets that sent me reeling into spasms of culinary euphoria cram my thoughts. This river supports many millions of people along its shores, influencing them and the very fabric of their societies, feeding and sustaining life throughout its epic passage. Before I left England, I knew the trip would be fascinating but I had not imagined for one moment the significance that it served in people's everyday lives and the vital role it played in a spiritual sense. I'm still pondering this, as we breach the brow of a hill and then before me is the wide river of ice that it springs from. I leap from my horse, secure it and scramble up the grey, rocky scree, momentarily losing my footing, before reaching the top and peering down at a tiny stream that flows from the creek below me. A sudden wind whips up, as I scuttle down towards it, then a blizzard of snow sweeps down in a dramatic prelude. I kneel at the source, cup my hands and sip its pure life-giving water. I've made it. I let out a scream of exultant delight and thank the river for all it has provided me. I thank it for the people I have met, their open kindness, colourful culture and for guiding me safely to this point but most of all I thank it for the dazzling array of culinary highlights it has laid before me. I doff my hat, stand up straight and raise a salute to this magnificent wild river.

Bibliography

Buckley, Michael. *Tibet*, Bradt Travel Guides, 2006

Davidson, Alan. *The Oxford Companion to Food*, Oxford University Press, 1999

Gargan, Edward A. *The River's Tale*, Vintage Departures, 2003

Keay, John. *Mad About The Mekong*, Harper Perennial, 2005

Mansfield, Stephen. China, *Yunnan Province,* Bradt Travel Guides, second edition, 2007

Mekong Conservation Project, Irawaddy dolphin

Osborne, Milton. *River Road to China*, London, George Allen & Unwin, 1975

Paddock, Richard C and Demick, Barbara. *LA Times*, Khun Sa, November 2007

Various authors.*The Rough Guide To South East Asia,* Rough Guide, 2005

www.bbc.co.uk, BBC, Life/The Natural World/Plants:Bamboo

www.directfood.net, Blue Diamond. The History of Mono Sodium Glutamate

www.leafgovso.co.uk, The Hui Nationality People, Bai

www.TuochaTea.com, Puer Tea Online Resource

www.guardian.co.uk, Noah's Ark of 5000 rare animals, Watts, Jonathan, 26 May 2007

www.akha.org

www.wikipedia.com